THE MEANING OF THE MOUNTAIN

Lord, who shall dwell in Thy tabernacle and who shall rest on Thy holy mountain? He that walketh without blemish and worketh justice; he that speaketh truth in his heart; who hath not used deceit in his tongue, nor hath taken up a reproach against his neighbor . . . they who praise the Lord working in them, saying with the prophet: "Not to us, O Lord, not to us; but to Thy name give glory."

— Prologue to the Rule of St. Benedict

THE

MEANING OF THE MOUNTAIN

A History of the First Century at Mount St. Scholastica

by Sister Mary Faith Schuster, O.S.B.

BENEDICTINE STUDIES

HELICON: BALTIMORE · DUBLIN

Imprimi Potest:
 Mother M. Celeste Hemmen, O.S.B., Prioress
 Mount St. Scholastica, Atchison, Kansas
 July 3, 1963

Nihil Obstat:
 Louis Hauber, S.T.D.
 Censor Librorum

Imprimatur:
 ✚ Edward J. Hunkeler, D.D.
 Archbishop of Kansas City in Kansas
 July 5, 1963

The *Nihil Obstat* and *Imprimatur* are official declarations that a book
or pamphlet is free of doctrinal or moral error. No implication
is contained therein that those who have granted the *Nihil
Obstat* and *Imprimatur* agree with the opinions expressed.

This volume is the sixth in a series entitled *Benedictine Studies*
sponsored by the American Benedictine Academy and published
by Helicon Press, Inc., Baltimore, Maryland 21202.

Library of Congress Catalog Card Number 63-19401

Typography and design by Frank Kacmarcik

Printed in St. Paul, Minnesota
 by the North Central Publishing Company

Dedicated
to the Prioresses of
Mount St. Scholastica Convent
1863–1963
and to the parents of all the
Sisters of this Community

FOREWORD

It is with great pleasure that I introduce the story of the first century at Mount St. Scholastica Convent. The hundred years show the record of individual human beings working out their salvation by the grace of God. They also form a chapter in the history of the United States of America. Indeed, they link the old world with the new and the new with the future work of Christ's Mystical Body.

Last autumn during the Ecumenical Council, I visited the tombs of St. Benedict and St. Scholastica at Monte Cassino, and I reflected on how fleeting time is. It was my only visit outside Rome. A century is a long time, I thought there, but it is very short in terms of the ages. I prayed there at that tomb for the Benedictines of the Archdiocese who have been such a blessing to the Archdiocese.

The emphasis at the Council was on updating the Church, updating it to meet the challenges cast by evil and the weakness of man. I ask Mount St. Scholastica, at the beginning of its new century, to help update the Church by trying to live so holily that the world will believe God has sent Christ.

✠ Edward J. Hunkeler, D.D.
Archbishop of Kansas City in Kansas

PREFACE

I knew I never could really tell the whole story of the meaning of the mountain. But the moment came in time when its daily life had suddenly become history, when the first century at Mount St. Scholastica was over. In a land over which Spanish explorers had passed 300 years earlier, a small group of Sisters who had come to stay in 1863 had left behind them a living home.

Legend, perhaps even history, had held that a Benedictine monk was with Columbus on his original voyage. But the Benedictine Sisters who came to Kansas were the first Sisters to bring the heritage there. In telling their story, it has been important therefore to look at that heritage. It has been important, too, to try to choose among the written accounts and the thousands of oral stories those things which most significantly carry the thread of the common life and of the convent's essential spirit.

But I have not been able to tell the whole story. Much of human life is a struggle and at its best a victory. It is understood fully by God alone, and is somehow protected by Him. There is no real written record of why two of the seven founders returned "to the world" after three years of pioneering, and we do not really need to know. It is important to know why the others stayed and what God built with them. There is, then, enough to tell a story but not enough to violate a privacy. It is that way with the living. It is good it can be thus also with the dead.

In reliving the century, I have tried to be faithful to fact and, in spirit if not in name, to all who gave their help and their lives to build the great human city of Mount St. Scholastica.

I wish to thank Mother Alfred Schroll and Mother Celeste Hemmen, who commissioned and encouraged the work; the Most Rev. Archbishop Edward J. Hunkeler, who gave his blessing; Abbot Cuthbert McDonald, who opened the St. Benedict's Abbey Archives to me; Monsignor William T. Curtin, who permitted the use of Archdiocesan Archives; Sister Grace McDonald, of happy memory, who shared with me the Archives of St. Benedict's Convent, St. Joseph, Minnesota; the librarians of the Kansas and Missouri Historical Associations; the Rev. Colman Barry, O.S.B., the Rev. Peter Beckman, O.S.B., the Rev. David Kinish, O.S.B., who served as readers of the manuscript; the Sisters of St. Paul's Priory who gave me hospitality when I was checking the final copy; and the many Sisters of the Mount St. Scholastica community who helped me.

Mount St. Scholastica is today a majestic succession of buildings ranged in succeeding architectural styles on a hill in south Atchison. It faces the rising sun and is framed in the evening against the Kansas sunset. This book is a loving and reverent attempt to tell its story and to find its meaning.

Sister Mary Faith Schuster, o.s.b.

July 6, 1963

TABLE OF CONTENTS

THE MEANING OF THE MOUNTAIN

Section One

THE BEGINNING

A little girl was swinging from the fresh smelling rafters of new wood being hammered into place for the new convent. It was a summer evening, and the sun shone bright on the river flowing far below, the river she could see by picking her way through the hazelbrush and peering carefully down the high banks.

"The Sisters are coming. The Sisters are coming."

"What are Sisters?"

The little girl stared. No one she played with really knew what Sisters were. That was part of the surprise. But they were coming to teach her and the people were building a house for them. The parish was having a social to pay for the house. There would be ice cream, and lightning bugs playing around in the grass, and summer moths around the lantern-lighted stands; and the world was quite full of happiness. The papers being printed in the town were full of the Civil War, but she did not even know what either word meant. She went on swinging.

The little girl was Mary O'Keefe and she was swinging a long time ago. But then the history of Mount St. Scholastica begins a long time ago.[1]

Indeed, anyone who would know the history of Mount St. Scholastica Convent, Atchison, Kansas, must begin in the city of its dead, which the little girl herself was to enter. We know what people have been and, in a sense, what they have really done, only when we know how they have died. Every work of art on earth has a beginning, a middle, and an end. Not until we have seen the end do we really know the person or the art his life has really made, or how enduring has been the work of his hands.

A trip to the city of the dead on the slight elevation to the south of Atchison, Kansas, is best made during the early June retreat, when the community of Mount St. Scholastica most shares with the dead — when it, too, is asleep momentarily to the sounds of Time and alive to Eternity.

In the early June community retreat, one walks down the winding drive bordered by spruce and peonies: the trees of the dead because their leaves do not fade, and the flowers of the living because their blossoms flame and die. The gardener will be cutting grass, the whir of electric blades blending peacefully with the nearby gardens of long standing and with the graves of people who died before a single light bulb went on in America. The founders of the convent were not afraid of progress or of the future. They came down the Mississippi River on a boat because they believed in both the eternal and the temporal future.

Clover blossoms border the higher parts of the winding drive, the pasture land which skirts the cemetery and melts into the common world. This is an uncommon world, the land of a people who by an act of the will, consecrated by the Church, gave over to God during life all their weaknesses, strengths, needs, talents — the sum total of their humanity and their capacity for Divinity.

If one leaves the cement drive at the tenth station and crosses through the rich green, one meets the grave of Sister Rita Callahan, eighty-one, teacher and seamstress, who died in her room at the close of an ordinary day — Sister Rita who made the stations many times a day for her friends who might be too busy or who were sick; of Sister Basilia, who died at the foot of the Crucifix on her way to the dining room; of Sister Gaudentia, who was always quiet gladness; of Sister Prisca, smiling cripple for thirty years; of Sister Mary Peter, sacristan, the only Sister for whom the first chant after death was not the *Miserere* but the *Te Deum*.

One could index the kind of ailment from which they died, for it makes a difference in the kind of lives they lived. But for the moment it is all caught up in a total. The birds sing and the wind blows over fresh cut grass. Bees hum. There are wild roses among the clover.

The visitor walks past the rows of graves: Sister Cajetan, who kept the college halls spotless with her crew of cleaners, and whose memory comes back with every awareness of fresh wax when feast days near; Sister Mary Anne, oldest Sister in the cemetery. Her life began in 1805. She came as a widow to the convent and seemed always to be sewing.

Sister Dorothy's grave is near the sidewalk. She died in 1930, one of the first Sisters in the community to earn a Master's degree.

Sister Teresita Snoddy, who died as a very young Sister, saying, "Jesus, You love me"; Sister Ephrem, who made lace albs; Sister Remigia Gassman, talented musician; Sister Wenceslaus, teacher, bookbinder, whose face had only one expression — quizzical wonder at life; Sister Modesta Burns, who tended the sick; Sister Mary Salome, who wanted to teach until she died and who did so, waiting to suffer her stroke until one spring evening after school had closed, May 21, 1956, when she was returning from a trip to her trunk.

They are all here, inauspiciously reminding one of the importance of the daily work of the hands and mind in a community and of the lasting quality with which the personality of the workman touches the work. They are all here in rows, the graves of different, lovable, human Sisters, buried with hands folded and with wreaths on their black veils.

Two novices are here, and grave upon grave of the young who died in years when tuberculosis was an incurable, inscrutable disease; and Sister Luitgard who lived through seventy-eight years of the convent's first century and died at the age of ninety-six.

Somewhere amid the rows is the grave of Sister Gertrude Winter, musician, choir director, classical scholar. "Why don't they come?" she asked an hour before her death. "Your niece is on her way." "I don't mean Maxine. I mean Jesus and Mary."

They are all here, the relics and the memories of more than 200 Sisters who bear the names of great saints to which they themselves add a lustre. Benedictine saints from a vigorous past come to life here because some American nun carried their names. Edith, abbess, daughter of Oswy, the Anglo-Saxon king; Hilda of Whitby, who encouraged Caedmon; Adelgund, who would be forever buried in a Benedictine martyrology except for the Kansas girl who at seventeen in the old days of early wisdom taught Abbot Martin his fifth grade catechism.

Richtrude, Edeltrudis, Ebba, Ethelburg, Ositha — the old names of centuries ago have not been strange names when given at the altar to personalities who with their lives built Kansas, Iowa, Missouri, Nebraska, California, Colorado, and Mexico convents.

With the American born Sisters are those who came at Abbot Boniface Wimmer's request from Eichstätt, Bavaria, with its 900-year-old history — its own story reaching through war and peace back to Walburga, niece of Boniface, who was himself a contemporary of Bede, who was only a generation from Augustine of Canterbury, who was one generation away from Benedict.

And there are those who later left a native land.

"Do you miss your home?"

"I knew I would never see my mother again when I left. I said to God on the ocean: 'You are my only home,'" Sister Valentine Rosenwirth remarked before her death.

At the Crucifixion group in the cemetery, the visitor is on top of the world with only the slightly sloping fields beyond and the sky above. Here one can see the spires of Mount St. Scholastica. This is the city, these are the roof tops, this is the spirit which the dead have built.

Sister Rosalia Krieger of Baltimore, city of the white marble steps, procurator of the monastery for so many years, helped to leave quite a city behind when, as her gravestone announces, she went to the Eternal One in 1929.

Looking down, one sees a bridge over a small creek. In the creek banks are rocks from the old novitiate building, torn down in 1937 to make room for the Chapel of Mount St. Scholastica. Now the rocks give direction to the stream of water, which has mirrored the sky for a hundred years to meditating retreatants. The rocks, the bridge, the pasture, all speak. Place was sacred to St. Benedict. Let the clothing and footgear of the brethren be suited to the place, he said.

The look down the hill takes one to the common blessings of the convent, past the strawberry patch, the vegetable and flower gardens, the apple trees, to the home that the dead have built and left for the living. The Convent, the Infirmary, Marian Hall, Benet Hall, St. Scholastica Chapel, St. Cecilia's, the Administration Building, Kremmeter, Riccardi Center, St. Catherine's, Marywood, Our Lady of Wisdom Library — most of it is visible from here.

The visitor walks up another row of steps. There are four graves here under the Crucifix.

The eye travels down the stones: Mother Lucy Dooley, 1924–1950; Mother Aloysia Northman, 1897–1924; Mother Theresa Moser, 1884–1897; Mother Evangelista Kremmeter. Born, Feb. 2, 1833. Died, June 21, 1909. Prioress, 1863–1884.

One hundred years roll back. The world is as new and the whole hill of Mount St. Scholastica as clear of buildings and as brown with autumn trees and vegetation as it was that November 11 when Mother Evangelista came, with a great sense of the present and the gift of the centuries in her heart and mind and hands.

1. For the original account of this incident, see Sister Hildegard O'Keefe, *Manuscript History of Mount St. Scholastica*, 1913, in the Convent Archives.

THE GIFT OF THE CENTURIES

The lives of St. Benedict and St. Scholastica are a sacred part of human history. The two saints are everyone's, for they were people who did eminently well what everyone wants to do, and in so doing they became fellow human beings to all men. They never intended to found a way of life, just to find one for themselves, when she consecrated herself to God from childhood [1] and he went out to the hills from Rome as a student to find peace.

But from that prayer in solitude which St. Benedict made around the year 497, there did spring a way of life. His Rule, written for those who sought the peace he found, provided first an inner plan of the soul — with humility, obedience, silence, courtesy, work of hand and mind, prayer in private and in public as the path by which a man might go to God. It provided also an outward structure whereby men could live together, and a certain spirit and organization which could be adapted to life outside a cloister.

At the end of his life, St. Benedict visited his sister at some point between her convent and his monastery. There is a special beauty in the fact that they were old people then. They talked all afternoon of the things of God, and when evening came she asked him to stay longer. He declined because his Rule legislated that everything should be done by daylight and monks should not stay outside their monastery unless there was no avoiding the stay. Then she made one of the most famous prayers of history, folding her hands on the table and bowing her head. The serene sky, in an instant, was clouded,

8

the lightning and thunder broke, and torrents of water flooded the stream that separated the place from the monastery.

"God forgive you, Sister! What have you done?"

"I asked you for a favor and you said no. I asked God and He said yes. Return, if you can, to your monastery."

And, says St. Gregory, whose *Dialogues* are the principal source of the life of Benedict, because of the raging torrent which made passage impossible they spent the night speaking of heavenly things. Three days later, from his room in Monte Cassino, St. Benedict saw a dove fly past his window and knew that his sister had died. With his monks in procession he went to her convent and brought her remains to the Abbey for burial in a double tomb, part of which he reserved for his own body. Shortly afterwards, standing and praying in his Oratory, he himself died. Since then throughout history their stories have been linked and their influences inter-related.

Certain fundamental ways of looking at life and of doing things had been written into St. Benedict's Rule and solidified into tradition by his long life as Abbot. The Rule makes no reference to troubled Italy, to barbarian hordes wanting conversion. It is a plan for men to order their lives, to return "by the path of obedience to God from whom by the sloth of disobedience they have departed." It prescribes for what St. Benedict calls "schools of the Lord's service," almost as if he is playing on words and contrasting these schools to those of human eloquence and career-designing which had left his own heart and mind empty. It makes practical provisions: that goods of the monastery be sold more cheaply than obtainable elsewhere, that guests be treated as Christ, that the poor be given more than usual attention, that children be educated with care, that when monks must transact business in the outside world they be attired a little better than usual, and that living by patience, penitence, and charity the monastery go to sleep each night in peace — everyone asking pardon before retiring for any injury given and the Abbot reciting the *Pater Noster* aloud at Vespers so that its petition for mutual forgiveness echo through the house.

He did not intend to found an Order, thinks Abbot Cuthbert Butler in *Benedictine Monachism*. He seems rather to be saying things anyone would say who had time to think about how Christians ought to live.

To the monk's personal life he gave special care. The cultivation of humility was to be a striving up a twelve-rung ladder; all difficulties were to be "dashed at once against Christ." He took Cassian's precept that men ought to dash temptation against the rock, and personalized the rock. He presumed, remarks Owen Chadwick, that man is apt to fail, that no monk ever passes far beyond the novitiate, that all men are beginners, that triumph comes from increasing union with Christ. In this presumption, "Benedict transformed Cassian by placing the spiritual life more within the context of grace." [2]

Within his own lifetime, St. Benedict sent monks into Gaul, but the great exodus to pagan lands came a little later. It was St. Gregory the Great who, within fifty years of St. Benedict's death, sent a branch of the Order to England with directions that they should not destroy paganism but should baptize it. One of the group, the tall and stately Paulinus, explained the meaning of life to the court of Edwin of Northumbria, and the Venerable Bede caught the importance of the scene in a passage of literature always new even to those who have read and reread it. In a drafty courtroom, the King sat with his council of seventy wise men. Edwin presented his guest and asked if he should be heard. One of the king's priests, Coifi, answered: "O king, consider what this is which is now preached to us; for I verily declare to you, that the religion which we have hitherto professed has, as far as I can learn, no virtue in it." There is the basic honesty of good men in the scene, and there is the beauty of the reflective thinker, for another of Edwin's chief men added, introducing the English sparrow forever to literature:

This present life of man, O king, seems to me, in comparison of that time which is unknown to us, like to the swift flight of a sparrow through the room wherein you sit at supper in winter . . . but after a short space of fair weather, he immediately vanishes out of your sight, into the dark winter from which he had emerged. So this life of man appears for a short space, but of what went before, or what is to follow, we are utterly ignorant. If, therefore, this new doctrine contains something more certain, it seems justly to deserve to be followed.[3]

England heard the monks. The native Anglo-Saxon kings gave their lives fighting for their faith against those who attacked it out of fear or ignorance or human weakness, but Augustine's monks were not asked to give theirs, and within a century England entered a "Golden Age." Men like Edwin and Oswald and Richard, kings of small areas, were good and noble rulers. Within this first century after Augustine's coming, Bede and Boniface and perhaps the author of the *Beowulf* poem were born and flourished. Benedictine convents were established and attained a high level of effort in God's service. St. Etheldreda of Ely, one of the earliest English nuns, was to be a tie with the twentieth century.[4]

By 700 A.D., the island was almost entirely Christian and ready to look to the needs of other lands. Germany was one such land, and to it went St. Boniface, the famous field-man among Anglo-Saxon monks. In 716 he left his abbey in Hampshire for Frisia, a territory northeast of Holland. He returned to England in 717 to be elected abbot, only to beg that his resignation be accepted. Then back to Frisia and Germany for forty years.

He was a lover of learning as well as of souls. Whether he knew the Venerable Bede personally or not, he loved his writings and asked for copies of them. He asked the Sisters of English convents to copy the Scriptures too, in beautiful letters so that they would attract the people. After forty years of converting and organizing the Church on Roman lines, the great archbishop died, martyred with thirty companions by a yet unconverted tribe. It is said that he met his murderers with a book in his hand, held it instinctively above his head, and was hacked in two by the nonbelievers, leaving them no memory of resistance or violence. The book was *The Advantages of Death*, by St. Ambrose.

Near the end of his life, about 748, he had invited Sisters from England to help. Abbess Tetta of Wimbourne sent a number, among whom were Chunihild, Berktgild, Chunitrud, Tekla, Lioba, and Walpurgis or Walburga. Their names sound harsh to the American ear. But they were rich names, related to English families rich in courage then. Walburgis or Walburga was a niece of Archbishop Boniface. Her name accumulated stories of the miraculous from the beginning, for even in the passage from England to the continent the sailors thought it was her prayer that had stopped a storm at sea. She became such a symbol of goodness in Germany that the German pagan May-day feast was Christianized and re-named "Walpurgis Eve." Goethe puts one of his famous *Faust* scenes on that day.

Walburga was the daughter of Richard, thought to be an Anglo-Saxon king, who died on a pilgrimage to Rome. At Wimbourne she had lived among a community of 500 Sisters who chanted the office, studied Scripture and the Fathers of the Church, Latin, the ordinances of the Church, Latin classics, and sometimes Greek. The nuns were manuscript copyists. They took care, too, of their own convents, of fields, mills, gardens, and stables. They did spinning, weaving, tailoring, tanning, and cobbling. They made vestments for the altar. Their religious life included the rite of consecration of Virgins. In Germany they taught school, dispensed medicine, food and clothing, and maintained hospitals and inns for travelers and guests. Their convents, says the biographer of St. Walburga's convent, were "removed from the world in an extensive solitude, but midway between the people of the mission field." One writer records that St. Lioba "opened her house to all without exception . . . prepared their meals and washed their feet." [5]

In 761, thirteen years after her arrival in Germany and seven years after the death of St. Boniface, Walburga was made Abbess of Heidenheim, a convent built by her brother Wunibald. She was a good superior. The suffering and the poor were welcome at her convent and she went out herself to care for them. An old biographer supplies the detail of her going at night to the bedside of a sick girl, "commanding the furious barking dogs to be silent." [6] Perhaps the distance of centuries makes this look more miraculous than it was, but in any age it looks brave. The child recovered, and the parents offered gifts to Walburga, but she refused, saying the credit was not hers.

Her early biographers tell more stories of her goodness. She was mild, brave, and prayerful. She died February 25, 779, at the age of sixty-nine, and her brother, Bishop Willibald, buried her at the monastery church at Heidenheim where a stone sarcophagus depicts what people thought of her. On it angels are shown holding a crown above her head. She is holding book and staff. When Willibald died a few years later, his body was interred in his cathedral in Eichstätt.

Nearly a century later her relics were moved by the bishop to Eichstätt, to the church of the Holy Cross built by her brother. About 150 years later, Count Leodogar von Lechsgemund und Graibach fulfilled a vow by building a Benedictine convent near her tomb. He brought Sisters from the Convent of St. Ehrentrud near Salzburg, with Abbess Imma, their Superior, to begin the venture. From this convent, founded in 700 by St. Rupert of a Frankish Merovingian family, Sisters brought the oldest stream of Benedictinism in Germany to meet the spirit and tradition of St. Walburga and St. Boniface. Sisters from neighboring convents also came to help form the new community, which began in 1035 and has always been known as St. Walburga's convent.

Eichstätt went through many vicissitudes in the next 900 years. From the tenth to the fifteenth centuries it kept its position as a strong convent, but in the fifteenth it became more of a home for noble ladies than a cloister in the original sense. Bishop Von Eyck then became its benefactor. He instituted a reform, calling Abbess Sophia from Marienberg in the Rhineland to help. After the Council of Trent, observance at the convent was made stricter and a specific half hour or hour daily was set aside for meditation, in addition to the Office, the reading, and the provision for private prayer which St. Benedict had made.[7]

The seventeenth century was externally stormy. St. Walburga's had rebuilt and consecrated a new church by October 12, 1634. But that year saw the famine and terror of the Thirty Years War reach the convent. Invading Swedish soldiers swarmed the neighborhood of the Bavarian convents, and St. Walburga's repaid Marienberg by now giving hospitality to its Sisters in the wake of the armies. The Swedish generals spared the church when the Sisters begged for its safety, but the convent and barns were burned. One lay Sister, not bound to the recitation of the Divine Office, promised that if her life were spared she would say the Office the rest of her life. She was spared and kept her promise.

With the help of Emperor Ferdinand of Austria, cultured "Holy Roman" emperor, the convent was rebuilt and by 1646 all the Sisters could again be housed in it. Now, writes the Rev. Stephen Hilpisch, O.S.B., in his *History of Benedictine Nuns*, the practice arose of prefixing the name "Mary" to the new name which each Sister received at the reception of the habit. Eichstätt Sisters also took "Anna," and many American Sisters have wondered why. The extra name, never used but written on the formula of vows, was to honor the Emperor Ferdinand who had helped and whose Empress was named Maria Anna.[8] In Atchison the extra name would lead to the establishment of a community nameday celebration every July 26.[9]

A course of peace and fervor followed. Abbess Adelgund was one of the superiors who directed the community. Emperor Charles VII said of her, remarks the convent's historian, "There is nothing wanting to this abbess other than a title of nobility; she has everything in her that makes such a person noble." He entrusted his daughters to the convent for education and gave to the Abbess and her successors a pectoral cross on a blue ribbon which "from that time on, with the approval of the bishop, has been worn by the abbesses on solemn occasions." [10]

"The zeal of the convent," writes Sister Grace McDonald, "carried it safely past the perils of the French Revolution." [11] But other troubles were ahead. During the Napoleonic wars the convent property was secularized and the convent forbidden to receive novices. For twenty-seven years no new members were admitted and when in July, 1826, King Ludwig I of Bavaria sent word that he intended to restore the convent, only eight nuns were there keeping up the Divine Office and the ways of religious life. Abbess Michaela had died on May 23 of that year, and Frau Willibalda Schmittner, the subprioress of what was then known as the "dissolved convent of St. Walburga," tried to find ways of helping in the restoration. Revenue was a problem. Well meaning officials suggested that the

Sisters sell St. Walburga's oil—which exuded from the relics and to which miracles had been attributed over the centuries —or that they undertake a brewery, or live from the cultivation of gardens. The first proposition was sacrilegious; the second, inappropriate; and the third impractical for the handful of aging nuns.

King Ludwig found a better way. He had a sincere love for the traditions of Germany and he encouraged the Sisters to take up the work which first brought them to Bavaria. He gave the girls' school of Eichstätt into their care. New postulants entered, and on October 16, 1836, three novices received the habit. They were named Ludovica for Ludwig, Theresa for his Queen, and Edward to honor the cabinet leader, Edward Schenk. Eight days later, October 24, the school opened.

The Sisters remaining from the days of secularization did not live much longer. Prioress Willibalda died soon after the opening of the school. Sister Deocara Hinterreiter, as novice-mistress and subprioress, helped give the old traditions to the young, one of whom, Sister Ludovica, was soon Prioress. At her early death, Prioress Edwarda Schnitzer was elected, in 1849. She had been only thirteen years in religion, but had formed some conclusions which she wrote in her diary:

In a convent it is well to follow the old traditions, centuries-tried usages, since they have been established to serve all times and conditions. Each generation should esteem and hold fast to those customs which older Sisters, who conscientiously observe the Rule, practice. In this way a convent will be able to retain a firm footing.

The oldest custom at the convent named for the niece of St. Boniface was soon to be tested. Boniface Wimmer, the bearded monk who had been in the United States only three years, came to the Eichstätt parlor in 1852, asking for Sisters. The Prioress wrote of the reactions to his visit:

Although I could not do this without sacrificing something of my own convent . . . I gave my consent because I saw the finger of God and hoped that God would reward our convent for such a sacrifice and would give all its members still greater zeal.[12]

The community began a retreat for guidance. By June 11, 1852, the first three American missionaries had been chosen and left the motherhouse for Bremen where they took the boat for the United States. Mother Benedicta Riepp, twenty-seven years old, novice mistress and teacher at Eichstätt, was named the Superior. Sister Walburga Dietrich, an older woman, instructor in needlework and a daughter of a businessman, and Sister Maura Flieger, a farmer's daughter, were her companions. They arrived on the steamer *Washington* in the New York harbor in the evening of July 3, slept quietly in their anchored ship, and walked off the gangplank with some wonderment the next morning to the booming of fireworks.

Less than a century later, in 1945, the Lady Abbess Benedicta von Spiegel would be made an honorary citizen of the United States for handing over the city of Eichstätt to American troops. But on this July day, 1852, the three Sisters only knew they had come to an excitable, slightly noisy, and apparently vigorous land to preserve in it the faith of the fathers among German immigrants who were now part of the American excitement.

The scene was new to them. They had gone through a novitiate which, according to St. Benedict, should "try the spirit to see whether it truly seeks God, is eager for the work of God, and for obedience." They were in solemn vows. At old St. Walburga's they had kept strict enclosure. They had come to be missionaries. There were adaptations and changes before them and the challenge of keeping the ancient spirit as well. Something entirely new was opening to Benedictines in this America. In black habits, with their veils lined in white, the Sisters knew the thrill of the immigrant. They stepped on to the New York sidewalk. "Let not the son of the free man be preferred to the son of the freed man," Benedict had written long ago. Bedloe Island did not yet have its giant Statue of Liberty, but the waters were there where it would be erected in a few years, and it was July 4.

How would they fare in the new land?

The nuns of St. Walburga's had come from Eichstätt and its long history reaching back through Walburg, Boniface, Augustine, and Gregory to the young girl and her brother who had wanted God so long ago in Italy. History was behind them, far across the water in the walled town they had forever left.

16

But it was equally before them. The wide plains and hills of America were ahead.

Their founder would have told them that their only real cause for joy would be if they found the answer to their search, that without a consciousness of God after a while everything on earth has already happened, and that it is only the quest for Him which can be trusted to fill a life.

They stepped off the gangplank and became part of the new world.

1. Cardinal Ildephonse Schuster, in *St. Benedict and His Times*, suggests that St. Scholastica may have been the first of the two to seek an answer to life's desires in total consecration, and may have been the inspiration of her brother before he was hers.

2. Owen Chadwick, *John Cassian. A Study in Primitive Monasticism.* (Cambridge: University Press, 1950), p. 176.

3. The Venerable Bede, *Ecclesiastical History of the English Nation* (New York: E. P. Dutton, 1930), Bk II, Chapter 13, p. 91.

4. In a church dedicated to her, the only pre-Reformation Catholic church in London today, Douglas Hyde received the gift of faith. Mr. Hyde tells of his visit to the small church, kept Catholic through the years because it was attended by the Spanish embassy. The editor of the *London Daily Worker* sat in a back pew, troubled and musing, in the summer of 1947, when a working girl came in to pray. The sight of her face when her prayer was over led him to try what she had tried.

5. *Spring and Harvest*, translated by Sister Gonzaga Engelhart, O.S.B., from the German of the Nuns of St. Walburga (St. Meinrad, Indiana: The Grail Press, 1952), p. 20. This history of St. Walburga's was published in German in 1935 on the occasion of the Eichstätt convent's 900th anniversary.

6. *Ibid.*

7. There were Jesuit confessors and retreat-masters, says the historian of St. Walburga's. Perhaps they were remotely responsible for the emphasis which the first Superior of Mount St. Scholastica placed on the particular examen.

8. Emperor Ferdinand III (1608–1657) was "a scholarly and cultured man, an excellent linguist, and a composer of music." His first wife, Maria Anna, died in 1646. See *Encyclopedia Britannica*, 1961 edition, Vol. IX, p. 166.

An interview with Mother Domitilla, Boulder, Colorado, September, 1962, led the writer to the discovery of the origin of the extra name. The Convent of St. Therese, Boulder, is a mission of St. Walburga's, Eichstätt. "The name Anna," Mother Domitilla said, "is to honor the wife of an emperor who helped us."

9. "Gaude Mater Anna," and "Ballad of St. Anne," written by Sister Chrysostom Koppes and Sisters Mary Dennis Collins and Aquinas Guilfoil, and sung by the community, are an interesting product of a 300-year-old act of gratitude.

10. *Spring and Harvest*, p. 33.

11. *With Lamps Burning* (St. Joseph, Minnesota: Priory Press, 1957), p. 5.

12. Letter to the King Ludwig Mission Society, quoted in *Spring and Harvest*, p. 43.

THE COMING

The first sight that meets the visitor at Mount St. Scholastica Convent is the larger-than-life statue of Saint Benedict, facing the front door from the convent corridor. Marking the invisible line which divides and unites the cloister and the world, it pictures St. Benedict as a mature monk and is itself the gift of the first Benedictine priest the pioneers met on American soil.

On July 8, 1852, a wagon carrying Sisters and luggage drew up before St. Vincent's Priory, Latrobe, Pennsylvania, among the Allegheny hills, and a lay brother noticing it announced: "Father Superior, here comes a wagonload of trouble."[1]

A bearded man with deep, shrewd eyes looked up, and Boniface Wimmer welcomed the Benedictine Sisters to the United States. The three Sisters, the Eichstätt novice-mistress, a teacher, and a housekeeper, were quite conscious of the importance of the moment. They had the Holy Rule, the Eichstätt custom book, and the resolution to stay in this new land. The green hills welcomed them. Pennsylvania was a beautiful state. They were ready for America.

St. Vincent's was a briefing interlude. After a few days there as guests, they set out on a five-day wagon trip through wonderful wooded country to St. Mary's in Elk County, where in a building abandoned by the School Sisters of Notre Dame they established St. Joseph's Convent, the first Benedictine Convent in the United States. Within their first year they were joined by two more groups of Sisters from the Bavarian motherhouse and by twelve young girls who received the habit October 16, 1853, in the first reception ceremony held by Benedictine Sisters in America.

19

But the focus of Atchison history was to be on the next group of postulants, those who received the habit February 10, 1855, for among them was Mary Ann Kremmeter, twenty-two years old, who had come to the United States with her parents from Neu Ulm, Bavaria. She shared an ambitious religious life with her companions, and one of them as a very old Sister left a record of it:

The young Sisters were now instructed in their religious duties, especially in the recitation of the Divine Office. Rev. Father Benedict taught them a little Latin and to their great delight they began to pray the Office with the Sisters. At 3:30 the signal was given for rising — Matins and Lauds were prayed; and in winter, in a cold room. And with what zeal they chanted the grand Office of the Church! Their fresh, youthful voices rang out, making St. Mary's resound with the praises of God. Yet, now while I am writing this, the remembrance fills my heart with joy.[2]

Mother Benedicta knew how to start a convent. She seemed to know how to keep people happy. She began with a whole convent which prayed and sacrificed and rejoiced. At the very first Christmas there were presents — the common fare which was to be served as breakfast was a "gift" from God.

On March 21, 1857, the community held its first ceremony of solemn vows. Boniface Wimmer, designated by Bishop Young of Erie to receive them, must have heard the ancient formula for the first time on new soil with deep emotion. Two of the newly professed Sisters he would remember with particular pride in a report to Rome a few years later.

For in the summer of 1857, five Sisters left St. Mary's to establish a convent in Minnesota, and Sister Evangelista Kremmeter and Sister Gregoria Moser were among them. It was a mission venture as well as an attempt to find a part of the United States where Benedictine life could more quickly flourish. Mother Benedicta Riepp herself headed the group, conscious of the need for growth if Benedictinism was to survive and convinced that the spot in Pennsylvania lacked the scope they needed. She was young and not very strong, but she had not given up one continent without the hope of really gaining another. Her thoughts were racing ahead to whether there would be Sisters for tomorrow and opportunity for them to expand. Sister Evangelista responded primarily to the missionary call of the farther West. She wrote: "There are girls here [in Minnesota] fifteen years old who still do not know the alphabet or the Ten Commandments, much less the Our Father . . . In this land where everything is still primitive and the people unlearned, much good can be done."

But Minnesota offered them all — Abbot Boniface whose big dream was best fulfilled by it, and all the Sisters involved — a particular and strange kind of trial. The whole organization of Benedictine convents had to be worked out not in words so much as in people's lives. Boniface Wimmer thought the young convents of young Sisters ought to be under the centralized control of the monk responsible for bringing them. It was not a selfish and stubborn opinion. He viewed weightily his responsibilities in introducing cloistered religious whose houses had choir obligations to America, brimming with people whose children, if they could be reached, cried out for education. He knew the work had to be done, but he feared the Order's losing its essential character and he wanted to keep a close finger on all he had started. His intense self-scrutiny was revealed in a letter written twenty-eight years later to the Abbot of Atchison:

The trouble for me comes from the answer to the question: did I work in the right *direction*? viz., did I do my work as it ought to have been done? Would it not have been 10 times better, if I had settled down somewhere with a few of my followers and commenced a religious life according to the rule of St. Benedict, living a life in retirement with them, devoted to prayers, to the praise of God, to mortification and self-denial, to occasional preaching of the gospel too, than assuming or rather presuming to establish monasteries and colleges and thereby running the risk that often comes while I myself and my companions might become or appear to be worldly minded, giving little edification and turn out to be a bogus kind of monk, not warm and not cold? [3]

Mother Benedicta, in a great country calling for the harmony of prayer and work, thought convents organized autonomously but with some allegiance to Eichstätt, and guided by bishops, would better serve the church. She battled tuberculosis and worry and, without meaning to do so, Abbot Boniface himself, to begin the convent as she thought she should,

21

leaving very few words of her own to vindicate her in the misunderstandings which distance and slowness of mail occasioned. Within a century, the largest Benedictine convent in the world and its many daughterhouses would testify that her choice of Minnesota had been blessed. But Abbot Boniface, looking upon her activities in the midst of his own busy round of vast works, thought she had exceeded her authority in moving to Minnesota and commissioned Sister Evangelista to assume the superiorship of the community there. St. Benedict's Rule had given the Superior authority to employ a kind of excommunication toward rebellious monks, and the forthright Abbot wrote energetically from Pennsylvania that the young and gentle Sister Evangelista apply the stringent remedy to the foundress.

Sister Evangelista transcended trouble with simple wisdom and disarmed the Abbot with a question: "How could I treat my own Sisters thus? If your orders must be complied with, I will feel constrained to leave and seek to secure salvation in a stricter order . . . With all the other points of your ultimatum it will be our endeavor to comply."[4] She won the point. The Abbot remained her life-long friend and gratified religious father.

In 1862, the troubled young foundress died in peace. Mother Benedicta left behind her a community which had grown from five to twelve members, and had survived a good deal of history in its five years at St. Cloud. Sisters who lived with her and priests and bishops who dealt with her believed in her humility and singleness of purpose. Novice-mistress at Eichstätt, she had brought to this country the spirit, the Rule, and some of the customs she had herself learned in the old convent behind the high walls. She had brought a willingness to adapt and a sense of mission, and a kind of fearlessness of pain. Sister Evangelista, who had witnessed her effort and her early death, had studied superiorship in a hard school and would need to remember all the lessons.

Hundreds of miles to the south an ambitious town was building itself along the Missouri River, and a handful of Benedictine monks had begun a college in Atchison, Kansas. In January, 1863, Prior Augustine Wirth began planning a school for the Atchison townspeople. Educationally, Atchison was an interesting town, composed of Irish and German Catholic immigrants, Lutherans, New England people come west, and southern families moving out of the war area. It had an optimistic tone, a taste for fine things. John J. Ingalls, the author of one of the "opportunity" poems, was editor of its paper for a time, a paper which quoted Carlyle, Emerson, Newman, and the poetry of Thomas Hood in the same pages that commented on horse-thievery, rainfall, and local news.

Prior Augustine engaged a Jesuit to preach a mission, one result of which was to be sufficient enthusiasm to build a school, and Father Demetrius Smarius did so with success.[5] Then Prior Augustine borrowed money to build the school and on one of his trips to Chicago must have spoken personally with Mother Willibalda of St. Cloud, who went to Chicago to discuss the venture.

All summer and autumn there was the excitement of new wood and of hammers pounding at Second and Division Street in Atchison, and in the autumn of that 1863 the twelve Sisters at St. Cloud drew straws as to who should occupy what was at least one of the first real convents really built for Benedictine Sisters in the new world. Novices, too, had a chance at the straws. They fell to Sister Evangelista, appointed superior by Mother Willibalda, and Sister Gregoria, who had made profession with her at St. Mary's; to Sisters Amanda Meier, Adelaide Lejal, and Ehrentrude Wolters, who had gone as postulants from St. Mary's to St. Cloud; to Sister Dominica Massoth, who had entered at St. Cloud; and to Sister Scholastica Duerr of Alsace, a novice.[6] Mother Evangelista was just thirty years old. All the rest were in their twenties.

At St. Cloud the Mississippi River flows evenly to the edge of the city. There are tall water weeds. The landscape is flat and the water quiet. The stagecoach, in 1863, left for St. Paul at some point on the main thoroughfare near the river. It is hard to believe that the travelers boarded a coach when they could have taken a boat, but the manuscript history says they did so and that the trip wearied them sufficiently to necessitate resting several days at St. Paul. The first history says they rested "probably with Benedictine Sisters," for, it continues, the monk negotiating the trip had to terminate leave-taking in order not to miss the boat. The monk was the Rev. Thomas Bartl,[7] and the Abbey cashbook, after a century, records in clear script that 600 precious dollars had been given him for the "passage" of the pioneers.

But there is no written record of Benedictines being in St. Paul in 1863, and it is more probable that the Sisters it was so hard to leave were the same St. Joseph hospital nuns who had received Mother Evangelista and the pioneers from Pennsylvania six years earlier.[8]

It is highly interesting to try to follow the route of the Sisters to Kansas, and a little difficult, for an account says that they visited in Chicago on the journey south. That means most probably that they traveled by boat to Rock Island, Illinois, then by Rock Island train to Chicago for a visit, then back by train to Rock Island and south to Hannibal where they boarded the new Hannibal-St. Joseph railroad to the very banks of the Missouri River near Atchison. The whole trip has a human stamp. The Chicago Sisters would then have included several with whom Mother Evangelista had shared convent life, for the Chicago foundation had been made a year earlier from Pennsylvania and included in that November of 1863 Sister Nepomucene Ludwig and Sister Adalberta Glatt, who had been fellow Sisters of Mother Evangelista and Sister Gregoria at St. Mary's.[9]

Then, with the cross-Illinois trip over, the Mississippi River awaited. In her book, *With Lamps Burning*, Sister Grace McDonald remarks the universal kindness of Mississippi River captains to Sisters. Because of war tensions, these Sisters wore bonnets rather than traditional Benedictine headdress. But the dyed shawls and black habits, the custom of staying together, and perhaps the captain's own keenness and sympathy must have led him to know their identity. For remembering the trip years later, one of the pioneers gave the convent's first historian the following material:

The meals were good and the Sisters were kindly treated by captain and crew. One day after dinner the captain requested the Sisters to sing. Sisters Adelaide, Dominica, and Amanda began and all joined in. What they sang I do not know, but it must have been pleasing for the captain furnished an extra treat as reward for the concert.[10]

No one thought to record the name of the captain or of his boat. It might have been Captain Sheble of the *Effie Deans,* Captain James Ward of the *Sucker State,* or some hospitable master of the *Hawk Eye State,* the *Northerner,* the *Canada,* or the *New Davenport.* The river lines, in low water, were also using the *New Muscatine,* the *Pembina,* the *W. L. Ewing,* and the *New Savanna.*[11]

The boat docked most probably at Hannibal, Missouri, where the seven Sisters took the newly completed Hannibal-St. Joseph-Atchison railway, of which Atchison citizens were then so proud, with its direct connections to the Atlantic. The Sisters reached Atchison at eleven o'clock on an early November evening, ferrying across the Missouri River. They were traveling into a golden season, for the *Champion* had noted on November 6: "Fine Indian summer weather succeeded the inclement fury of last week." It was the feast of the great St. Martin, dear to St. Benedict, and the nameday of the abbot who would be one of the convent's great spiritual directors. The day looked backward and forward, but its accent was on the present. Was it that night itself, before retiring in the clean new convent, that Mother Evangelista made the entry on the title page of the foundation's first account book: "St. Scholastica Academy, Atchison City, Kansas, November 11, 1863"?

Atchison was a promising town of rapid growth in the midst of a country which had all the problems of growth. That night, an hour before midnight, James Kennedy and Lambert Halling, carpenters for the Abbey, were swinging lanterns up and down the street in front of that newly built convent. Their march had several causes.

The city of Atchison was coming of age quickly. It had been laid out by an association from Platte County, Missouri, and the first sale of lots held September 21, 1854. The seal of the state had been designed by Senator Ingalls. The city had grown to more than 5,000 in nine years. It had tasted westward expansion and civil war. It was abreast of national turbulence and of its own. Its paper, that year of 1863, had recorded the catching of horse thieves, the echoes of war, and an awareness of racial injustices. Two of the items which Atchison people had read that year seem too lively not to include. The editor included, June 20, 1863:

Scott, one of the horse thieves caught below town, in company with Williams and Wilson, has been permitted to join the 9th Kansas, and we learn that he is anxious to do his duty. If he does, it will be better than to have hung him.

Only the length of a century in between makes the item humorous, if that really succeeds, for when one really looks at what was happening it is easy to understand why Mother Evangelista found the Atchison children sometimes restless.

An eye for national coverage and a reflection of interesting editorial sympathies are shown in the other item, August 8 of the same year:

One of the Roman Catholic priests of Newark, N.J., told his flock some days since that if he should at any time hear of the perpetration by an Irishman, of any outrage whatever upon any coloured citizen he should immediately seek out and protect in his own house the person so assailed.

The town had turned out on December 2, 1859, to hear Abraham Lincoln talk at the corner of Fifth and Parallel Streets on "The Issues of the Day." Those issues, with their repercussions, were later felt. On December 18, 1861, Prior Augustine had written to King Ludwig of Bavaria: "Across the river is Missouri, in rebellion against the United States government. No ship can sail on the river, so we are cut off from other states." [12] In the same year, on April 18, 1861, the steamboat, the *Sam Gaty*, had arrived at Leavenworth under the Confederate flag and the captain had been forced by the people to substitute the *Stars and Stripes*. The Atchison paper, on April 11, 1863, had printed Mr. Lincoln's statement: "We have grown in numbers, wealth and power as no nation has ever grown. But we have forgotten God." It had also printed his announcement that Thursday, April 30, 1863, would be a day of "national prayer and humiliation."

It was to this city, aware of the world and energetically at work putting up sidewalks, that the Sisters came. And there was religious prejudice too. Efforts had been made indeed to keep out bigotry. As early as December 16, 1859, Joseph P. Carr had addressed the Festival of the Ladies of the Baptist Church with these words:

In our own happy land, peopled as it was by refugees for conscience' sake — by Puritans, Huguenots, Catholics, French — those who would sacrifice all but their God — it may well be expected that there should be found many evidences of the faith that is in us . . .

The *Champion* had given generous space to the words. But the war had brought restlessness and fomented all manner of misunderstanding. Mr. Finney, the wharfmaster, had heard of threats to burn down the house if Sisters came.

That house stood at Second and Division Streets, a stately little frame building with two classrooms, living quarters, a small room which could be used for a chapel, and a graceful cupola topped by a cross. It looked like a convent. It had cost $4,150. Besides the personal safety of the Sisters, it was important that the house be protected. For $4,150 was not easily come by, nor had it, of course, been yet come by at all. Abbot Boniface was to comment with sympathetic humor:

The people adopted a unique plan to pay for it. They founded a society of one hundred fathers of families who are contributing fifty cents a month. Unless it increases its membership eight to ten years will pass before they will cancel that debt.[13]

But the Sisters were aware of no worry that night. To the swinging of the friendly lanterns, they reached the convent at eleven o'clock. Across the street was the first Abbey Church, a wooden structure but a real church. There were seven new beds in the convent and seven new tin basins. There were friends who were glad they had come. As long as they lived they would remember the stagecoach, the river, their singing as they came, and the fact that lights were lit for their arrival.

The Compline prayer in the new convent had a special significance: *Visita quaesumus, Domine, habitationem istam et omnes insidias inimici ab ea longe repelle.* "Visit, we beseech Thee, O Lord, this habitation and repel all the influences of the enemy."

The prayer to St. Joseph, too, was fitting in the new convent named for him: "Grant that as we venerate him as our Protector on earth we may be found worthy to be aided by his intercession in Heaven." For fourteen years, although the school would be called St. Scholastica, the convent's name would be St. Joseph. The evening prayer to St. Benedict also had a comforting sound this night: "Protect me, I beseech thee, O glorious father, this day and every day by thy holy blessing that I may never be separated from our blessed Lord and from the society of thyself and of all the blessed."

The Romans venerated household gods. Even the pagan Romans would have understood the Sisters' asking the help of Joseph and of Benedict as their first night in their new convent closed about them. Christian Rome, the Rome that sent Augustine to Canterbury, would have rejoiced for additional reasons.

The young Superior must have looked out over the darkness of the nine-year-old town that evening with joy and hope. She had come to the convent with resplendent grade cards from the national schools of Bavaria. She had made solemn vows. She had traveled the rickety trains and had been a passenger on the river boats. She had known great people who held religious life precious in pioneer days among people whose language they could scarcely speak. She had seen the Rule of cloistered Eichstätt adapted to educational lifework. She had learned the pain which stems from misunderstandings among the just. In the country of freedom to which she had come there had been for religious communities very little peril from without. For the early Benedictine Sisters, sensitive and eager, accustomed to rigorous daily schedules, the suffering had been of a different nature. The misunderstanding between Abbot Boniface, whom they revered for his zeal and great ideal, and Mother Benedicta, whom they loved because they knew her, would have refined souls quickly.

It must have been so for young Mother Evangelista. Photographs of her show a whimsical, gentle, strong face. Her small diary, of some seventy-seven entries between 1866 and 1901, might have been written by a novice, for it contains only resolutions to try for holiness. Its first entry, made three years after this night in Atchison, was: "The love of Jesus keeps me from fearfulness." This must have been something of her sentiment, as she looked out over the nine-year-old city from her new house that night of November 11, 1863. Outside, making friendly shadows, Mr. Halling and Mr. Kennedy still paced the street. And later, when the community tore down the first convent, it took to the new grounds the cupola which shone white against the glow of their lanterns as they swung them in the night.

1. Manuscript account by Sister Nepomucene, St. Mary's, Elk County, Pennsylvania, written August 26, 1913, and later incorporated into the centennial history of that community, *One Hundredth Anniversary of the Benedictine Sisters, 1852–1952.* Sister Nepomucene was one of the early postulants admitted to that community.

2. *Ibid.*

3. Letter of Jan. 12, 1885. St. Benedict's Abbey Archives.

4. Quoted by Sister Grace McDonald, O.S.B., *With Lamps Burning*, p. 31. The letter, dated August, 1857, is in the St. John's Abbey Archives, Collegeville, Minn.

5. The mission was commented upon by Atchison's *Freedom's Champion*, Jan. 10, 1863.

6. Sister Hildegard O'Keefe, *Manuscript History of Mount St. Scholastica*, as told by Sister Amanda Meier, 1913. MSS Archives.

7. Peter Beckman, O.S.B., *Kansas Monks* (Atchison: Abbey Student Press, 1957), p. 76.

8. Sister Grace McDonald, O.S.B., *With Lamps Burning*, p. 23.

9. *Catalogue of the Nuns and Convents of the Order of St. Benedict in the United States*, Sisters of St. Mary's Convent (St. Mary's: Herald Printing House, 1903), p. 57.

10. Sister Hildegard O'Keefe, *Manuscript History*, no pagination.

11. For the names of the boats and captains, I am indebted to the research of Ruth Ferris, Missouri Historical Society, St. Louis, and to Lois Fawcett, head of the reference department, Minnesota Historical Society, St. Paul, Minnesota.

12. St. Benedict's Abbey Archives.

13. Quoted by Rev. Felix Fellner, O.S.B., "St. Vincent Archabbey: Center of Missionary Activity," *Benedictine Review*, IV (July, 1949), 29.

MORNING

Kansas in November is not quite like any other state in the Union. For almost 400 miles west of the Missouri River in Atchison its brown fields stretch, framed in the eastern part of the state by trees and broken by small creeks, rising like a golden blanket in billows of wonderful wheat in summer, limitlessly brown and beautiful in late autumn.

Along the river itself, Kansas matches Missouri's high bluffs with hills of its own. The bushes along the river are tall and brittle in the sharp wind, and ducks must have been accessible there to the rifles of Lewis and Clark. In the evening, a blueness falls over the hills and leafless trees, and the sunset never seems so beautiful as when the world is bare. "So will everything be clear to all of us on judgment day," Sister Desideria, convent baker and assistant novice mistress, would say years later to postulants looking out from the fourth floor balcony. Then she would add: "And like the falling leaves that rest on earth, our souls will have gone home to God."

Mother Evangelista and her six companions could not envision the present fourth floor balcony and postulants meditating there before the rim of garden and sky. The morning after arrival dawned for them on a rutted trail leading to woods and fields. The Sisters attended Mass in the Abbey Church. After the Mass they were served breakfast in the rectory. Brother Luke did the honors with generous monastic portions of coffee, bread, butter, and the sorghum syrup known in the area. That day, November 12, was unpacking day; then came the feast of Benedictine All Saints, and Brother Luke etched his hospitable face on history

30

forever by serving a genuine banquet. Otherwise, the Sisters dined in their own new convent, and frugally, for the Eichstätt tradition of poverty was real and the four thousand dollars became their own responsibility, as the Abbey was fighting financial battles which would have completely overcome Mother Evangelista even to know.

The first Mass offered in the Sisters' chapel was celebrated by Father Thomas Bartl, the missionary who had brought them from Minnesota and who later earned such praise in that book sparing of praise, *Kansas Monks*. It was Sunday, November 16, feast of the Patronage of the Blessed Virgin Mary.[1] Father Thomas' sermon after the Mass was accompanied by extremely appropriate gestures, as the following account written from pioneer memories suggests:

First Mass was celebrated in the Sisters' convent on the feast of the Patrocinium of the Blessed Virgin. The celebrant was Rev. Thomas Bartl of saintly memory. At the close of Holy Mass, the Sisters sang: "Jungfrau wir Dich Grüszen." Father Thomas, who was obliged to leave immediately for a mission where he was to say Holy Mass, gave the Sisters a short instruction and exhortation while at the same time packing the necessary articles into the satchel which lay prepared beside the altar. One of the Rev. Father's remarks seems particularly well-chosen — that of the need of the heavenly mother's protection, of which the first Mass being on her feast seemed to be a guarantee.[2]

The mission for which Father Thomas was packing may have been Bendena, where he was building a church at that time. There, says the *Bendena History*, "He was loved, honored, and remembered by the children and grandchildren of parents whom he comforted in the trying years when the war's red wave swept over the land. . . . He joined a small army of workers, assisting in quarrying rock, mixing mortar, and even carrying hod. He appeared a frail man, but he had the zeal of Paul and the industry of Patrick. The church, begun in 1861, was completed in 1865."

From the beginning of the Kansas nuns, Kansas monks tried to help them. In their small and struggling Priory, with its own blend of missionary, educational and liturgical apostolates, they made an enduring contribution. They might worry and bluster a little, as Prior Oswald Moosmuller did in the early seventies, concerned as he was over the difficulties which this blend of cloistered and missionary nun had in observing *clausura*. But they wanted the seven pioneers to be real Sisters, and they gave solid spiritual strength, faithful guidance, and wonderful human kindness, along with financial help when they could, temporal advice, and opportunity for educational work. Convent chronicles, with the faithfulness to detail for which they are famous, record only once in the long century when a chaplain was unable to come for the morning Mass, and then the snow lay mountain high on the two miles of hills between Abbey and convent in days before the snow plow.

Opportunities for educational work were less than three weeks away. Prior Augustine had asked for the Sisters to start a school, and he meant immediately. When he begged the Ludwig Mission Society for funds to begin a school for orphans, he was not merely seeking a sensitive spot in the society's burdened heart.[3] There were orphans in Atchison, but all the children were orphans of Catholic education, and farmer families were ready to bring them in by buggy or wagon at the first sign that the cross of St. Joseph's really protected a school. Not Catholics only, but non-Catholics as well, were knocking at the door of the two English-speaking and five German-speaking Sisters. The city was education-eager, as the *Atchison City Union* had borne witness, four years earlier, June 4, 1859:

Atchison City is four years old — numbers some four thousand inhabitants, and is rapidly increasing in wealth and population . . . Industry, self-reliance, and associated effort are the marked characteristics of Atchison. Idleness and prodigality, the concomitants of poverty and crime, are rarely found within its borders; but in the place of these, the hum of industry, and the sound of the hammer and jack plane are heard in every direction. Standing on a promontory in this city, we counted sixty-five new buildings in progress of completion.

In the midst of these industrial elements we see emerging other civilizing and happifying elements — Religion, Science, and Letters. Churches for religious worship are being built — a wholesome system of Education has been perfected, and as the legitimate result of these benign influences, Order, which is "Heaven's first law" is visible and supreme everywhere.

Something of that optimism had spilled over to mingle with the optimism the young Sisters had brought, and on the first day after their arrival they wrote in their account book the first expenditure under the date, November 12, 1863: "$335.00 for textbooks." It is not hard to hear the pioneers saying to one another that first morning when sunlight broke over their new world: "The first thing we must do is to order books."

There were 124 Atchison Catholic families to serve. They had helped to build the convent school. One festival had netted $250[4] and now the building stood hopefully there out of a tangle of hazelbrush, above a lane that led down through the trees to Commercial Street and Mr. Dolan's store.

In the city and its surrounding farms, there was interest if not total approval. There were families like the Dolans and O'Keefes, the Glancys and Robinsons who took the proprietary interest of those who understand. The O'Keefe children had swung on the ropes and beams of the new convent under construction during the summer evenings. One of them, Sister Hildegard, prefaced her manuscript history years later:

The honor of attempting to tell the story was confided to the writer not as a reward of any superior skill or ability, but rather on account of her close relationship with the institution from childhood. She had watched the laying of its foundation, the rising of its walls, and had often enjoyed a swing from its beams, using the ropes and pulleys of the workmen, which older or more ingenious companions had improvised into swings. It was the writer's privilege, too, at the age of seven years, to be numbered among the pupils of the "Old Convent," at the very outset and thus especially to be brought into touch with the actual founders.

The Dolan family was on guard from the first, Mr. Dolan himself carrying baskets of groceries to the convent until enterprising postulants arrived who were not yet bound by enclosure and who could be sent with bonnet and basket down the hazelbrush lane to the store.

There were others who helped, in rather wonderful ways. There was no furniture in the house, except for the seven new beds. The Sisters ate their first meals off packing boxes until one day when Mary Barry, the aunt of the O'Keefe children, came to the back door with something and saw dishes being washed in a pan set on boxes. The result was that her nephew, Eugene Barry, was dispatched to carry Miss Barry's own dining room table into the Sisters' convent.

None of these small details reached the wider public. Instead, the *Champion* announced with all the dignity of John J. Ingalls' pen:

The first session of St. Scholastica's Academy for young ladies will begin on the 1st Monday of December. This Institution is situated in this city, on the corner of Second and Division Streets, near the Catholic Church. It is under the care of the Sisters of St. Benedict, and the patronage of the Rt. Rev. J. B. Miege, Bishop of Leavenworth. All communication relative to the Institution should be addressed to Sister Ehrentrude Wolters, O.S.B., Directress.[5]

School opened and the young ladies came. There were forty-three day students and one boarder named Minnie Wright. The Sisters had their problems; five of them did not speak English as well as they would have liked. Many of the children were non-Catholic and it must have been hard for Mother Evangelista to refrain from teaching the faith to them. But the *Champion* faithfully reported on December 10:

The female academy of St. Scholastica under the care of the Sisters of St. Benedict and the patronage of Rt. Rev. Bishop Miege, is in successful operation. The discipline is parental; the course of instruction is comprehensive and thorough; the number of pupils is large and rapidly increasing. Every arrangement to secure the comfort and health of the scholars has been made, and the institution is one of incalculable advantage to a new community like ours.

Some of the scholars were very small. There was little Mary O'Keefe, who would become one of the school's great teachers and the convent's great women. Some came a distance from the country in the early cold morning. Bridget Glancy, left inside the convent by her father long before school opened, is reported to have gone to sleep in the warmth and literally to have fallen into school the first day when the inside door was unlocked.

Life outside the convent moved on briskly. Two days before school opened that December 1, the *Atchison Champion* had printed the Gettysburg Address, given two weeks previous, on

November 19. The Indian summer had changed to bitter wintei and the snow was high. Then a strange battle broke out.

On December 24, an author using an interesting pseudonym wrote the editor:

Probably because your attention has been so entirely occupied by the improvements going on in the business part of the city, you have neglected or forgotten to notice a new building which, even if it is some distance from Commercial Street, is notwithstanding as creditable to the originators and as much an ornament to our young town, as any yet erected within its corporate limits.

I refer to the new Convent, a large and tasteful edifice on Second Street near the Catholic Church, and to be, or already occupied by the "Sisters of Charity," as a girls' school. This institution, with St. Benedict's College, will give great educational advantages to city and country, will add to the diffusion of intelligence and create a higher and purer standard of morals in the community. With well informed people, the character of schools of that Order is too well known and appreciated to require a word of approval.

Before the Sisters of Charity any one, whatever may be his or her individual religious belief, well must feel a reverence which a sceptred monarch would fail to evoke. In the plague-stricken city, on the blood-stained battlefield, by the deathbed of the fallen outcast, and in the cold and cheerless apartment of poverty, she is sure to be found as a ministering angel to smoothe the pillow of the dying, ease the pang of the sufferer, and relieve the necessities of the needy. Here is no negative good, no charitable parade for popular applause but an active, unostentatious, ceaseless career of benevolence. Her whole life is one continued sermon.

> Sisterhoods of pity,
> Sisterhoods for ever going
> Through the dark and winding street,
> With their dark robes meekly flowing
> To their mercy-winged feet,
> Ever free and open handed
> Giving to who e'er demanded.

Then the writer identified himself as a non-Catholic by concluding:

Ever true to their well-earned title of "friends of the poor," angelic women, though in your religion a heretic, I bow with lowly reverence before your noble and unselfish character.

Signed, "Imprimatur"

35

"Imprimatur" had called upon all he knew of Sisterhoods, borrowing generously from records set in the United States by Daughters of Charity, Sisters of Charity, Ursulines, and Sisters of Mercy to champion the seven people struggling for educational survival and linguistic competence. Of St. Walburga's march in the night, 1100 years previous, to the bedside of a sick German girl he knew nothing, but there seems something beautiful in the fact that he linked all Sisters in his compliment to these few.

The column called for editorial comment: "We have on several occasions," the editor remarked in the same issue, "called public attention to the beautiful edifice mentioned by our intelligent and most welcome correspondent." He went on to say that the tribute was worthily made to "these noble women who repeat in a sordid age the pious deeds of those who were first at the cross and last at the grave of Our Blessed Lord."

The eloquence of "Imprimatur" and of the editor for the Sisters was not universal. The same issue, December 24, slapped the paper for having mentioned the school at all, a writer signed "Protestant" holding that

The times seem rather inauspicious for the American press to give particular prominence to the efforts of convents . . . in the cause of education. This age is purely American . . . We are Protestants; Americanism is Protestantism . . . Catholicism in attempting to impart education . . . must teach men how not to think and also indoctrinate them with Protestantism. It is a contradiction in terms. Education with all its adjuncts is Protestantism. In fact, Protestantism is education itself.

The rest of the paper interestingly revealed that the weather was detestable with hail and snow, that there had been no mail east of St. Joseph for two weeks, and that to cross the Missouri on ice was safe.

By January 7, the weather was twenty-four degrees below zero and there was an answer for "Imprimatur," his opponent stating that Catholics, as dogmatists, "shackle thought." Two weeks later, "Imprimatur" was back saying that freedom of thought is the prerogative of the human being, but one which is "ever restrained, hedged around by laws, customs, and necessities; yet never more so in Catholic than in Protestant communities." He went on to say that Catholic education has prepared minds in "every field of philanthropy, science, and art for the benefit of our race."

On January 28, someone named "College" entered the fray, but only for one appearance. He said that the man signing himself "Protestant" is not Protestant at all but an infidel, that "no good ever comes out of controversy," but that blunders such as "Protestant" makes cannot pass unnoticed in the nineteenth century. He challenged the assertions that the Church fetters minds and concluded: "Herewith I stop and shall not answer one word more, no matter what he may say."

The battle between the two non-Catholics continued until March 10. "Imprimatur" noted, March 3, that the ignorance and barbarism ascribed to the Middle Ages were not the fault of the Church but came from causes she could not remove. Indeed, he said, she was the guardian and protector of education and he did not find through history that Protestantism had improved morals.

"Protestant" increased in bitterness and finally stopped with closing remarks on March 10. The St. Patrick's Day issue was happily free of altercation. The Atchison papers themselves never explained why the controversy ended. Perhaps the story which an elderly Atchison resident remembered hearing contains the answer.

Word came sometime that winter that the city mayor and prominent citizens, moved by the paper battle or not, had decided to hold a meeting to determine whether the Sisters should stay. The seven Sisters held their own council. Before their visitors could hold the meeting, they issued written invitations to them, inviting them to visit their school.

The day arrived and the interested Atchison citizens came, with their wives. Mother Evangelista and her Sisters displayed their textbooks and needlework. They had plans to teach Atchison girls to read and write, to play musical instruments, to do fine needlework, to paint and fire china. Several of the Sisters were musicians.[6] One was a good violinist. They played and sang for the visitors.

They took their callers through that part of the tiny school which was not *clausura*. They explained their hopes, which with the cooperation of Atchison people would materialize. The guests were sincerely delighted and lost all fear. Then Mother said, "We have one more room to show you." And she led them to a place where a buffet supper had been prepared.[7]

All during the preparations for the visit and the battle in the papers, the Sisters had prayed the Litany of the Blessed Virgin every day that they might be permitted to stay in Atchison and that they would grow in number. Their first feast of St. Benedict in Atchison dawned on serene days, the danger over, the bitterness of the few gone. Spring moved into the city early. On March 31 a train of fifty wagons left Atchison for the West. April made up, said the observant *Champion*, "for the vile, intolerable November weather." By May 19, "the prairies assumed a beautiful green, the flowers and shrubbery were in bloom, and trees donning their summer dresses."

The first school year in Atchison was nearly over.

1. The Patrocinium of Mary, established by Benedict XII, was held in the Papal States on the third Sunday of November and in other countries at a date designated by the Bishop, says the *Catholic Encyclopedia*. The United States must have concurred with the Papal States, for the third Sunday of November fell on November 16, in 1863, and in establishing November 11 as the date of the pioneers' arrival this date has been helpful.

2. Sister Hildegard O'Keefe, *Manuscript History*.

3. The Prior wrote his letter of petition on July 11, 1863, feast of the Solemnity of St. Benedict. He said: "I have begun to build a Sisters' house. Up to now, we had no school for girls, because we had no building. If it were not absolutely necessary to build a house, I would not have undertaken this difficult task. I feel responsible before God, to dare all to bring this undertaking to completion and all the more now, when so many fathers have died in battle, when so many children have become orphans. If we do not look after them, and instruct them in our holy religion, they will be lost to the church." (Photostatic copy in St. Benedict's Abbey Archives.)

4. "The Catholic Festival for the benefit of the convent will be held on Tuesday evening. Admission 50 cents; Children 25 cents," said the *Champion*, Oct. 29, 1863. The issue of November 5 announced the result.

5. The convent Archives have no extant correspondence with Bishop Miege. The arrangement to bring the Sisters to Atchison from Minnesota must have been made by oral contact with Prior Augustine.

6. The second entry in their account book was $352.70, for a piano.

7. Interview with Mrs. Agnes Robinson Cawley, Summer, 1960, whose mother was one of the early students.

MOTHER EVANGELISTA

While the verbal battle had raged in the papers, and the winter had raged outside, there had been a good deal of joy in the convent. The Sisters had received their very first postulant, Mary Bradley, of County Tyrone, Ireland, at the close of their first month of school, December 27. They had had their first Christmas. They had risen at midnight for Matins, and the *Stille Nacht* had been sung for the first St. Scholastica Christmas. It would be sung for ninety-nine more consecutive years in the community's first century, always in the tongue for which the notes had been composed.

In the spring two happy events occurred. On February 10, the first feast of St. Scholastica in the new city, Sister Scholastica Duerr made the first profession of vows to be spoken by a Benedictine sister there. And on May 8, Barbara Moser was received into the novitiate. The younger sister of Sister Gregoria, she had been baptized in 1847 in Pennsylvania by that rugged friend of Abbot Wimmer, Henry Lemke.[1] Now an Irish-born and an American-born candidate formed the first novitiate of the granddaughter house of Bavaria.

In August of 1864, Abbot Boniface Wimmer visited. He liked what he saw and wrote to Rome:

Last fall seven Benedictine Sisters arrived here from Minnesota. Across from the Priory they have a neat convent which was built under Father Prior's direction. Their boarding school has twelve girls from the best families in the State, and forty-two day pupils from the town. They lead exemplary lives.[2]

Their lives included a few details of which he did not approve, however. "When they started this foundation," continued the Abbot with some spirit, "a Father who believes that he has a special mission to reform the Order influenced them to rise at midnight, to recite the whole Office in choir, and to abstain from meat. . . . I explained to them that this Father has no faculties from Rome to make new Statutes and counselled them to return to their former observance." Although the old rigor was removed, something of its spirit stayed always and the first Sisters left a great bravery as their gift to those who followed.

The Kansas elements helped. Both cold and heat were severe and the prayer traditional then for the putting on of shoes took on particular significance: "Oh Jesus, I will walk in the way of Thy commandments and of obedience. With patience and silence, I will endure heat and cold, hunger and thirst after Thy holy example."[3]

There had been heat and cold by August of 1864. There had been hunger and thirst. There had been the establishment of community patterns which would last a century: the cutting of a piece of bread at the beginning of each meal into three small pieces to remind one of the Trinity, the daily Our Father and Hail Mary for the Sister next to die.

The seven founders had founded a home.

They were themselves of divergent backgrounds. Sister Gregoria Moser, twenty-seven, of New York, was a musician. Never strong, she was yet to live longest of all, dying in 1923 after having been confined to her room for eighteen years before her death. In the end, having received Holy Communion and being enjoined not to rise for Mass, she asked that her door be left open so that she could attend Mass from the second floor. She died during Mass on the feast of the Sacred Heart.

There was Sister Amanda Meier, twenty-six, of Altdorf, Baden, for a time subprioress and novice-mistress; Sister Scholastica Duerr, twenty-two, tailoress, tall and thin, the first to establish the long tradition of making religious habits for the Abbey novices. There was Sister Dominica Massoth, first novice-mistress.

There were Sisters Adelaide Lejal and Ehrentrude Wolters, who both resumed secular life after a little more than three years of pioneering. It was said that either one or both were musicians who played for the public at the convent's first reception of the mayor and Atchison citizens and that one or both heard comments on their "wasting their talents in a convent." A letter in the Abbey Archives from a brother of Sister Adelaide asks Prior Augustine to help her return to the convent since she is "so young," and oral tradition is that she led an exemplary life in works of Christian charity. Sister Ehrentrude, too, used her experience to do good, going to teach in a school in Minnesota.[4] Both of them spoke English a little better than the others and somehow allowed themselves to drift apart from the group. Their places were in a sense taken by Sister Boniface Bantle and Sister Gertrude Kapser, who also came from Minnesota and who stayed.

Mother Evangelista herself, if the picture in the convent first corridor is true, had a small face not unusually beautiful but very strong, with eyes that seem to have taken the measure of things. The only Sister living in 1962 who had entered under her rule, Sister Luitgard, remembered only that Mother was kind, that she did not say much. Sister Stella Slattery, who had also remembered her well, liked to tell of Mother's way of settling arguments. She would say to one of the disputants, "You be quiet." And to the other, "You give in." That rendered the victor humble and the loser obedient, and restored harmony.

For a Kansas sister in a world of new opportunity she had a great sense of the first reason for her being. She could tirelessly comb the countryside beseeching alms for her school and her convent but her motives sound like St. Gertrude's and her diary could have been written at any of the great saint-making convents. In a letter to a former fellow-Sister at St. Joseph, Minnesota, she wrote:

Please very often ask for me the intercession of Mary and Joseph that their Divine Son may ever be with me, especially in my Lutheran Kansas, where one does not as in St. Joseph enjoy little innocent children, but a wild unbelieving youth. Therefore you must recommend us daily to the Hearts of Jesus and Mary by means of the prayers you daily send heavenward for all heretics and unbelievers, especially for the poor Kansas children.[5]

Her battle to manage the English language fast enough may have partly conditioned her view of the wild, unbelieving youth, but there was another very real reason. Atchison children in 1863 and 1864 were often children whose fathers were in service or constantly on call to guard against local violence. The days were nervous even for adults.

She had no particularly romantic view of religious life, but she knew its foundations and its real beauty. The rest of that letter to the Sister she had so loved in Minnesota read:

One thing I ask of you, never forget to show great courage under every cross and suffering, but give your younger sisters in religion the good example, and then you may hope for great consolation and everlasting beatitude beyond the grave. Oh how beautiful it will be when in Paradise in the presence of Our Holy Father St. Benedict and our dear Mother Scholastica we will all meet the deceased Sisters of our Holy Order. No eye has seen or ear heard what is prepared for those who carry the heavy yoke of the Master to the end. The Bell calls for the Examen, so I recommend you to God's protection and that of St. Joseph. Your sister in religion, Evangelista, OSB, of the perpetual Adoration.

There was a postscript. "Pray often for me on your knees."

By 1865, when this letter was written, the heavy yoke surely included the problem of poverty. Finances would haunt Mother Evangelista until the end, but she conquered them by begging and by saving, and she seems never to have made them paramount. She never quite caught up with them, but neither did they ever quite conquer her, and they do not haunt that revelation of her inner life, her small diary.

The Abbey across the way was itself in financial rigor. The surrounding country was not wealthy. The scheme to pay the debt with a society of families contributing fifty cents a month was impossible. Prior Augustine had told Mother that the Missions-Verein of King Ludwig of Bavaria would help. So she began, March 26 of 1864, a series of letters to that society which would continue as long as she was in office. They sound like Orations a little, beginning with the reason for confidence, containing the statement of need, and closing in the name of the Lord Christ.

In the long story of what one nation has done for another, no one has probably counted what the Mission Society of Bavaria did to keep Mount St. Scholastica in existence, but year by year in small but steady sums the help came. Mother Evangelista's first letter, to the chairman of the society, read:

St. Scholastica Academy
Atchison City, Kansas
March 26, 1864

Most Honored Mr. Lebling:

The Rev. P. Augustine told me that you are a great friend of the Benedictines and that you are doing much for Missions. For this reason I dare to ask you to be our intercessor with the Missionsverein. Every beginning is difficult but the beginning of a new Convent is especially difficult since usually everything is wanting. That is the condition here. I would certainly not have the courage to ask for anything if the need were not so urgent. Trusting in the words of Our Lord: "Ask and you shall receive," I am sending this petition to you and ask most humbly to help us in any way you can.

Respectfully,
Your devoted servant,
M. Evangelista Kremmeter
Prioress, O.S.B.
St. Scholastica's Convent

The other letter, to the entire committee, spells out in more detail the need for furniture, utensils, piano, chapel equipment. At her desk in some corner of St. Joseph's, the first superior marshalled the only world she knew to help her. In sums of three or four hundred dollars annually, the Society responded.

On her own part, Mother Evangelista undertook begging tours. There are records of collections taken in Atchison, Seneca, and Richfountain, Missouri, a settlement on the way to St. Louis generous with small donations and with vocations. The account book tells, too, of donations from friends: the Rev. Father Kuhls, that great founder of St. Margaret's Hospital, in July of 1867 gave seven dollars. A note of January, 1868, says interestingly, "$49.75 by strangers"; and October 4 of the same year, "$50.00 by a stranger from California." Families of the Sisters and the periodic appearance of the name "James Kennedy," the carpenter who guarded the convent on its first night and stayed to help it until he died, also decorate the early books with devotion.

On its own part, the community kept to an economy program.

When shoelaces broke, they were sewed together. The cook saved a spoonful of sugar aside every day for a Sunday pie. There was butter only for the chaplain's breakfast and for the students. One has the feeling that had the hardy Father Thomas Bartl and his successors known this, there would have been no butter bill at all except for the meals of the little girls who filled the boarders' dining room with their morning silence and their noonday chatter. The Sisters had black coffee and soldiers' crackers for breakfast. The boarders had buns or bread.

The furniture is interesting to contemplate. Each sister had a narrow wooden bed, a chair, and a home-made chest of drawers. The latter was a cracker box which stood on end and had a cross division forming upper and lower compartments for clothing, shoes and slippers. A tin basin crowned the top, while a gathered calico curtain covered the contents. The mattresses, like those used by people in the surrounding country, were home-made containers of shredded corn husks, and one of the interesting treats of the year was to get a trip to some farmhouse to pick those husks. Rosaries were made with seeds from the water-lilies in Sugar and Bean Lakes.

There was a certain grace to it all. Daily life had the dignity of being codified in the custom book which Mother Evangelista wrote herself, based on Eichstätt but touched by Kansas plains and skies and ways of living. It had the dignity of being enclosed in a prayer routine and of being considered very important. And there were light touches and glad occasions.

Festivals at St. Benedict's parish were gala affairs, the Atchison *Champion* reporting that on August 25, 1864, a two-day fair would open for the Sisters' Academy with a brass band to play each night. The band could be heard for twenty-five cents and the supper could be purchased for another twenty-five cents. And while the Sisters did not attend the fair, they could hear the band across the street in the pleasant summer air.

In the same early days, August, 1865, one of the convent's most interesting postulants entered — a widow named Mrs. Carey who received the name Sister Mary Ann, who took up a life of humor, prayer, and knitting. She was sixty years old, and no one who knew her ever forgot her. She brought her savings of $200.

The academy's embroidery department began making beautiful things, which swelled the family income a little; the boarders' section of the convent contributed some to the fund for living and filled the house with interesting people to teach. And when the struggle between debits and credits became too uneven, Mr. Dolan had a way of knowing and came up the hazelbrush lane laden with supplies.

The school was growing. There were twenty-seven boarders when it opened its second term and a large day school. It was decided to separate the two groups. The plan must have had some good features but it divided the students, doubled the teaching work, and somehow separated the interests of the Sisters a little. Sister Adelaide had charge of boarders; Sister Ehrentrude of the day students. More teachers were needed. Two new novices had indeed received the habit in February of 1865, the expense account "for serge" brightening the ledger amid the wood and butcher bills. But they could not yet teach and in April, 1865, Mother Willibalda came from Minnesota, bringing with her Sister Gertrude Kapser, twenty-six years old, from Bavaria, and Sister Bernarda Auge, Canadian-born, twenty-five years old.

It was on this trip that convent history touched national history in a particular way. Mother Willibalda and the two Sisters, reaching Hannibal, Missouri, found the city preparing for a massive procession. Sister Hildegard records:

On their way the Sisters were detained at Hannibal, Missouri, for two days, the funeral cortege of President Lincoln having reached that city at the same time as the Sisters, which event afforded them the sad privilege of attending the obsequies of the martyred President. In what these ceremonies consisted we do not know, but they must have been impressive, for the event was a life-long remembrance to them.

It is hard to verify this story. Accounts of the funeral cortege westward do not mention Hannibal, but a Rock Island route from Chicago to Springfield might have taken a detour through Hannibal, and the story seems too important to be wrong. All northern cities held some ceremony on April 20, the day of formal funeral ceremonies in Washington before the body of

Lincoln was brought West. The Sisters reached Atchison on May 11.

When Mother Willibalda returned to Minnesota after perhaps a month, she took with her as companion seven-year-old Nora Cotter, a boarder whose mother had died and whom the Sisters had taken with her sister to educate. The father had given the convent a small farm in return for the care of his children. When little Nora returned after a year she spoke more German than English. Years later she enlivened novitiate recreations by recalling her account of her first confession in English. To escape the fruit of some misdoing, she had told a falsehood. When time came for confession, she tried to find a way to make the deed sound less wretched, but the German "Ich habe gelogen" was relentlessly clear. She turned with relief to the stranger tongue.

Sister Bernarda returned to Minnesota at the end of the year, only to die of tuberculosis, January 28, 1868. *The Northwest Chronicle* said of her:

The fatal disease which brought her to her grave was consumption, which she contracted some years ago, while laboring for the glory of God, in a convent of her order lately established in Kansas. Sister Bernarda spent her youthful days in St. Paul where she was known as a most exemplary, pious Christian maiden.

October of 1865 brought two other persons to Atchison — Sister Boniface Bantle, twenty-six, native of Wuerttemberg, professed four years, and eleven-year-old Lena Northman. Sister Boniface, coming down the Mississippi from St. Coud, went all the way to St. Louis to bring to Atchison for education the small sister of Fathers Ulric, Bede, and Wolfgang of St. John's Abbey. On the cross-country boat which brought them up the Missouri to St. Joseph, the only food served on Friday was liver. Sister Boniface persuaded the conscientious little passenger to eat something by saying, "Eat it, child; it isn't meat. It's liver."

Sister Boniface died March 4, 1897, of pneumonia. Had she lived four months longer she would have seen the child she brought up the Missouri elected Mother Superior of the community.

The year of 1866 and 1867 brought the greatest sorrow. Sometime that year Sister Ehrentrude, says the chronicle briefly,

found an excuse to go East on business, accompanied Lena
Northman as far as St. Louis, laid off her religious dress, and
returned to the "world." Sister Adelaide soon followed her example. The year was a critical one and its whole picture cannot
be reconstructed. In May, Mother Evangelista had received into
the community Sister Augustine Short of St. Mary's, Pennsylvania, who presided over the Academy for fourteen years. As a
novice she had been Mother Benedicta's companion to Eichstätt.[6] She earned highest praise from the *Champion* for her
conduct of the school and with a Miss Horan, a graduate of
Notre Dame College, Indiana, as the convent's first history says,
set up a partial high school course. Whether her coming and
the changes it involved affected the two earlier Sisters or
whether she came because they were wavering, no one knows,
and Mother Evangelista told no one's struggles. One scans in
vain her diary for particulars. Its first entry, January 2, 1866,
says only:

Tuesday. Lord, you know that I love You. I shall gladly suffer all
without complaining. The love of Jesus keeps me from fearfulness.
On March 21, 1857, I made my profession at St. Mary's. Abbot
Wimmer.

The entries of that year's early months deal only with her own
effort:

Jan. 11. Man must fight with himself much and for a long time, before he can overcome himself perfectly and learn to direct his whole
inclination to God. Jan. 12: The subject of my examen shall be often
during the day to recall the presence of God. Jan. 17: How have you
observed your solemn vows? How the reverence toward the Holy
Rule? March 5: I desire that everybody be silent about my faults;
that everybody interpret everything I do in the best light; that no
one refuse me a service; but, how do I treat other people? March 7:
Wherever I turn myself I find Thee, O my God, present. Grant that
I may not offend Thy holy Presence in thoughts, words, or actions.

From April to the end of the year, there is more specific concern
for the community:

April 5: St. Joseph, my chosen patron, pray for my spiritual children.
April 26: My Jesus, come to my aid. Dec. 13: I have a great fear
that my mind unaccustomed to tribulations might sink into the depths

of despair. Dec. 15: The care of souls is a difficult and frightening office. Dec. 16: I felt too downhearted to write. Dec. 17: I made the resolution to bear patiently every hard word for Jesus' sake. Dec. 21: When, O my Jesus, shall I behold Thy beautiful face? Dec. 22: My dear Mother, thou hast to save me. Dec. 23: Who shall separate me from the love of Christ.

In the spring of 1868 an event of unusual sweetness occurred. Bridget Glancy, the convent's first day student, entered the community on February 29. She was the daughter of Michael Glancy, whose name occurs and recurs for gifts of house and lot, money, food, and kindness. Her parents had dedicated their first little girl to the Blessed Virgin. Now she entered the convent.

But more was to come. Her best friend, Lena Northman, now a little more than thirteen years old, had been haunting Mother Evangelista for permission to follow her. She had permission from her mother in far away St. Louis. She had memorized the Magnificat. She was quite ready. In an absent moment, perhaps, in answer to the question, "Can I enter on St. Joseph's day?" Mother Evangelista had said, "Yes. Yes." So on the morning of that day, March 19, when the Sisters and girls left the tiny chapel to go to their respective dining rooms, Lena Northman followed the Sisters. In the refectory, she prayed as all did, and her former classmate Postulant Bridget seeing her, protested the impropriety of the green and white uniform amid all the black. Mother Evangelista came to the end of the table. "You are in the wrong dining room, child."

"Oh no, Mother. I have entered."

She was persuaded to return to the Academy until noon when, with the customary formalities, she returned to stay.

The two postulants were clothed in the habit on August 15 of the same year, Bridget Glancy receiving the name Sister Agnes. To Lena Northman Mother gave the name Aloysia. Both novices, so vitally part of the convent's first years, lived long lives. Until the last days of her own, Mother Aloysia would love to tell how Sister Agnes, "tried to keep me in line." And Sister Agnes whom Michael Glancy and his wife had dressed in blue for Mary in country days in wild Kansas, died August 13, 1932, and was buried on the feast of the Assumption.

In autumn, 1868, Father Louis Mary Fink, now Prior of St. Benedict's, bought a small two-story frame house near the convent. It was a grocery store, the lower story of brick and the upper of frame painted brown. It became known as the Brown School, the first real parochial school the Sisters had. Sister Agnes, only two weeks a novice, taught the boys out of the wisdom of her eighteen years and the lessons learned from her father and brothers. Sister Dominica Massoth, one of the original pioneers, taught the girls.

Sister Aloysia waited a little longer for public performance. Mother Evangelista wrote in her diary: "On May 27, 1869, Sister Aloysia played for the first time in the new church." By that time the Abbey's brick church across the way had arisen and a second era had begun.

Most of the convent's stable patterns were set. The decade of the sixties was over. Growth and change, loss, poverty, faith, courage and humor had marked it, and the lines of the future were ineffaceably projected. While concerning itself with subsistence and with progress in its own ventures, the convent had cultivated a largeness of view. Mother Evangelista proudly gave $10 to the new Abbey church and wrote an occasional $5.00 for alms in her account book. She had anchored her small convent in the spacious life of the church. The heads of her Sisters were bowed at the close of each meal, in imitation of St. Scholastica's effective prayer, and according to a custom so old at Eichstatt that no one knew who started it: "O my God, I beseech Thee to reward, comfort, and deliver all Christian souls, to give to the faithful departed peace and rest; to grant the whole Christian world peace and union, and to our Holy Father and us all life everlasting." One can never relive or even gather all of the past, but the things that matter most can often be found.

Abbot Boniface, on his visit in August, 1864, had worried about the health of the Sisters. In 1866 he petitioned and received permission from Rome for them to substitute the Little Office of the Blessed Virgin for the Divine Office, a compromise he considered absolutely necessary. Intended to be only temporary, it really took from them their most precious possession and caused them to have to struggle hard to claim their very status as Benedictines. All of this was ahead, though. Now the decade was closing over a convent from an ancient tradition in an old world trying to keep essentials alive in their service of God in the new.

1. A parish priest whose Benedictine vows Abbot Boniface received, Henry Lemke came to Kansas in 1855, the first Benedictine in the state He had a short but interesting career here. His story is told in *Kansas Monks*, and he is depicted in fresco above the altar of the Abbey Church.

2. This letter is quoted by Felix Fellner, O.S.B., *op. cit.*, p. 29.

3. From the notebook of Sister Luitgard Mengwasser, O.S.B., who remembered the old days.

4. Sister Pauline Anderson, "Early Memories of the Convent," 1945, Manuscript, MSS Archives.

5. The letter, dated May 31, 1865, is in the Archives of St. Joseph, Minnesota. Mother Evangelista had the spirit which Bishop Miege had hoped for Kansas missionaries to have when he wrote Abbot Boniface in 1857: "My great hope is to see before many years your venerable Order in the highest degree of prosperity in Kansas . . . Kansas will be an immense field for missionary labor . . . The number of lost sheep cannot be counted; and the evil will increase daily unless Our Lord sends me true laborers for His vineyard." Letters of Jan. 6 and June 11, 1857. St. Vincent's Abbey Archives.

6. Sister Regina Baska, *History of the Congregation of St. Scholastica* (Washington, D.C.: Catholic University of America Press, 1935), p. 82.

THE 1870'S

The Franco-Prussian War was in progress, grasshoppers were taking over Kansas fields, the panic of 1873 was spreading its shadow over the nation, young girls in new Benedictine habits were measuring up to classroom responsibilities, and little girls in green dresses and white pinafores were going to classroom, chapel, and dining room, learning arithmetic and McGuffey's Readers, music and German and Latin and manners. Remembering the procession, Sister Hildegard was to comment later: "And an attractive bunch they were."

The community added only fourteen new members during the seventies, but their memory is in benediction: Sister Benedicta Rudroff and Sister Mechtildis Neuner, Richfountain, Missouri; Sister Walburga Weber, Bohemia; Sister Angela O'Gorman and Sister Antonia Schmees, St. Louis; Sister Joseph Jacobs, Prussia; Sister Frances Kraemer, Vienna; Sister Patricia Dore, Limerick, Ireland; Sister Philomena Livings and Sister Cecilia Murphy, New York; Sister Hildegard O'Keefe and Sister Agatha Robinson, Atchison; Sister Rosalia Krieger, Baltimore; and Sister Edith Stein of the convent's first outside mission, Seneca, Kansas.

The Academy prospered. The festival of July 2, 1873, was anticipated by the Atchison *Champion* thus: "The worthy Sisters of St. Scholastica Academy are certainly in league with the elements." And the next report said of the scene:

Just dark enough to show off the handsome illuminations and just light enough to dispense with overshow; just warm enough to enjoy the entertainment without toiling with a fan, and just cool enough

51

to keep back perspiration and watch the starry canopy overhead. It was comfortable and magnificently grand.

The grandeur included an opening address, a drama entitled "No Cure Could Pay," a farce named "A Precious Pebble," and the valedictory for the school year by Elizabeth Sheehan. Taking part in the evening's starlight program as Faith, Hope and Charity, were M. Ostertag, Jennie Stringfellow, and A. Hurd. The *Champion* eulogized:

Saint Scholastica Academy is a modest unpretentious unit if ever one existed. . . . Sister Augustine, the directress of the Studies, is one of the most finished and ripe scholars there is in the West. . . . The Mother Superior possesses one of the most amiable and kind dispositions that can be described and is one of the most perfect ladies we have ever met. Sister Aloysia, the teacher of music, is one of the finest musicians in the country.

The school was a lively one. Its annual commencements were civic occasions. One of them, 1874, saw Alice Dolan receive the premium for encouragement; Lizzie O'Gorman, fourth class, for penmanship and geography; Maggie Normile, third class, for geography; Fannie Glancy, third, for grammar; Nora Cotter, third, for reading; and Leslie Shaughnessy a kind of grand prize for grammar.

It was true that the Academy had prospered. On March 19, 1873, it had been incorporated as an educational institution under the statutes of the laws of Kansas.[1] But not everything was as bright as the *Champion* saw it. "Did you get any more scholars in the Academy or are you nearly without any?" Prior Louis Fink wrote on February 6, 1871, to Mother Evangelista from Chicago, where he had gone to recuperate from illness. "Don't be troubled about the future. God will do His part — only let us do ours and everything will turn out well."[2] The rest of the letter, interestingly enough, advises Mother to give works of penance to a Sister wavering in her vocation. One is awed to learn that the Sister he mentions lived to a long and happy old age. "When one is busy for God," the Prior said, "she cannot be worried by the Evil One."

By 1872, the community had purchased some new lots and money was needed to reduce the debt. Mother Evangelista wrote the friendly Mr. Lebling of the Mission Society. Her need, which seems so small now, was huge then. Schools where children would not hear of their faith were to her corrupting schools. She said:

April 15, 1872

Very Honored Mr. Lebling:

Confiding in your compassionate heart, I dare to submit a most pressing request. I am writing that, by the wish of the Rt. Rev. Abbot Boniface Wimmer of St. Vincent, Pa. With a heavy heart and hesitatingly I am asking if there would not be some hope that the St. Ludwigsverein would give us some help, even if it be small. I am almost certain, that if Your Honor has a few dollars to spare, you will give them to a poor Benedictine Convent. We are now twenty Sisters and the present building is too small because we have a number of boarders with us of whom many pay very little for their tuition. We do this in order to keep them from going to the corrupting schools and to give them a Christian education. There is also a debt on the buildings, due to the purchase of some lots of land and which we have not yet been able to pay. It is hard for me to be such a persistent beggar, but for the greater honor of God, I am asking again for your help, without which we cannot carry on. We are not forgetting what you have done for us in the past and we count you our greatest benefactor without whom we would not have received help from the Missionsverein. In the name of my community, I promise to remember you in our daily prayers, especially at the Holy Sacrifice of the Mass. In the hope that you grant my request and send us help soon, I am

Your Honor's most devoted servant in Christ,

Evangelista, O.S.B., Prioress

Not only Mother Evangelista, but Prior Oswald Moosmuller (who had succeeded coadjutor-Bishop Fink), was pleading vehemently for a new building on a new location.[3] Prior Oswald thought the Sisters should be across the town from the Abbey, and he said so. They were now too far from the business district, too close to the parish church, too distracted with reasons for violating enclosure. In fact, commented the stern Prior to Abbot Boniface, these Sisters did not seem to know what it meant to be Sisters.

But Mother Evangelista had not dared yet to hope for self-contained grounds farther away, with chapel facilities adequate for convent and school, without dependence on the parish-Abbey church. She was trying only to do the possible, to add to the old building and to pay current expenses. She was a good letter-writer, able to communicate total viewpoints as well as needs, to make subtle references to sacrifice and to appeal to highest motives. Her account to the Mission Committee of poverty and Kansas fever among the Sisters, on February 13, 1874, concluded:

May the Lord be praised for this! I have lately made a cursory survey of the cost of the planned building making it as simple as possible. It would need $3000. That took all the courage out of me because we still have a debt of $2000 on the old buildings. If the good Lord would send better times, we might be able to do the work next year. I trust in the word of the Lord: "Knock and it shall be opened to you; ask and you shall receive." This quotation gives me courage, to bother you again, honored gentlemen, with my begging. God reward you a thousandfold for all that we have received from you. I myself and my Sisters are offering several Communions and oral prayers for our benefactors in Munich. Though far from our home, we are equally near to God and to our loving Mother, the Church. Your kindness will forgive, honored Gentlemen, if I again come with a begging letter.

Begging for your continued favor to my poor convent in far America, I am filled with deepest gratitude.

Your devoted servant in Christ,
M. Evangelista, OSB, Prioress

The answer to the letter was another affirmative. But she spent the money not on a new building but to enlarge the parish school, explaining that the number of German settlers had steadily increased. Her tact in ascribing the reason for swallowing up the benefaction so quickly is equaled only by the dignity with which she asks for more, and by her ability to describe a Kansas winter with snow two feet high, wood priced at $500 for the season, sickness among cattle and horses. She seems to be looking out of a window as she writes:

The bad year killed the winter wheat and the sickness among the horses and cattle hurt the business in everything. Perhaps you have read in the papers about these plagues and know that it really is bad and sad to see the omnibus coming, drawn by the slow oxen. And she says bravely, "I would not dare to tell you all this if I were not convinced that your generous heart cannot get angry . . . grow not weary if I come with too much insistence." She promises the customary recompense, a novena to the Immaculate Conception and to St. Joseph for Mr. Lebling and sung High Masses for the Committee and his Honor, King Ludwig. The faithful committee continued not to grow weary and the texture of convent life went on.

Sometime in the early part of the decade, Abbot Boniface questioned the validity of previous profession ceremonies. For in a letter dated November 15, 1872, Bishop Fink asks: "What Sisters' vows did Right Rev. Abbot say to be invalid? And what reason did he give for his opinion? Let me know by letter."

The answer is not extant, but convent archives contain re-profession formulas of Mother Theresa and Sister Clara Bradley and of Sister Dominica Massoth, who had made profession at St. Cloud. It is interesting to scan the yellowed paper and to read the formula of vows made by the first Sister to enter in Atchison:

I, Sister Mary A. Clara Bradley, County Tyrone, Ireland, do hereby promise in honor of Almighty God, the most Blessed Virgin Mary, our most Blessed Father Benedict, and all the saints, poverty, chastity, obedience, and amendment of my life according to the Rules of St. Benedict, our constitutions or statutes, in the presence of God and the saints whose relics are here present and in the presence of the Rt. Rev. Lewis Maria Fink, OSB, Bishop of Eucorpia, i.p.i. Coadjutor of the Vicar Apostolic of Kansas in the presence of the Ven. Mother M. A. Evangelista Kremmeter, Prioress of this Convent and in the presence of you, Venerable Sisters, that I will persevere in this order truly believing that I will never be permitted to leave it by my own will in the name of the Father and of the Son and of the Holy Ghost.

This profession of religious vows I have made and in the presences do make in case of any defect in my profession I have made on the 10th of February, 1867. In testimony whereof I have signed this with my own hand in the Chapel of St. Scholastica's convent this ninth day of February in the year of Our Lord, 1873, on Septuagesima Sunday in the City of Atchison, Kansas.

This may have been only a conventual ceremony, for there are formulas apparently read on the next day, February 10. The wording is revised to read:

I, Sister Mary Ann Clara, do hereby promise, in honor of the Almighty God and the most Blessed Virgin Mary, our holy Father St. Benedict and all the saints poverty, chastity, obedience, and amendment of my life. According to the Rules of St. Benedict in the presence of God and the Saints whose Relics are here present and in the presence of the Venerable Mother Evangelista, Prioress of the Convent, and in the presence of you, Venerable Sisters, that I will persevere in this order truly believing that I will never be permitted to leave by my own will and that only in case if it should ever happen the Superiors of the Order were forced to expel me on account of my bad morals and faults I would be free from my vows and obligations and from leading a monastic life. I have written this with my own hand in the Chapel of St. Scholastica Convent, February 10, 1873.

The ceremony of this February 10 was accompanied by as much dignity as possible, preceded by a week's retreat and conducted according to the Pontifical.[4]

But the refrain of temporal poverty did not stay long out of the affairs of the day. The convent shared it with diocese and state. Bishop Miege himself, that fine man, was in South America in 1872 and 1873 begging for money to cut the debt on his cathedral. Bishop Fink wrote of him:

Bishop Miege is at present in Chile — from where I got a letter a couple of days ago. I wrote to him yesterday; I will try to mention you and yours especially in my next, God willing; his next move may be to Buenos Ayres — Montevideo. Rio Janeiro too if the Lord do not interpose serious difficulties. I hope you will not forget him and his mission in your prayers and will also pray for me.[5]

The state of Kansas itself was in a sorry plight. Grasshoppers had literally stripped the fields, and many families, wrote Prior Oswald to Abbot Boniface, had literally but one meal a day. Mother Evangelista, writing the long-suffering Mission Committee in April, 1875, combines her plight with the general one, saying:

April 4, 1875

Respected Committee:

It is late in the evening and I just returned from a visit to the Blessed Sacrament where I prayed for all our benefactors in Germany. . . . In my last letter I told you I would use the money sent me through Abbot Wimmer to pay off a debt. To my sorrow I

56

must confess that the plan was frustrated through a bad year of harvest and plague of locusts and worms, and a severe winter which ate up every penny that we saved.[6]

This, honored sirs, is the reason why my plans did not carry through. I was forced to use the money to buy wood and food. Every day, young strong Germans come begging, because they have had no work for months and are starving and depend on what they can get from the people, who are themselves poor. His Excellency, Bishop Fink, who celebrated the feast of St. Benedict in our chapel, told me himself that he was several weeks going around begging for the poor in Kansas. Now it looks as if the heavenly Father will punish us still longer by sending a severe frost that destroyed in a few days the greater part of the winter wheat. Now swarms of grasshoppers are eating everything up – a black mass is all that can be seen.

The farmers would gladly leave Kansas if they had enough to move and money to buy something else. The industries, too, are entirely stopped. That warns us of bad times. My poor little convent, too, suffers very much . . . About six months ago, I took in three young girls who have talents for the English and could be trained to become teachers. Of course everything has to be furnished them gratis. If we refused to take them, they might have gone wrong in this country where the faith is still so weak. It is heart-rending to see so many children who could be educated for better things, if only means were at hand.

. . . Sending you heartiest greetings through Mary, Queen of May, who will intercede for me and my benefactors, I remain very respectfully,

Your grateful servant in Christ,
M. Evangelista, O.S.B.

The Committee must have responded loyally, for February of the next year finds Mother Evangelista at her desk asking for $1200 more. Such letter-writing was not her whole life, but it was a kind of constant under-structure along with her prayers and these, said those who remembered, accumulated.

The summer of 1876 brought two events of a different nature. In the parched and blackened season of grasshoppers, Atchison observed the centennial of the nation's independence. A parade began near Ostertag's blacksmith shop with, in the words of the *Champion*, "a conglomeration of unearthly sounds that could make pandemonium ashamed." [7] The reporter continued: "Over 50 locomotives with steam up . . . every bell in the city rang the tidings that America had seen 100 years of freedom and prosperity." St. Joseph's bell atop St. Scholastica's Academy was loyally among them.

The other event was the taking of the convent's first missions — St. Ann's in Seneca and the mission school of the Assumption three and one-half miles from it.

"The convent in Seneca is named St. Ann's," Mother Evangelista wrote proudly in October to the Mission Committee, "and three and one-half miles from Seneca is the mission school of the Assumption. The name of this place is Wildcat. There were actually many wild cats around there and it is not too long ago that they were actually seen there. I am very happy to tell you about these new schools of our holy religion in this far away North America."

The Seneca people built a small convent and a schoolhouse forty feet long. Sister Dominica Massoth, the Superior, wrote cheerfully and realistically of its early days, wishing she had her Atchison desk but noting that the people were doing all they could do.[8] Those who traveled to Assumption mission school rode merrily in Mr. Rettele's wagon through the fresh countryside every Monday morning, returning Friday afternoon to spend the week-end with the town Sisters. The beauty of both missions was the zeal of the parishioners for the school and for their faith. Visitors to Seneca today are still shown the Stein home where the children gave up their room so that the Sisters could have a place to stay until the convent was finished.

Of the convent school itself the *Champion* was still saying: "Year by year this grand institution is bringing up a reputation that nothing will ever erase." And the convent announced its own educational purposes in January of 1877:

> To cultivate the heart, to form and cherish good habits, to prevent evil ones, in fine, to exercise a truly maternal care over the morals of the pupils no less than over their intellectual and physical development are paramount duties kept constantly and sacredly in view by the Sisters. Charges for tuition and board are very moderate. Terms will be furnished on application.

What the paper said was quite literally true. A certain Ellen Robinson was one of the first students, in attendance from 1863 to 1868. Tim Finnegan, a workman at the Abbey, saw

Ellen and prevailed upon the pastor of St. Benedict's parish to invite the boarders at the academy to the early summer social. The pastor did indeed invite them, but Ellen Robinson refused to come, saying: "I won't meet Tim Finnegan until I've been introduced to him." She spent the gala evening at her needlework and books and Tim's friend, the pastor, had to resort to another suggestion. When school had closed, in early July, he sent his workman Tim to the Robinson farm on an errand and advised him to ask for a drink of cold water at the back door.

Mrs. Agnes Finnegan Cawley, Ellen's oldest daughter, told the story on a visit to Sister Mary, a younger daughter of Ellen and Tim whose request for cold water was not in vain.

The years passed. Then came a new opportunity and a new era. St. Benedict's Priory was raised to the dignity of an Abbey and the Rev. Innocent Wolf chosen its first abbot on September 29, 1876. A few months later, July, 1877, a stately mansion at the south end of town was put up for sale.

1. Years later, Sister Augusta Parle, then Scholastic-Mistress assembling archive material, was to say to the Scholastics: "Today I handled the original copy of the incorporation."

2. MSS Archives.

3. See photostatic copy of Prior Oswald's letter to Abbot Boniface, St. Benedict's Abbey Archives.

4. "I will be there — God willing. You will please to have them make a good retreat of about a week, have them drilled according to the Pontifical . . . for I will follow it — and remind me of it before the feast, in case I might forget. Our Organist you will hardly get — he has gone to Chicago and may stay there." Letter of Bishop Fink, November 15, 1872. Mother must have asked for the Cathedral organist, since Sister Aloysia was among those making vows.

5. *Ibid.*

6. That Mother Evangelista, Bavarian born, saw the high-flying pests under their older, more Biblical name, suggests that the scene of bare Kansas fields held even more than its ordinary bleakness for her.

7. The *Champion*, July 8, 1876.

8. Letter from Sister Dominica to John Intfen, a pupil, August, 1876, given to the Atchison Archives by Andrew Baumgartner, nephew of Mr. Intfen.

PRICE VILLA

Environment has always been sacred to the Christian because it encloses the time and place where salvation is somehow worked out, and it tends to become almost a part of man. An entirely new era in the life of Mount St. Scholastica opened with its transplantation to a mount. Every step of history since 1877 has left some touch on some piece of wood, brick, or stone still visible there.

"Slow as was the growth of the little community, yet it was hampered by stint of space," writes its first historian with the flavor of one who remembers the grand event which changed everything. "Luckily . . . at this juncture . . . what was known as the 'Price Villa' property was put up for sale, and to the amazement of all was purchased by the Sisters for the sum of $20,000." And Sister Hildegard concludes: "This certainly was a visible act of Divine Providence who . . . had put it into the heart of Mr. John M. Price of Atchison to erect a grand mansion on a most beautiful site south of the city and surrounded with 28 acres of woodland and meadow." Divine Providence had also put into the heart of Abbot Innocent the faith to put into the heart of Mother Evangelista the courage even to think of $20,000 at one time.

Mr. Price had built the Villa in 1872 and had spent five years beautifying it. A small son had been born, had died, and had been buried there and his small grave, surrounded by a rail fence, seemed to make the place still their home and to give it an especially human significance.[1] A turn in political events made it inexpedient for the Prices to keep the home, so with

60

its spacious ground and trees, its lovely floors and stairways it came to be Mount St. Scholastica's. Convent, city, and diocese were more or less shaken with excitement at the very idea. Mother Evangelista wrote briefly and happily to the bishop.

St. Scholastica's Convent
June 30, 1877

Right Rev. Louis M. Fink, D.D.
My Lord Bishop:
Would you kindly give us your permission to purchase Price's Villa? The terms of sale would be twenty thousand ($20,000); however, M. F. Bier assures us we may confidently hope to get it for sixteen thousand ($16,000) . . . We are terribly in earnest about buying this property, but should you deem it best to withhold your consent, we shall try to be resigned. Recommending myself and my community to the Bounty of your prayers, I remain

Yours, obediently and with profound respect
M. Evangelista, OSB

The letter is in the convent Archives because the Bishop sent his answer by annotating the letter itself. Before doing so, however, he wrote another letter which drew the following reply from Mother:

July 7, 1877

JMJ
Right Rev. Louis M. Fink, D.D.
My Lord Bishop,
Your favor of yesterday is received and in reply to your question as to whether we had consulted the Rt. Rev. Abbot regarding the purchase of the Villa, I hasten to inform your Lordship that it was by his advice I wrote you on the subject, and he thinks we shall by no means let the opportunity slip, as we may never have another such offer. We have been over to look at the house and found it altogether suitable for a convent and school — far more so, than the house we live in. The distance is only two short miles and Rt. Rev. Abbot himself says, would be only ten or fifteen minutes ride. As to the money, we have had several offers, at the low rate of from six to seven per cent.

Mentally to contemplate the excited community roaming in exploratory fashion through St. Cecilia's (then Price Villa) in its youth is to think one tastes something of those years. The Bishop must have caught all the freighted adjectives and adverbs resulting from the visit, for on July 9 he gave his answer: "Well, if you are so terribly in earnest about buying this property and if you think you can pay for it honestly, I have no objection." He added: "As soon as you shall have your charter and by-laws in order before signing them officially, I would like to see them. Consult Father Abbot. LMF."

From then on, events moved rapidly. In nine days, with the help of Abbot Innocent and friends among the laity whose names still are not conclusively known, the Sisters bought the building. They set up their by-laws that very day, July 16, and held the first meeting of their board — Mother herself, Sister Theresa Moser and Sister Amanda Meier. The last Mass was celebrated that July 16 in the old convent. Then for nine days more they moved, Tim Finnegan's hayrack helping to repay what the old convent had given Ellen.

On July 26, 1877, Mass was celebrated at the new convent on its acres of beauty. Mother Evangelista recorded it in her diary: "July 26, left the old convent." The faithful Atchison *Champion* shared and reflected her enthusiasm, noting on July 20:

The Purchase of the elegant place at $20,000 is a financial stroke that the Order will be proud of. Their many friends are aiding them materially in making the payments . . . One staunch admirer and noble friend who wishes his name suppressed donating $5,000 to the enterprise.

First to say Mass in the new convent was the Rev. Raymond Daniels, O.S.B., chaplain, in a converted parlor now the Music Library of St. Cecilia's.[2] Then three weeks later, on August 17, the *Champion* published the following notice:

The Benedictine Sisters have purchased Price Villa, St. Scholastica Academy. The course of instruction embraces all the branches necessary for the acquisition of a refined and solid education.

A photograph of the new Academy with horse and buggy in spirited mood on the driveway accompanied the advertisement.

But days of poverty were ahead and the very growth which came with the new site admitted a new visitor — death.

Price Villa was beautiful but it was heated by grates and fireplaces only and, writes Sister Hildegard, "while the system was attractive and comfortable it left a large portion of the building unheated." The community needed a furnace, but it could not afford furniture for the huge mansion, and for people deeply in debt a furnace was out of the question.

Help came from a familiar source, but in an unexpected amount. James Kennedy, the carpenter who had swung his protecting lantern that night of the Sisters' arrival, gave Mother a check for $1,000, involving most of his savings. Now the community had a home that was warm. So did Mr. Kennedy, who lived to an old age occupying a small room in what had been the stable of Price Villa. When he was old and blind, Sister Benedicta Rudroff ministered to him, Sister Adelaide Cass read to him from the daily papers, and the Chaplain brought him Holy Communion.

From 1877 through 1882 Mother Evangelista solicited funds in the neighborhood and wrote frequently to the Mission Society. She speaks of four candidates who will receive the habit through help given by the society, and of the ever present need for fuel, warmer clothing, interest funds. Bishop Fink, asking the same people for help for his diocese, once closed a letter: "If you would have something to spare, I beg you to help me. In closing, I recommend to you the request of the Sisters . . ."

The very growth of the convent had made the needs urgent. Mother described them thus, on January 9, 1882:

There are now 24 Sisters and 18 novices and 4 candidates in this convent. These were poor when they entered and could not pay the expenses of the novitiate, in most cases. Our convent is so small that the Sisters have to sleep in the attic. The kitchen and the dining room, both for the Sisters and the boarders, are in the cellar and are poorly furnished.[3]

To read the letter is to understand the story, in the convent's oral traditions, of the novice, Sister Ethelburg Glancy, who asked: "Why is Mother crying?" and was told, "Because there is not enough for the Sisters to eat." According to the same story, Sister Ethelburg told her father on his next visit to the convent, and the Sisters never went really destitute again.[4] Michael Glancy had given the first daughter, Bridget, with a grace, but he had not destined the younger one for the convent. He resisted mightily when she asked to go, but at a word that the convent was really hungry he joined the Glancy farm in conspiracy with the Dolan grocery store to help the family of Sisters and students.

Even during those days life at Price Villa presented a serene and ordered picture. Mountains of white handkerchiefs and of ruffled aprons and skirts kept Sister Mary Ann Carey at an ironing board, her green knitting basket momentarily put aside; candidates carried water from the creek; the aroma of fresh bread came from the round house which had been the playhouse of the Price children; and Sister Benedicta Rudroff repaired and made shoes and created wax fruit from molds. Sister Mary Ann, the little Irish widow who entered at sixty-one, did not so much assimilate the culture, as sociologists would say, as she added to it a configuration of her own. In her seventies she helped with dishes in the kitchen. There were mountains of them, and when Sister Agnes Glancy as novice-mistress sent the novices to help her, Sister Mary Ann forgot or transcended the rule of calling people "Sister" to shake her head happily and say, "Ah, sweet Agnes."

Orchards of apple, peach, and cherry trees decorated the north side of the convent. Roses and evergreen trees and a much loved linden tree completed the picture. Within, on the first floor were the primary classroom, a museum and musical instrument room, Sister Aloysia's music room and guest dining room combined, and two parlors – one used for presenting plays.

On the second floor were community room, classrooms, a Directress' room, infirmary, novitiate, and the Superior's room, a small alcove off the community room. One classroom was public test room. Here all the Sisters were invited to listen to the fruit of their common labor and to make comments at the close of the oral examinations.

The third floor held a chapel on the south side, with three altars, and a dormitory on the north. In what had been the Price Villa ballroom the Sisters prayed. Here Sister Pauline tells of coming when she applied for entrance. Pictures of St. Benedict and St. Scholastica, now in the convent refectory, were in that chapel. Altars of St. Joseph on the convent first floor and of the Blessed Virgin on the convent third floor were in that chapel also. Here life focused.

Death began to visit the convent in the 1880's and the crowded quarters, basement work, and sparse diet hastened its coming. "The general tendency of the human mind is to belittle the importance of the individual life," writes Abbot Vonier,[5] but to look at the stories of those first deaths is to have the tendency corrected. From 1880 to 1885 the community witnessed the deaths of Sister Dominica Massoth, aged forty; Sister Bertha Cotter, twenty-three; Sister Cecilia Murphy, twenty-four; Sister Ethelburg Glancy, twenty-two.

"She was held in high esteem by the people of Atchison, and the children said she was a saint," wrote Sister Pauline Anderson of Sister Dominica, who died December 26, 1880. "They said that while she was praying before the statue of the Infant Jesus that was in the first grade class room, the Infant spoke to her."[6] Sister Dominica loved her pupils and their parents. "Greet your parents for me, and may the Blessed Mother take care of you," she wrote from Seneca to the Intfen children in Atchison, and they preserved the letter for sixty-five years. She had been also the first novice mistress.

In September, 1882, Sister Bertha Cotter died. The little girl who had been taken to the convent when her mother was burned to death, who had been Mother Willibalda's traveling companion in the summer of 1865, the community's first lay teacher in the convent's first mission of Seneca, and later the novice regaling young members with stories, had also been academy directress for one brief year on Sister Augustine's return to the East.

"She was one of our promising young Sisters," Sister Pauline concluded.

The third of the early deaths had a different tie with community history. Sister Cecilia Murphy, twenty-three, died in March, 1883. Sister Pauline writes:

She was the sister of Rev. Denis Murphy of St. Benedict's . . . She was beautiful, everyone said, but she had never had her picture taken. The year she died she was teaching singing in the Parish School in Atchison. This was her last obedience . . . Rev. Ambrose

Huebner buried her, and preached a short sermon. At the end of the sermon he said, "Let us pray for the one who will take her place."

Then Sister Pauline, writing from the vantage point of sixty-two years, said, "I made up my mind that I would be that one and try to stand at the head of the class as she did. Father said in his sermon that she always stood at the head of the class."

There was special pathos in Sister Cecilia's illness and death. Young Sister Hilda Booz, commissioned to care for her, was so busy during the day that at night sleeping near the invalid she worked out a code with her that if Sister Cecilia could not sleep or grew too ill she would press Sister Hilda's hand. So the sick kept watch too, that the well might sleep and be able to work.

Sister Ethelburg Glancy was the fourth and last to die during Mother Evangelista's regime. Born in Leavenworth, Kansas, on the feast of St. Scholastica, 1862, she made triennial vows on January 1, 1883, and perpetual vows on her deathbed, April 9, 1884. She died twenty days later. She was the gifted and tender-hearted young sister who had asked, "Why is Mother crying?" The memory of her death was fresh when Sister Pauline entered a few months later, and the latter records:

She had great struggles with the Evil One on her deathbed. She denied or acknowledged accusations which he brought against her. She had the Sisters sprinkle Holy Water, first at one place then at another in the infirmary. It certainly filled the Sisters with great fear and made them more exact in all their obedience. At the last she became calm and died peacefully.

Sister Luitgard, who had entered in 1883 and had received the habit February 10, 1884, was one of the awed young novices called. "Oh Sisters, be sure and acknowledge your faults if you do anything wrong," Sister Luitgard recalled the voice and the words.[7]

With the burial of his twenty-two-year-old daughter, Mr. Glancy, who had so long understood the life of the community, gave a crucifixion group for its cemetery. High winds later upset its foundations, and it was simply buried. But when in the 1930's some graves were moved and a new set of statues installed, the corpus of the crucifix was found unharmed and was placed in the convent refectory, where it presides over the sacred small observances of fidelity and love, so integral to monastic life from the beginning. That Sister Ethelburg would leave behind a memory of the importance of exact observance and of humility, when she could so easily have stood for the joy of perpetual profession which was certainly hers on her early deathbed, seems one of the proofs that through the early members of a house, Providence makes a path for the future.

"Their lives are not really over, even on earth," one of the volunteers for the new Colorado daughterhouse said in 1963. "Looking at their early gravestones, I resolved to volunteer, to do maybe what they would have wanted to do."

For all the seriousness of those last years of Mother's rule, the life was happy. Asked if those days were hard, Sister Luitgard always said, "No. We were happy." Occasionally the community would take lunch under the linden tree, sing songs, and tell stories. The laundry had to be done at night so that the kitchen stoves could be free by day. Sister Ida Seeger, chief cook, always provided lunch. The workers would rise before midnight in order to have lunch before work and yet not break the fast of Communion days. Stories cluster around those lunches, which were sometimes doughnuts cut in two the horizontal way in order to make them reach. Once Sister Cunnegund, then a postulant, was awakened with the injunction: "Praised be Jesus Christ," and to soften the hard blow of midnight rising, the caller said, "It's time for lunch, Margaret." "I thank you, but I do not care for lunch," Margaret answered politely and prepared for further sleep, which of course did not materialize.

Sometimes amid the splashing of water the Sisters became aware of Mother Evangelista's face watching them from the doorway with understanding and devotion. They loved their ideal, but they loved her also so much that motives intermingled, and they offered to do without sugar in coffee and butter on bread. Sister Pauline remembers:

Some benefactor gave the convent a barrel of sorghum, so it was bread and molasses and later either butter or molasses, but not both. Even when I was on mission, with Sister Hildegard O'Keefe, it was either-or, but not both . . . In the first place it was done out of love for Mother Evangelista.

Sociologists say that social actions are first concrete and personal and then become concepts and part of institutions. Tracing a convent's history fills one with awe, for one finds how simple and how real were the beginnings of what is so often just labeled "tradition," or "the spirit of a house." That everyone serve one another in a convent, that all work is noble — these are beautiful theories. But on one of those nights long ago a novice learned them quite concretely. Sister Amanda, the novice-mistress, had special need because of the crowded house and multi-purpose rooms to tell the novices to avoid the parlor if they were to make their novitiate worthily and find their own thoughts. She told them that the Evil One tends to take his stand there in order to make novices unstable. One of her charges, Sister Philomena Livings, listened with rapt attention. That evening after prayers she heard distinct noises in the parlor. She said nothing but resolved to have courage and investigate. Hearing the noises again the next night, she armed herself with holy water and crept into the parlor. "Why it wasn't the Evil One at all," she told Sister Amanda, "but Mother herself cleaning the room." [8]

The days had a curious combination of poverty and largesse. On one begging tour in Kansas City, Mother Evangelista stopped at St. Joseph Hospital, where a young woman said to her, "Who will take care of my little girls when I die?"

"We will," Mother said. "Don't worry. Be at peace. We will take them and educate them. We have very small girls in our school and they are happy."

The young woman did not die, but she did send her daughters to the Academy and they never forgot the words that had comforted their mother. One of them, Mrs. Frank Dolan of Kansas City, Missouri, then Eleanor Sweeney, recalled the story seventy-nine years later. One of the children who came to the academy when there were only four graves in the cemetery, she remembered only happy things: good food, good teachers, hard work, being loved.

The year 1883 brought the convent its third mission outside Atchison. A letter from Bishop Fink, March 17 of that year, said:

Rev. Mother:

Father Pichler wants and needs Sisters for next year. I hope you will be able to accommodate him with a small colony of them. If you cannot, I am sorry for it, as I then will have to get other Sisters there. I thought by concentrating your forces and getting the loan of one or two for a couple of years you could make out. Have a little more energy, try to get candidates and matters will shape themselves accordingly. You should have several places so as to get candidates and to have a chance of changing your Sisters and get a little revenue by degrees; otherwise you cannot do much. Consider these hints and let me know as soon as you can. Yours respectfully,

Louis Mary Fink [9]

In the history of the St. Joseph Sisters of Concordia, *Footprints on the Frontier*, Sister Evangeline Thomas wonders why this school, tentatively offered to them, was given to Atchison. One reason was that Mary Cass, the Hanover parish lay teacher, entered the Atchison convent that summer. Perhaps it is of greater human interest, though, to find another reason in the Bishop's very real knowledge of Mother Evangelista's weary spirit and great need.

In the spring of 1884, the convent took a different kind of mission. When Abbot Innocent asked for Sisters to take over the Abbey and College kitchens, Bishop Fink wrote again, saying, "Help the good abbot all you can." Sisters Clodescind, Frances, Ida, and Martha went to be St. Benedict's first Sister cooks, to establish the long tradition of hundreds of loaves of bread and all the other activity which made the kitchen warm and perhaps helped to keep boys in college and novices from wavering too early.

Another matter occupied Mother Evangelista. Her small community was one of the many Benedictine houses experiencing the need for great unity and cooperation among themselves. She attended a General Chapter of Benedictine superioresses in Chicago, July 19, 1881, and was elected to the imposing position of Mother General. She returned telling of a headdress which was worn in England and was much simpler than the Eichstätt style. The simplified veil was adopted in 1884. But extensive results from the chapter were slower in coming.

On Mother Evangelista the sheer accumulation of the convent's needs became heavy. Price Villa was, as everyone could see, an outgrown home. There was not room for the additional candidates who were so greatly needed. The Academy seems to have been doing fairly well under Sister Aloysia who had succeeded Sister Augustine Short on the latter's return to the East.[10] The building of a new convent was raising the shadow of further debt. Many real worries, which no diary reveals for she kept all confidences, preyed on Mother Evangelista and in the summer of 1884 she went for a rest to the place where her religious roots had been most deeply entrenched. The visit to St. Joseph, Minnesota, was not a going to asylum, however, but a going to an old home for refreshment and retreat. The Atchison community watched her go with love; Minnesota received her in the same spirit; Atchison would welcome her back with lighted candles and wreaths of jubilee. In the meantime, Bishop Fink appointed Sister Theresa as superior in her place. Mother Evangelista returned, but in the winter of 1884 she asked the community to accept her resignation.[11] By this time they had already moved into the new St. Scholastica's convent, a very plain structure, but one which permitted really separate quarters for convent and academy. Involved in something of a new era occasioned by new surroundings, the Sisters accepted the resignation.

They had never made the mistake of under-evaluating her although there were many matters in which she did not know absolutely everything. Mild and kind in the memory of those who knew her, one who prayed much and searched her own soul, she had always known the meaning of her vocation, and she presents a remarkable picture of a foundress who never considered her convent to be anything but a fully fledged convent with all the responsibilities and privileges of real religious life. She had felt responsibility to and for the whole Christian world and had introduced the pattern of prayer, reverence, and courtesy taken for granted now in the convent's daily observance. She had placed most emphasis of all on the Mass, always mentioning it as the means of recompensing her benefactors.

Her small diary, in delicate German script, records praying for the Abbey Prior in the days of the Abbey's heavy debt. It records love of her own family in a significant entry of May 2,

1871, which suggests that her brother has died: "To suffer or to die. For my dear brother Joseph. Till we meet again in Heaven." It records awareness of benefactors, remarking on May 26, 1876: "Today, on May 26, 1876, I learned that Professor Belki (who had been music instructor to the Sisters) died yesterday." It shows her faculty of always remaining the dedicated Sister, no matter to what magnitude exterior pressures gathered: "Suffer with patience. Battle with resignation. Love with a pure heart. Let it cost what it may. It can never be bought at too high a price. I will dedicate myself to the service of God forever."

She loved community observance and meaning in everything, establishing in her small convent the Eichstätt practice of having the Superior serve table on Holy Thursday in imitation of Christ. "On Holy Thursday, March 29, 1866, I served my venerable sisters at table. The weather was favorable." She set for herself a high goal: "April 1. Easter. At every Holy Communion I will ask God for a special grace. This exercise will make convent life more meaningful."

She established everyday customs which gave a joy to life, such as visiting the Sisters at St. Benedict's College kitchen on Easter Monday and calling it her "Emmaus." She prayed for her benefactors: "Today I offered my Rosary for my benefactors." She loved the Blessed Virgin: "What will become of me, if I be not a very good child of Mary." And she longed for God. "When, O my Jesus, shall I behold Thy beautiful Face?"

She was able to give herself completely to her community without losing her own personal identification with Christ. The last entry, made in 1901, sums up the attitude of her life: "Lord, when I arise from sleep, when I go to church, when I go to my work, grant that everything is done aright."

When Mother resigned in 1884, the community had two buildings connected by a windowed passageway. It had an academy and six parochial schools: St. Benedict's and Sacred Heart in Atchison, Seneca, St. Mary's outside Seneca, Wathena, and Hanover. The convent's first constitutions had been sent to Rome for approval and plans for a congregation were being prayed for and made. There was the strong and stable help of the Abbey across the city. There was Mother Theresa Moser, one of the convent's very first students, to succeed her, and all the way across the world important people in Rome were thinking about this small convent.

In her twenty-one years as Superior, she had received fifty-two postulants who persevered in the community until death; she saw the loss of only two professed vocations. These were the two extremely young co-founders, one of whom had made her perpetual vows after less than a year's novitiate, the other after only a year and a half. During Mother's time, the procedure of entrance was regularized to include a triennial vow period.

She celebrated the silver jubilee of her own profession in 1882, wrote the first Book of Customs, and tried to look ahead without losing the present. Her devotions were deep and simple — to the Mass, to St. Benedict and St. Scholastica, and to St. Aloysius. She went to the Novitiate herself on the six Sundays before his feast to pray in his honor for all young people dedicating themselves to God. There was no room for conflict in her spirit. Eichstätt had had some impress of Jesuit spirituality, and this may be reflected in the attention given by her to the particular examen, but all traditions blended well in her. The struggles of mission days did not change the quality of her life. "Oh we prayed — and a lot," Sister Luitgard used to say, smiling.

She was gentle but not weak. Sister Pauline Anderson, who was received by her, comments that some had wished Mother Beatrice Blakely of Nebraska had been sent to Atchison, since the Nebraska foundation seemed to prosper more visibly. But if she was mild and inclined to let life grow more slowly, she was also sure and patient. Her diary with its small blue pencil sharpened with a knife has a small picture of Mary on its inside cover. In German and in English, it mirrors the young woman who knew the one language and learned the other and who grew to be an old Sister so beautifully.

She who was set to rule others never stopped her guard on herself. She asks herself in her diary one Sunday, June 14, 1866: "How was your conduct today?" and answers sadly, "Ordinary." She cared for people: "Little Agnes Dougherty [a boarder] left the convent on the tenth of March, 1871. She was here for 6 years and ten months."

For all her meekness, there was steel in her. She knew: "If you

desire to be crowned, fight manfully and in thy patience endure."
And, "The more you prepare yourself to suffer the wiser you act
and the greater merit you will heap up." She took the twelfth
degree of St. Benedict's ladder of humility seriously: "March
7: Wherever I may turn myself, I find Thee, O my God, present.
Grant that I may not offend Thy holy presence in thoughts,
words, or actions." She understood community life: "He who
possesses true love of neighbor knows true sympathy and under-
stands the art of excusing the shortcomings of the faltering
Sister."

After her resignation, she lived to see the convent grow to
more than 300 Sisters, to record the dedication of its new chapel,
and to note on June 13, 1901: "I occupied St. John's cell in the
new convent."

While the convent under her never knew violence or starva-
tion, it knew extreme poverty, overcrowdedness, and the work
of daily sacrifice. The matter of financing its every undertaking
fell primarily to her in the years from 1863 to 1884. She did what
she could do. And then she asked for help, from the people of
Missouri and Kansas as well as from the fine King Louis in
Bavaria who had revived, restored, and extended Benedictinism.
She always wrote his society as if she expected them to understand her language.

She delegated others to ask for help and sometimes one forgets
how much she had to give as well as to receive. Sister Clodescind
used to recall her trip with Sister Amanda to neighboring farms.
One farmer in the St. Patrick's rural vicinity near Atchison gave
them potatoes and ultimately his daughter, for the young Sister
Clodescind did the smiling and spoke so warmly of serving God
that the girl who was to become the convent's famous Sister
Eleanor McNally packed her clothes and came to stay.

Mother Evangelista was humble, ladylike, and filial toward
the dignitaries of the Church, and her letters to them lend grace
to the convent Archives. And when in 1884 she went back into
the ranks of the simple Sister she had no difficulty. She had borne
the blessing and the cares of authority without ever ceasing to be
a simple Sister.

Whatever had been the concerns which she had subordinated
to greater ones, we have no record of their inmost nature. There

must have been some kind of pain which caused Sister Augustine Short after fourteen years as Directress to return to the East, and there was worry of some nature which sent Mother herself north to rest and think and pray. But she was Mother and bore the trials of her family. And she was Sister and allowed the trials to be only part of the gigantic pattern of life she had vowed to God. Her own life she finished: for some time as member of the Council, for a few years on the missions, and then in starched apron washing breakfast dishes with Sister Amanda Meier where the only exterior sign of her dignity was a little embroidery on the checked apron and the awe of entering postulants. She died on the feast of St. Aloysius, whom she loved, June 21, 1909, during the superiority of the little St. Louis girl she had received into the academy and then, after much early importunity, into the convent.

She slipped imperceptibly but eternally into Atchison history, so much a part of its daily life and ideal that no special tag marked the small rocking chair which used to be behind the dispensing table in the room where temporal wants were supplied. But that small chair was her chair and when someone happened to remark the fact, it was rescued from daily life and established in the Rare Books room, together with her Bible — much read but unfortunately immaculately free from annotations, together also with the account book and the diary which tell together part of the story of the convent's first era.

Today an almost ordinary face looks down on the convent corridor from her picture. In a sense there is a message from that face to all who walk past it. In her diary she says one Saturday: "Immaculate Mary, I recommend to thee all those who love thee, especially those of whom I have charge."

A Mother foundress forever keeps something of her charge.

Perhaps her supreme victory really was that she saw her own life in terms of Heaven and she built her convent on the promises of Christ.

1. A few years later, with the approval of the parents, Mother had the little coffin removed to the city cemetery. Those early years had a tie with daily life which somehow entered the convent's very tone. One morning during the first decade, the Sisters found an abandoned child on the porch. They followed Abbot Innocent's advice and took it to city authorities, but

they never forgot and watched the growing-up of the child with prayer and hope.

2. What to do with the old convent was something of a question. In a letter to the faithful Mr. Lebling, January 16, 1878, Mother Evangelista tells of transforming it into St. Benedict's Parish School and asks for financial help. She tells the Society that the community had banished the thought of selling the house for fear a saloon would be made of it. In contemplating her letters, one notes their constant if sometimes subtle apostolic note. This one has the gentle assumption that the Mission Society would not want a building once used as a convent turned into a saloon but would want to contribute to a parish school.

3. To the Cathedral Canon, Rev. Dr. Kagener, who now seems in charge of the donations from the Missionsverein.

4. Interview with Sister Luitgard Mengwasser, Summer, 1961, who was a novice with Sister Ethelburg.

5. *The Collected Works of Abbot Vonier* (Westminster, Maryland: The Newman Press, 1958), Vol. I, 178.

6. *Biographies of Deceased Sisters*, first entry, written about 1945.

7. Interview, Summer, 1960.

8. *Memories of Early Days*, Sister Stella Slattery.

9. MSS Archives.

10. Sister Augustine died at St. Walburga's Convent, Covington, Kentucky, in 1902.

11. A letter from Abbot Innocent to Abbot Boniface at this time suggests that both the community and the Abbot feared a breakdown for her.

THROUGH THE SIGN OF THE CROSS

While Mount St. Scholastica was building its life, paying its bills and dreaming of expansion, preparing its teachers, and framing its customs, the world outside was going its larger way.

Some idea of what that larger way was and of the manner in which the Sisters fitted their home into it could be made clear by looking at the world through the eyes of the bishops in whose diocese the Sisters lived and under whose jurisdiction they were most kindly treated.

The Sisters came to Atchison when it had been for thirteen years a Vicariate under John Baptist Miege, S.J., a friendly, refined pioneer whose administration was marked by zeal for the Church, understanding of religious life, love of people, loyalty to his adopted country, and the ability to remain himself. He was residing at St. Mary's, Kansas, when the Sisters came to Atchison. His cathedral was a log church there.

There is no extant correspondence between Bishop Miege and the St. Cloud community or the Sisters who came from there to Atchison. But the notices in the *Champion* that the new school was under his patronage are significant. His correspondence with Abbot Boniface reveals his attitude toward the Benedictine Order, and his letters to and about Louis Mary Fink suggest that he left the Sisters' spiritual and temporal guidance largely to the Atchison Prior and his successors.

The bishop's attitude toward the Abbey and Prior Louis is reflected in his comment when the latter was made his own Coadjutor Bishop. He wrote to the Jesuit General in Rome:

At last I have a Coadjutor. He is a worthy man, fearing God and the devil, and serving the Good Master with all the generosity of

76

a true son of St. Benedict. He is nearly six feet tall, with a beard a foot and a half long, but as thin as a rail.[1]

His appreciation was reflected back in the answer from the Jesuit General:

I congratulate you on having at last a Coadjutor such as you have desired, a man religious, prudent, pious, full of apostolic zeal, knowing the country, eager to go ahead with the good works you have begun and able to bring them to a happy issue.[2]

Already as Coadjutor, Bishop Fink presided at reception ceremonies and made profession occasions solemn and beautiful. In 1877 Bishop Miege resigned. His successor's episcopate from that year until his death in 1904 is a continued story of efforts to strengthen the slowly growing convent and place it strongly within the vast fabric of the Church. His letters, honest, humorous, were stamped by his belief that things of worth were done with the sign of the Cross. *Per Signum Crucis* was his motto. He did not romanticize the Sisters, but he understood them and helped them.

In 1878, one year after he took over the see of Leavenworth, the bishop wrote to Rome, painting a clear picture of what was happening at the small convent. He said:

Most Holy Father:

The Bishop of Leavenworth in the State of Kansas in the United States of North America humbly places the following matter before you:

In this diocese there are religious houses, or groups of pious women, called Sisters of St. Benedict, who by an indult of the Holy See and according to the laws of the Church are flourishing among us. They make simple vows for three years after completing a Tyrocinium. Afterwards they make perpetual vows.

At the instance of the Most Rev. Abbot Boniface Wimmer, these religious women obtained the privilege for ferial days in the place of the Divine Office to recite the Marian Office. Very recently I approached the houses in this diocese under my jurisdiction to draw up plans for better governance and the establishment of certain rules tending to religious perfection.

The Sisters recite the Office of Mary every day — on ferias, feasts, Sundays, and through most of the year in place of the Divine Office. This privilege was granted (in audience to Boniface Wimmer)

June 10, 1866. In the elapsing years since, many sisters have received the habit and made vows. They do not know how to recite
the Divine Office, nor do they have copies of the Benedictine Brevi-
ary at hand; and they are poor. They have neither time nor strength
for reciting the Office. For the sustenance of the community and
according to the ordinance of the Superiors, they teach poor parochial schools and a school for children popularly called an "Academy." Some Sisters who are not able to recite the Little Office say
the Rosary, that is the whole Rosary in three parts with the Litanies.
In my heart I keep thinking that they are not really nuns because
they no longer take solemn vows or go to the Divine Office as was
customary for Benedictine Sisters. They are not obliged to it, especially since they are constituted under the Bishop of the diocese.
I have thought best to turn the whole thing over to the Holy Apostolic Chair and to supplicate your Holiness:

(1) That the aforesaid Sisters of the Order of St. Benedict established in this diocese be able to recite always and every day whether
Sunday, feast, or feria, the Little Office;

(2) That daughter houses and the mother house and those founded
in other dioceses enjoy this;

(3) That those engaged in servile work or without sufficient education to recite the Office of Mary in choir be able to say the Rosary
in three parts with the customary litanies;

(4) That Sisters in branch houses enjoy the same privileges.[3]

In May, 1878, Cardinal Simeoni answered. He agreed that
Abbot Boniface had obtained the permission but said that no
subsequent Decree could be found. He said that a Congregation for the purpose of uniformity among Benedictine convents
was the wish of the Holy See. He recommended that Bishop
Fink seek the approval of the Bishops in whose dioceses the
Congregation would be represented and perhaps call a chapter
of the Sisters themselves. He requested a complete report on
the spiritual and temporal state of the Sisters and a copy of
the proposed Declarations. The Bishop complied, and there
began the long self-study among the Sisters and their effort
to get into right words the blueprint of their house and their
hopes.

After several plans and several delays — one of them such a
simple thing as a smallpox epidemic in Covington, Kentucky —
six Benedictine Mother Superiors met at Chicago at St. Bene-

dict's and St. Scholastica's Convent, July 19, 1881, with Mothei Evangelista presiding. It was this chapter which chose the habit and headdress worn today, already adopted by the Chicago Benedictines at the suggestion of Bishop Foley. Four convents inaugurated the congregation — Atchison, Kansas; Covington, Kentucky; Chicago, Illinois; and St. Joseph, Minnesota.[4]

The Constitutions at home were finished and sent to Rome. Cardinal Simeoni, in a letter of November 28, 1883, acknowledged their receipt and praised the Bishop for his zeal. But he said that for lack of agreement among bishops and the other houses, consent for a congregation must be withheld. For further foundation of Benedictine convents, he said it would be sufficient to get the approval of the Bishops concerned. Meanwhile, Atchison's own proposed Constitutions went to a committee for careful study and the two-year scrutiny resulted in an important comment which as much as anything, perhaps more than anything else, shaped the formation of Mount St. Scholastica.

For fundamentally the thing of greatest importance in a Benedictine house is the prayer framework. A convent may say the Office poorly, but it remains the pattern by which everything else is regulated and this is each house's inheritance from the founder who made the search for God and the praise of God the cornerstone of his house and who wrote: Let nothing be preferred to the work of God.

A committee of four from the Sacred Congregation examined the Constitutions. They called in for consultation the Benedictine Abbot Romaricus Flugi. The committee sent its report from the Monastery of the Holy Cross in Jerusalem, May, 1885, signed Fr. Ant. MMC., Arch. Colossensis; Fr. Raim. Bianchi, O.P.; Fr. Gabriel; P. Valerianus Carella, with Dom. Gregorius Bartolini, Abbas Cisterciensis, Consultor.

The result was to reach the pioneer Kansas Sisters and to put back into their hands the Office book, to place them, pioneers or no, back in the mainstream of Benedictine life. The committee granted a "Decree of Praise." But it said the Sisters were organized more as a modern religious institute than as traditional Benedictines. Their basis was true Christian works of charity, while the substantial law of Benedictine life was the perform-

79

ance of the work of God, nightly and daily. The request to keep Wednesdays and Saturdays as meatless days simply drew the comment, perhaps from the Cistercian consultor, that Benedictines abstain altogether from meat.

Further, the committee raised real difficulties. It said that if there was to be a Mother General, she and her Council, like other councils in modern institutes, should have a separate house. The Sisters were moving away from the Order's idea to the Province idea, said the committee.

This was in 1885. Mother Evangelista had already resigned, and Mother Theresa Moser was prioress. Talk of a congregation slowed down for thought and appraisal. But within several years after Rome's answer reached the Bishop, in the parlor of Mount St. Scholastica Convent, Abbot Innocent Wolf began to teach the Sisters again to say the Divine Office and contributions of old, new, and various-sized Office books poured into the convent from various abbeys. One novice had a book almost the size of a dictionary. The Divine Office was resumed at Mount St. Scholastica on July 26, 1892, the feast of St. Ann, and has continued without interruption to the present time.

Further, the committee said, the distinction between Choir and Lay Sister was not Benedictine but European. But this decision had already been reached at the Atchison house. Sister Aloysia and Sister Theresa had requested years previous not to have to precede in rank those who were characterized as lay Sisters — although Sister Boniface Bantle, Sister Scholastica Duerr, Sister Clara Bradley, Sister Mary Anne Carey, Sister Benedicta Rudroff, Sister Antonia Schmees, Sister Frances Kramer, Sister Bernarda Protzmann, Sister Philomena Livings, Sister Cecilia Murphy, Sister Rosalia Krieger, and Sister Agatha Robinson were still listed thus in the 1879 Catalogue of American Benedictine Sisters.[5] And Mother Evangelista must have received tentative approbation from the Bishop to change the practice, for Lay Sisters had disappeared as a reality before the report came from Rome.

The community went to work on the Sacred Congregation's report. Bishop Fink faithfully wrote another request for approbation and just as faithfully complied with Rome's request for another report on spiritual and economic status and for a revised copy of proposed Constitutions. The Archdiocesan Archives preserve the Bishop's handwritten, often-corrected first draft of his reply, and one of his letters to Abbot Boniface admits that Sisters can take a lot of time.

The new Constitutions were completed and sent to Rome in 1892, at the same time that the Office was resumed. Its preamble said that the purpose was to define accurately how the Sisters of Atchison sought the glory of God and observed the Holy Rule, as well as the circumstances of the region permit. The Constitutions were printed for St. Joseph, Elk County, Pennsylvania; St. Benedict, Erie, Pennsylvania; St. Mary, Allegheny, Pennsylvania; St. Scholastica, Atchison; St. Benedict and St. Scholastica, Chicago; and Sacred Heart, Chicago.

Regarding the Divine Office, the revised rules said that it would be recited daily at the motherhouse by the Sisters and novices who could do so, stating a dispensation from the obligation and a substitution of the Rosary for those unable to participate because of weak health, five hours or more of classroom work, or other prohibiting conditions. Missions with less than four Sisters might substitute the Rosary for the Office.

The Constitutions dropped altogether the distinction between choir and lay Sisters. They kept the request for meatless Wednesdays and Saturdays and for a common novitiate for the six convents, and a Mother General who would reside at the house of which she was Mother. This edition was accompanied by a concise historical narrative written with appropriate comment by Bishop Fink. A translation of the Bishop's report makes good reading seventy-one years later:

THE REPORT

1. Historical Narrative

1. In the year of Our Lord, 1863, on November 11, seven Sisters from the town of St. Cloud in the diocese of St. Paul, Minnesota, called to the city of Atchison, came that they might found here a convent of their Order. There they found a commodious house built and prepared for them but burdened with a $4,000 debt. They lived a poor life indeed. But in the course of time they paid the debts, bought nearby ground, and built the small buildings which they found necessary. In the meanwhile they took a parochial school and an Academy for the education of young girls and they work much for the good of religion and the Christian people.

2. As the number of religious increased more and more daily, and the house which they lived in grew daily less desirable and was difficult because of many inconveniences, in the year 1877 they moved the convent to another place and house, with the advice of the Bishop, and there they annexed a large house with 28 acres for the price of $20,000 which might serve for the Sisters and the children being educated.

3. In the year 1884 with the consent of the Bishop they erected a large building of baked bricks where the Sisters and Academy girls could live separately. The erection of this building cost $12,000.

4. The community of Sisters, novices, students, and capitulars where Our Lord is served and Mass is daily celebrated are located in this more recent home, and for the present there is sufficient space for the living of the Common life according to the Rule and the Constitutions which I have sent for the approbation of the Apostolic See.

2. Temporal Status

1. The temporal status consists of buildings and grounds ample enough that they may live apart from secular people and have no molestation from them. The estimated price of the buildings with their grounds reaches $50,000 or more. The proceeds of the Academy, of the parochial schools and the work of their hands, they apply from year to year for the paying of their debts, the building of new buildings, and whatever necessity the here and now demands. The present debt is above $11,000, which will be paid. In the Academy this year were more than 100 girls instructed in the Catholic religion, the necessary secular sciences, and the arts.

2. There are now the following parochial schools: In Atchison, St. Benedict's and Sacred Heart; in Topeka, St. Joseph; in Kansas City, St. Anthony; in Seneca, Sts. Peter and Paul; in Hanover, St. John's; in the country of St. Benedict's, St. Mary's. All of these schools are located in my diocese.

In Nebraska City, diocese of Lincoln, in the state of Nebraska, the school of St. Benedict; in Kansas City, Mo., the school of St. Mary of Sorrows; in Council Bluffs, diocese of Davenport, Iowa, St. Peter's.

3. Personal Status

1. The personal standing of the Convent of St. Scholastica consists of 76 professed Sisters, four novices, and three postulants.

2. The Prioress is in charge of the community and there are other officials according to the Holy Rule and the Constitutions there established. A Mistress of Novices presides over the Novitiate ac-

cording to the constitutions sent to the Holy See. A Directress presides over the teachers and students of the academy.

3. The Community obtained incorporation by the civil State by which is established personal jurisdiction, in which the title resides, and through which it is administered as provided by civil law and the constitutions.

4. Religious Status

1. As far as I know, regular discipline, clausura, prayers and religious exercises are observed strictly and religiously according to the Holy Rule and the Constitutions. The Sisters enjoy the best of reputation among Catholics as well as non-Catholics. As regards the Novices, they are admitted to triennial and perpetual vows only after careful scrutiny and the consent of the chapter.

2. The Novitiate is lived according to rule; the novices are separated from the sisters and instructed by a teacher properly.

3. Sisters go out to teach in the parochial schools prepared in the sciences and in music so that they bravely labor with great distinction for the good of religion.

The Constitutions were acknowledged with commendation by a letter from the Congregation, July 26, 1893. But the requested congregation was not approved. The committee said that if the Atchison house itself should found houses in other dioceses, then it might present the Constitutions again to the Sacred Congregation. Until that time, Cardinal Simeoni said, the Sisters should keep the rank of third Order and each house function separately.

This decision led to a steady movement by other Benedictine convents toward uniformity. Mother Theresa's regime, as it unfolds, shows a steady tendency for convents of the Middle West especially to act together, and when the Constitutions were submitted again for approval, in 1908, the convents themselves knew better what they really wanted. The process was to be slowed by the war. Before it was completed, the story would bring into the stream of daily life on the hill in Atchison the interest, effort, and prayer of such men as Cardinal Simeoni, Bishop Ullathorne, Cardinal Gasquet, Abbot Innocent, Abbot Martin, and Pope Pius XI. But the march of their names began with the effort of Bishop Fink.[6]

Before it had all reached conclusion, Bishop Fink, of course, was dead. The tall giant of a man, whom Bishop Miege had loved, had by his guidance and hours of work turned a community's ordinary daily struggles into noble Latin words and helped put the Latin words back into the daily struggle. His honesty, devotion, humor, and hard work were all unfailing. When he requested Sisters to keep house for him at the episcopal residence he was kind and jovial to them, but he took them seriously, once reminding a monk that if he should forget or neglect to go to give a retreat the Sisters would not easily forgive the bishop. He sent his own nieces to learn English at the academy. He tried to set an educational pattern, writing a catechism for the children of his diocese and forming a diocesan school board in 1899 to set standards and promote ways of achieving them. His own ideas of religious life and of education were solid and profound. He made them work on Kansas hills and prairies and respected other people who were also trying to make ideals work.

He helped the convent get a foothold in its apostolate. Bishop and brother he remained, and the combination helped Mount St. Scholastica.

In the light of seventy-nine years later, it is pleasant to contemplate the writing and reading of the following letter which he received once at the episcopal residence:

> Mount St. Scholastica
> Atchison, Kansas
> Feb. 17, 1884

Rt. Rev. L. M. Fink, O.S.B., D.D.
Rev. and Dear Bishop,

I return you my most sincere thanks for allowing me to receive the habit this morning. I have no means to repay your kindness unless by prayers. I will offer up a Holy Communion for your intentions.

> Begging your blessing, I remain,
> Your affectionate child in Christ,
> Sister M. Adelaide, O.S.B., Formerly Mary Cass

To Mother Evangelista, he was always "My Lord Bishop," and the phrase fits the face which looks down on the convent first floor corridor, across from her picture. He had helped the convent, too, to live *Per Signum Crucis*. He lived to see the small, impoverished house he had shepherded become a beautiful series of buildings with a worthy chapel which he himself dedicated July 11, 1901, three years before his death. In Mother Evangelista's most harassed days he had written her: "Do not worry. Do your best and God will take care of the rest." His mark is on the simple and stable traditions of Mount St. Scholastica, and one of its proudest heirlooms is his comment to Rome: "As far as I know, regular discipline, clausura, prayers and religious exercises are observed strictly and religiously according to the Holy Rule and the Constitutions . . . they bravely labor with great distinction for the good of religion."

These words were high praise from so great a man.

But while he was writing them, the convent's second Prioress was in the midst of trying to actualize them. The first American-born Mother Superior was learning what St. Benedict had sympathetically known she would learn — what a labor one undertakes who undertakes the care of souls.

1. Archdiocesan Archives. Prior Louis had been prior since June 18, 1868. He was named coadjutor bishop in 1871.

2. *Ibid.* The answer of the General is dated, July 23, 1871.

3. The Latin original is in the Archdiocesan Archives. In fact, the Archives preserve several versions of this and later similar documents, showing the careful writing and correcting of each before its final mailing.

4. Sister Regina Baska, *The Benedictine Congregation of Saint Scholastica* (Washington: The Catholic University of America, 1935), pp. 128–130.

5. *Catalogue of the Nuns and Convents of the Holy Order of St. Benedict* (Latrobe, Pennsylvania: St. Vincent's Abbey, 1879), p. 44.

6. For Bishop Ullathorne's letter of 1880, written to the Mother Superior of Erie concerning the Congregation, see Sister Regina Baska, *History of the Congregation of St. Scholastica*, p. 141.

MOTHER THERESA

Between the founding days of Mother Evangelista and the gigantic achievements of Mother Aloysia, lie the twelve and one-half years of Mother Theresa, appointed acting Superior by Bishop Fink, July 5, 1884, and elected by the community six months later. As Sister Theresa she had had much to do in 1883 and 1884 with the moving into the new St. Scholastica's convent, but strictly speaking she built no buildings.

Yet during her administration the Divine Office was restored, the Sisters of another community affiliated with Atchison, the convent took four additional parochial schools, and Mount St. Scholastica's community grew from thirty-one professed Sisters to eighty. She received into the convent postulants who were to shape community history. She saw six young Sisters between the ages of twenty and twenty-seven die between 1888 and 1890, including all four Scholastics who made their profession on February 10, 1887. She tasted all the realities of convent living.

The missionary Benedictine Henry Lemke, with his awareness of history and his sense of mission, would have rejoiced to know that Barbara Moser, whom he baptized in Carrolltown, Pennsylvania, November 16, 1847, would become the second Mother Superior of Atchison Sisters. When the pioneer Sisters came from Minnesota in 1863, Sister Gregoria Moser was among them. Barbara, who had attended the school at St. Mary's in Pennsylvania, asked to transfer to the Atchison academy and came in the winter of that very first year. Before the close of its first term, on May 8, 1864, when she was sixteen, she asked for admittance. The convent's second postulant received the habit in the convent's first reception ceremony and made first vows with Sister Clara Bradley.

One day in her early weeks as a postulant, she went out on a mission. One of the Sisters was ill, and the doctor said she should have eggs. Even before the seventy's, the grasshoppers in the summer were stripping Kansas fields, the poultry yards of the farmers were barren, and the neighbors of the Sisters really had no eggs nor could find any. Barbara, because she was yet uncloistered, went alone in bonnet and shawl with basket to surrounding farmhouses for a long time and finally came to one farm where there was one egg. She bought it for fifteen cents and returned home triumphant. The cook and everyone else were happy, but when the egg was opened it was not good, and for what the poet Thomas Gray would call "chill penury," everyone cried.[1]

As a very young Sister, Sister Theresa felt responsibility for the convent's well-being and shared the responsibility with her relatives, for a letter from an uncle in Galveston, Texas, speaks of a donation of $146.70 which he hopes will "take care of your needs for a while." The letter supplies something of the temper of the people of 1866, and of families such as the Moser's who helped to build the church in America. Sending the money, April 12, 1866, Mr. Moser says:

I hope it will releive you from all troubles at present; please write to your other Sisters [two were Sisters at St. Mary's, Pennsylvania] and I will releive them also; please pray for me also, thank God that this horrible War is at an end, and hoping I shall have the pleasure to see some of you yet . . . Please answer forthwith if you got the money. Give my best respects to Mother Superior and Father Wirth.[2]

In another letter, June 19, 1871, the uncle tells of his children — from the oldest, a sculptor and marble-cutter, to the little girls who were good musicians and of whom he was very proud. He is happy because his oldest son is a "good Christian, going to Holy Communion once a month," and he closes with pride:

I have a complete harmony at home. I am not above bragging. Still I have not got enough to live independent, but I keep straight with my God and with the Law of the Land. No Constable or Sheriff will ever enter my home with a citation or execution or any suit whatever.

The last letter from this uncle, January 16, 1875, reflected back to the convent the contribution of such small things as teaching children to write good letters. It reflected too the values which an old man held dear:

It affords me great pleasure every time I hear from you. Your nice handwriting and your affectionate language — and then getting a letter from one of the Mosers. I am always a little proud of my Name because our ancestors had always been good Catholics.

As teacher of German and needlework, Sister Theresa was well known in the academy. As Procurator and novice-mistress she was already representing Mother Evangelista by Holy Thursday of 1884, which Sister Pauline Anderson remembers very well. Sister describes that day, and the summer and autumn which follow:

On Holy Thursday of the year 1884 I walked from 2nd and Division Street to Mount St. Scholastica on Holy Thursday afternoon, to ask to be admitted. I wanted to become a Benedictine. When I arrived I was taken to the chapel which was situated in what is now St. Cecilia's Dormitory. The altar was where the cupola door is now. A row of pews was on either side of the aisle . . . I went up the winding back stairs.

After I was there about a half hour someone came and took me to the parlor first floor southeast room. Mother Evangelista was not so well then, so Sister Theresa, procurator and novice mistress at that time came in to the parlor to meet me. I had an interview. She told me I should get my parents' permission and she would let me know through Sister Hildegard O'Keefe when I should come.[3]

Sister Pauline entered the community on July 6 at breakfast, and the postulant who had promised God to try to take Sister Cecilia Murphy's place remained to fill many posts of duty through a long life. It was a lively novitiate to which she came and over which Sister Theresa presided. Laundry days, without electric power, lasted from seven to seven. There was table-waiting, table-reading, dish-washing, baking, the cleaning of lamps and the carrying of kerosene and water for the four candidates and the three more who soon joined their active enterprise. Sister Winifred Mihm had the milking and the baking to do. As a postulant, when she put on her baker's cap, remembers Sister Pauline, she would pull it high in the center to make it look like a mitre. Then she was Bishop Mihm.

The convent had three cisterns in those days, upon which it depended for water supply, and the water supply depended upon the rain. When that supply gave out during the winter, candidates and novices gathered snow for laundry day and Mother Theresa herself presided over the conversion of the snow into water, filling the boiler on the kitchen range with snow and dipping the water into the tubs as it melted. In spring, summer, and autumn, the candidates carried water from "Crystal Lake," which disappeared when the builders blasted for rocks for the foundation of the new convent in 1900.[4]

The moving into the new convent of the 1884 and 1885 days brought a few changes.

There was a permanent chapel now, there was more room for novitiate and convent quarters, and there was a certain air of mystery which academy girls found interesting in the wooden lattice work grilling off the novitiate. A third floor dormitory with dormer windows completed the effect.

The first to make vows in the new chapel, April 6, 1885, were Sister Luitgard Mengwasser, Sister Irmena Tiehen, and Sister Adelaide Cass. Sister Pauline was among the group of four who were first to receive the habit there. They wore colored silk dresses, since not enough white dresses were about, and they pledged one another that all four would persevere until the end of life. Conferences and instructions by Abbot Innocent helped to make up for the lack of time for study.

Mother Theresa relied much on his help, and among the very few pieces of correspondence which she kept was the following note on the occasion of her first nameday as Mother:

> St. Benedict's College
> Atchison, Kansas
> Oct. 14, 1885

Ven. M. Theresa, OSB, Prioress
Ven. Mother,

Accept my best wishes for your nameday. May your patron saint be your model, guide and protectress during your life, and your comfortress in the hour of death. I shall pray that God may fulfill this wish, and for that Intention shall say Mass for you tomorrow.

Respectfully,

Innocent, OSB

Abbot

Perhaps because there is so little correspondence to guide one, Mother Theresa never gives one the impression of having been a particularly efficient Mother. But she was everywhere in the midst of the convent's life. These were the years when it was establishing permanent viewpoints, such as Sister Benedicta Rudroff's frequent statement, "Keep the Rule and the Rule will keep you," and Sister Loretta Gleason's, "When you die, show Our Lord your hands." There were always the poor, and Sister Boniface Bantle, in charge of the kitchen, was instructed never to refuse anyone. The lunch was put into paper bags, a cup of coffee accompanied it, and no poor person ever knocked in vain. On one occasion an entire family asked for dinner. Sister Boniface began the lunches, but Mother Theresa suggested that a table be set under the linden tree and herself prepared multitudinous pancakes for the crowd of little children and their parents.

The convent had a stately black phaeton driven by "Sweet William," a man who had been a Negro slave. His disposition was flawlessly cheerful, and he brightened recreation perhaps more than he knew. "You are tracking mud on the floor. Look back and see," Sister Ida protested once as he carried groceries in to the table. "I never look back, Sister Ida. Look what happened to Lot's wife," he grinned amiably.

The twenty-fifth jubilee of the community drew near. Remembering that the first Mass had been said on Mary's patronage, and that Price Villa had been bought on Mary's feast, the Sisters celebrated the jubilee on July 16, 1888, with a High Mass of thanksgiving and an afternoon lunch of bread and butter and coffee, with cookies and lemonade as optional. The faithful linden tree, its roots now ground somewhere into the earth under the present convent building, served as the setting. The Academy held its first formal public graduation that year and its first formal graduation in music one year later.

But not all of community life was exteriorly gay. Conditions were quickly becoming crowded again, dormitories were not heated in winter. The four young Sisters who made vows February 10, 1887, all died of tuberculosis within a year and a half. Parents began to fear to let their daughters enter. "You have to analyze this. They are giving it to one another," the doctor told Mother Theresa.

It is possible to follow one of the Sister's stories through the little sister who took her place and who recalled it seventy-three years later.

Sister Anastasia Rudroff was the niece of Sister Benedicta, shoemaker and garden manager, christened by Father Gerard Heinz for her generous deeds as the "golden Sister." The family had long been connected with the convent and the Abbey. Father Boniface Verheyen always stopped at the Rudroff home when he went to St. Louis to get rocks from the Gasconnade River for the Abbey Museum. He befriended the children who played with his watch and listened to his stories. Mother Evangelista had stopped there too on collecting tours.

Not quite twenty years old now, the novice Sister Anastasia was dying. Mother Theresa visited her often, in the spring of 1890, asking if she would like to make her vows before she died. "Yes, Mother, but not yet — I'm not quite ready yet," she said until Good Friday, April 4, when she received the Last Sacraments, made her first and final profession, and died at two o'clock in the afternoon.

In the summer of 1961 the writer of this book met Sister Lioba Rudroff near one of the convent's back doors where nasturtiums and ordinary summer flowers bloom. "Tell me about Sister Anastasia." The words were too sudden.

"Anastasia! You are too young. You don't remember Anastasia."

"No. But I have seen her name. She was your sister. I want to know about her."

And while the summer sun beat warm and bright against the convent bricks, Sister Lioba recalled sitting as a little girl of six at the dinner table with her parents on a farm near Richfountain, Holy Thursday, 1890. While they were at table, Sister said, a white dove flew in the open window with a small branch in its beak. It chirped a little and flew out. Her mother put down the dish she was placing on the table and said: "Anastasia. Sister Anastasia has died." And when the letter was mailed next day from Atchison, there was a dove with a branch in its beak pictured on the convent stationery. Both the girl of sixteen and the child of six who watched their mother read the letter said they would take their sister's place.[5]

The same Good Friday saw the death, also from tuberculosis, of Sister Ositha Lenherr, twenty-one. Her sister, Sister Austroberta, was also soon to die. Little Sister Ascellina Godfrey, whose mother after much importunity had permitted her to join at the age of fourteen, completed the quartette. Mother Theresa watched it all with agony, giving her own bed to the ailing so often that someone in the house was appointed by general consent to see that Mother herself have a place to sleep. Mother Theresa must have written her worry to her sister, Sister Martha in Pennsylvania, for there is an answer dated October 12, 1890:

I have been praying for your intention every day since you wrote asking me to do so, and if my prayers have not yet been answered, you must have patience till they are, or better still you pray real fervently for me that I may become more holy, then of course my prayers will be heard.[6]

At least one part of the answer must have come in new vocations. For 1890 saw the entrance of community members who would etch themselves importantly into Atchison's story: Sister Josephine Weber, Sister Genevieve and Sister Aurelia Scanlan, Sister Christina Luber, and Sister Clotilda Lee. And the new decade brought Sisters Johanna Mengwasser, Martina and Lidwina Masat, Juliana Oestereicher, Margaret Gillen, Barbara Schneider, Marcellina Sinnot, Lucy Dooley, Zitta Belter, Elizabeth Overton, Rose Scahill, Euphrasia Coleman, Colletta Vollmer, Stella Slattery, Matilda Mayer, Domitilla Wagner, Irene Nolan, Blandina Karman, Imelda Nitzel, Leocadia Wolff, Dorothy Dooley, Petronilla Willems, Beata Doll, Veronica and Appolonia Haug, Rita and Sylvia Callahan, Thecla and Monica Schecher, and Helena Brandmeier. Four of these — Sisters Josephine, Martina, Sylvia, and Veronica —

are living in the centennial year. "How can I die now, Lord? I have not yet finished those albs for Your boys," Sister Veronica was heard to say in the spring of 1962 when a stroke halted her lace-making. And like Peter's mother-in-law she rose and began ministering again.

Outside the convent world there was work for every Sister who came. Mother Theresa took four new missions — St. Anthony's, Kansas City; St. Peter's, Council Bluffs; St. Malachy's, Creston; St. Benedict's, Nebraska City.

The Nebraska City story was a special chapter. A small Benedictine convent had been built there in 1865 and had thrived, with Mother Beatrice Blakely of Pennsylvania as its foundress. After her death in 1884, the convent experienced poverty, instability, and turbulence. In July of that year, Bishop James O'Connor of Omaha drew the convent to the attention of Abbot Innocent, suggesting that it unite with Atchison. None of the succeeding superiors — Sisters Emmerana Buder, Gertrude Seiling, Frances and Cornelia Dougherty — could make the community prosper. Finally, after a series of negotiations, with the encouragement and blessing of Bishop Bonacum of the newly formed Lincoln diocese to which Nebraska City now belonged, eight Sisters were admitted to the Atchison community, December 13, 1888. One Sister went East.

The story exemplifies both the saddest and the happiest sides of religious life. Sister Emmerana, who governed the community for a time after Mother Beatrice's death, went restlessly from convent to convent after its amalgamation with Atchison. She died at the Abbey of Chiemese, Germany, July 17, 1902, after an illness which she bore with great patience and longing for God, and "with great, holy confidence," wrote Sister Margaretha of the Chiemese Abbey.[7] Somehow the sad part was that there had not been unanimity in the convent after the death of the Superior, but the beauty was in those Sisters who came to make their home in Atchison: Sister Maura Plattman, Sister Justina Mettman, Sister Cornelia Dougherty, Sister Agnes Murphy, Sister Benedicta Will, Sister Mechtild Stenger. "They were kind and patient Sisters," wrote Sister Pauline, who knew them all. And they helped take care of their new home.

In the threadbare days when the loss of even one chicken was a rather serious financial blow, Sister Maura Plattman kept guard one night from a window. Amid the sound of fluttering poultry wings, her voice went out into the night bravely: "You would not steal from the poor Sisters, would you?" The unknown thief would not and did not, but crept away unidentified.

Legends abound concerning the Nebraska City community, and when legends are known to be only legends they become a part of valid history. One story, related by Sister Stella Slattery, is that on the night of Mother Beatrice's death she appeared to Abbot Boniface who gave her his blessing, at which she disappeared. This particular legend is a bit eerie. Abbot Boniface, then an old man who had already worried much about the chain of foundations his inspiration and energy had set loose, probably did bless at least from afar the Superior who must have known the conditions which were going to make life in her community hard after her death. Mother Beatrice was greatly revered at St. Mary's in Elk County, which had sent her to Nebraska City, and her influence on the community she founded is discernible in the kind of Sisters who came from there to Atchison.

Maybe the coming of the Sisters to Atchison was the fruit of the blessing. If it was, it was a mutual one, for the story of at least one of them has the beauty of legend.

Sister Mechtild Stenger served four years as a teacher and mission superior.[8] She was not always a successful disciplinarian externally, for she was better at praying that children would behave than she was in forcibly bringing good behavior. But for her prayerfulness she left a lasting mark, and in her old age she helped establish in the new college at Atchison a tradition of unstinted hospitality. Her task was to keep the door, to make visitors welcome, and when her eyesight began to fail, to keep the towel supply fresh in the custodial rooms. Many a college girl used to wait deliberately on Friday nights just to speak to the bowed old figure with the wonderful smile and the quiet voice. It was somehow as if everything had been taken from Sister Mechtild so that she could be free.

One spring night in 1936, she walked in her sleep on the infirmary porch, lost her balance, and fell to the pavement below. The night watchman finding her, said: "Oh Sister, where were you going?" "I was going to see Jesus," she answered. After a day of suffering she died, April 1, 1936.

Events such as the Nebraska City story accumulated to show that some congregational organization was desirable. Then, from across the world came calls for help from Benedictine convents and this, too, called for some concerted action. In 1886, the convent secretary, Sister Angela O'Gorman, received the following letter from Abbot Boniface Wimmer, now an aged monk at St. Vincent's Abbey, turning his apostolic ear back to the Old Country's needs.

St. Vincent Abbey
Beatty P.O.
Westmoreland Co., Pa.
Jan. 9, 1886

My dear Sister Angela,

I have received the $30 you sent me for the poor Sisters in Subjago, and have forwarded to them $370 plus 305 plus 145 plus 158 . . . in francs 1897 plus 1564 plus 743 plus 895 equals 5000 francs. And little contributions are still dropping in so as to make me hope our Sisters can return to their cloister again. Rev. Mother Abbess acknowledged the receipt of the drafts and returned thousands of joyful thanks to all contributors. Among the Sister contributors, Atchison is second best. I am proud of it. Vergelt's Gott.

Thanking for the good wishes on the occasion of the new year, I beg to accept mine in return to Ven. Mother and all the Sisters, and to believe me to be in fatherly love,

Your Old Abbot Confrere
Boniface Wimmer

The trials of Italian convents in the years of unification and afterwards had stirred the old missionary to turn back across the ocean some of the charity which had crossed it under his beckoning. There is a flourish in the signature of the Abbot who, incidentally, did not reveal who held first place for generosity. Out of its small store,[9] the convent continued to give, and the Abbot's last letter expresses his gratitude. The letter is interesting, too, for its blueprint of hope for the future.

April 16, 1886

My dear Sister,

Received your letter and check for $250 and will make it right. I was for 2 weeks in Chicago where we intend erecting a Bohemian

Monastery at St. Procopius Church to which 3 Bohemian Patres of mine already attend. It gives me a good deal of work to do and to think about.

I have a great aversion against travelling and go not out unless forced by duty or business of great importance. Such a business is establishment of a monastery, more so of a Bohemian monastery.

I am since Jan. 14th already 77 years old and feel the burden of age hard. Still I can yet attend to my regular duties and enjoy comparatively good health of course not without troublesome infirmities which are necessary or at least very useful for anybody to practice and learn thereby patience and sympathy for the sufferings of others.

I would like to see Atchison once more; perhaps I get an opportunity. But I have not been even in Erie and St. Mary's for 5 years having been too much engaged in the South and at home.

Your family has wonderfully increased; mine, too, this is St. Benedict's blessing. I anticipate sometimes in my mind the glory of our holy Order when it will cover the plains and mountains of New Mexico, Colorado territory, and also the Southern states, engaged in Christianizing the yellow and black skins of those zones. . . .

With kindest regards to Sister Evangelista and all the other Sisters, I remain in pius remembrance at the altar.

> Sincerely in Christ
> Boniface Wimmer
> Abbot [10]

In 1893 Mother Theresa herself took the leadership in helping the still needy Sisters in Italy, writing to Benedictine convents on February 25 of that year:

We Benedictine Sisters have not yet made a unified effort for any purpose, but the present occasion gives all an opportunity to join in a good work. Each Community, separately, cannot help much, but many small amounts make a good sum. One dollar makes five lire, and one lira in Italy, goes nearly as far as one dollar here. Then, also, the Holy Father will see that there are many communities of Benedictine Sisters of whom he has never heard, and he will surely bestow on them a special care. As long as the Benedictine Sisters do not make themselves known to the Holy Father, they have to ascribe it to themselves if they are not cared for in particular. The special care of the Holy Father would bring on all houses a special blessing.[11]

At home the pattern of life went on, with occasional variations whose full story the Sisters did not always know. Sister

Genevieve Scanlan, convent chroniclist for almost forty years, records a stormy morning in the 1920's when chaplains were late for Mass and remarks that only once had daily Mass been missed in the convent's history. She may not have known, at least she did not give the details of that incident which occurred in the chaplaincy of Father Herman Mengwasser in Mother Theresa's days, who told the story himself.

The night had been a bitter one, and Father Herman, looking out on a snowbound world in early morning, decided that no human being could walk the two miles across town to the convent, particularly since it was not a "Communion" morning. So he said a private Mass at the Abbey. In mid-morning, Abbot Innocent asked a Brother to harness the horse and buggy as he himself intended to see Mother about some business. Father Herman, longing to stave off a crisis perhaps by a prudent word in advance to Mother, requested to go along to visit his sister, Sister Johanna. The Abbot said, "But you saw her only this morning." Hoping for a miracle, Father Herman remained silent.

The Abbot returned in the afternoon and said no word to Father Herman. The day came to a close, Compline ended without a word, and Father Herman, thinking the miracle had occurred, went thankfully to his room. As he crossed the threshold he said aloud: "Thank God, he didn't send for me!" "For what, Father? Why should he send for you?" said a voice behind him, a voice which Father Herman well knew.[12] Father Herman never forgot the conversation, in the warm room with the world white and cold outside, on how everyone needs the Mass, and he relayed it years later with humor and deep realization.

Every Sunday morning, from 10:00 to 10:30, the bearded Abbot himself came to the community room for exhortation. He sat in the midst of a circle of chairs and spoke of religious perfection and the life of the Church. Notes written closely together on small pieces of paper and carefully kept in the St. Benedict's Abbey Archives bring back the Abbot's voice: "Whoever is careless in education need not expect a reward from God, says St. John Crysostom." And, "Reverence a child as much as Christ Himself. Show confidence in children; do not suspect them; do not love them for your own sakes, though."

Annual retreats and retreats for profession were important. The retreat for final vows made by Sister Luitgard, beginning July 2, 1888, was conducted by Father Bede Durham of St. Benedict's. Her small notebook recorded:

Compared us to a rosebush. He said when we started the rosebush was planted, it just began to take root. When we got the Habit, the bush began to grow, the stems to get green. When we made Simple Vows, the bush began to have leaves on the stem and the little buds to show. Last vows the bush begins to open. At our death, the rosebush is in full bloom, the roses begin to open wide. Keep it in mind the rosebush has thorns. That means to have crosses and trials in your lives and death comes; all is over in this world. The rosebush dies, so your life goes that way. Your good works well performed will last; make the rosebush your model.

The summer of 1892 brought intensive practice for the Divine Office. Abbot Innocent himself taught the officials the rubrics first. Father Peter Kassens of St. Benedict's gave special lessons in Latin, and Father Gregory Huegle of Conception Abbey came to help the whole community with the chant.

The summer of 1892 also brought a visitation from Bishop Fink. His commendation was always pitched in a low key, as if he were always asking for even more. He praised the Sisters for "working hard and having a good will to do their duty as religious." He recommended continued faithfulness to community exercises and to cheerful obedience, "so much the more, as the Holy See seems to favor St. Scholastica's convent in a special manner, of which all should render themselves worthy."[13]

Listening most earnestly to that report were two people who soon acted on it with unusual vigor. In the fall and winter of 1893–1894, Sister Genevieve Scanlan, twenty-two years old and professed only one year, was faced with surgery for what was called "erysipelas of the bones." Remembering the event, Sister Genevieve recorded many years later:

I became very ill and we could not determine the cause of the malady. Finally Dr. Linley decided that an operation was necessary. Operations were rare events in those days, and I rather think that was the first one we had in the Community. He brought Dr. Shelly for consultation and it was decided that the operation take place the following forenoon. They called it erysipelas of the bone . . . Sister

M. Aloysia, then Directress of the Academy, made arrangements with the two doctors for the surgical feat. She came to me and said, "It would be splendid to undergo it without taking an anesthetic if you think you could stand it, for Dr. Shelly is not favorably inclined toward Catholics or Religious and I know it would please Dr. Linley." I told her I would gladly comply with her wish. She stood right beside me all during the operation and I clung tight to her hand. Dr. Linley, although not a Catholic, was very much pleased that Dr. Shelly should see a Sister prove that nature sustained by grace can endure bravely.[14]

Without faith, convents would be dismal places. In fact they would not, of course, exist at all. Mount St. Scholastica has always placed great store on the plain path of duty and love. But it has to have its legends of special favor from God, too, since it receives into its house those who sometimes do ask God for special things. Sister Genevieve was one of these. During this same illness of hers the community made a novena in honor of St. Walburga, and when Dr. Linley came to repeat the feat of operation without anesthetic for a third time he found it mercifully unnecessary.

He was very puzzled how the changed condition occurred [writes the victim, remembering]. Dr. Shelley had operated the first time, and these were also his first visits to the convent. After Dr. Linley's death, he became our regular physician and remained so till his death in 1928. He, too, was a loyal friend of the Community.[15]

In October, 1892, Sister Scholastica Duerr died. And on November 25, another influence left the halls and kitchen and chapel. Sister Mary Ann Carey, eighty-seven, died at night, saying, "O Jesus, receive my soul. Have mercy." December, 1893, brought the deaths of Sister Harlindis Plank and Sister Ermenilda Huber, both young. It so often happens in convents that Sisters really ask permission to die, as if for them the permission is a necessity. To the watcher the act may seem redundant, but they seem to get a special grace really to see Christ in the Superior. "May I die on Christmas Eve?" young Sister Ermenilda asked the harrassed Mother Theresa, who answered, "If it is God's Will." And so on December 24, the young face still so unwritten on by life took on the ageless look too soon, and Mother Theresa wondered, as Mother Evangelista had done, what could stop the procession.

In 1896 and 1897 Sister Modesta Moran, Sister Ottilia Shields, and Sister Milburga Striegl — all in their twenties — died. Sister Milburga was a novice. Sister Boniface Bantle, fifty-eight, died of pneumonia. Sister Mechtild Neuner, forty-one, and Sister Patricia Dore, forty-two, also died. Sister Patricia's death resulted from a heart condition. But the cause of most of the early deaths was tuberculosis. The cure was not yet found.

Smallpox added its complications to life. The year 1894 saw Mr. Kennedy's small cottage become the quarantine house, with Sister Philomena and Sister Agatha caring for the first victim, Sister Merwena. The chaplain, Father Eugene Phelan, visited the cottage daily, taking Holy Communion to victim and nurses. The epidemic struck other Sisters too, and as a result of it the Sisters discontinued the practice of wearing veils over their faces when they appeared in public, lest people think they were hiding contagion.

July of 1897 came and the community met to elect its next Superior. Mother Theresa declined re-election, and they chose Sister Aloysia Northman, forty-three years old, thirty-two of which had been spent at the convent.

Mother Theresa lived until June 7, 1918. By those who remember her she is described as a woman of dignity who kept Academy study halls, taught German, and loved beautiful things. The youthful sweetness of the face in the Eichstatt headdress, for an early picture is all the community has of her, never really left her. She was "jolly," the older sisters said, and in her older years chubby. Table linens still used on festive occasions for guests are the work of the little girl who came West at the age of sixteen, in 1864, to spend her life. She saw the convent which had eighty living professed Sisters at the end of her superiorship increase to more than 300 members.

Sometimes in the days of change and increase, there were times of loneliness for her. Except for her own sister, Sister Gregoria, who was an invalid, the last of the pioneers had died by 1917. One day Mother Theresa asked to go to the Abbey kitchen convent, saying she wanted to stay there for a few days. That kitchen, presided over by Sister Luitgard then, comforted

Mother Evangelista Kremmeter,
O.S.B. (1863–1884)

Mother Theresa Moser, O.S.B.

(1884–1897)

Mother Aloysia Northman,

O.S.B. (1897–1924)

Mother Lucy Dooley, O.S.B.

(1924–1950)

Mother Alfred Schroll, O.S.B.

(1950–1962)

Mother Celeste Hemmen, O.S.B. (1962–   )

Abbot Boniface Wimmer, O.S.B.

Abbot Innocent Wolf, O.S.B.

Ludwig I, King of Bavaria.

Abbot Martin Veth, O.S.B.

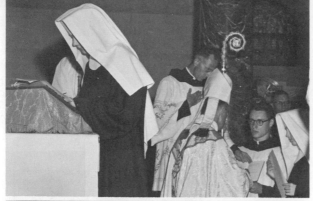

Profession Day

"Let him prefer

nothing to the

work of God"

Sister Luitgarde Mengwasser,

O.S.B., professed 78 years.

Died March 3, 1962

her. It was near the site of the old convent from which the sixteen-year-old postulant had gone merrily forth, shopping with Mary Bradley long ago.

In the end, Mother Theresa died on June 7, 1918, at the age of seventy-one. The child baptized by Henry Lemke had added four missions — three of which would be permanent — promoted the Academy, urged Benedictine Sisters in the United States to be mindful of the needs of the world, restored the Divine Office, admitted the Nebraska City community, served as novice-mistress and as Mother, told a multitude of beautiful stories to young girls in the Academy, made lovely lace, and admitted sixty-three Sisters to vows.

Mother's funeral expenses at the Harouff Funeral Company were $68.00, and to see the receipt in the Archives is to meditate on infinite things. Her uncle, P. H. Moser of Galveston, would have been proud of her work for the Church they both loved.

To one looking backward over her span of years as Mother, there seems not enough evidence to form any extensive judgment. Her letters are kind, dignified, and human, but there are few of them and there is no diary. Her only photograph is a youthful one, her veil and headdress immaculate, her eyes clear and untroubled. She does not seem so much to initiate or to shape events, to stamp the convent with her spirit; she seems somehow to have permitted great things to happen rather than to have inaugurated them. Yet she shared the convent work, wept for the sick, contributed to European communities when her own was in need, took an intelligent if limited leadership among American convents, and gave warm welcome to Sisters from another house, respecting their confidence and granting them love.

She stood at seventeen deathbeds. She was mild and kind and of a happy disposition. By her deeds and her reactions to the events Providence permitted to happen, she kept the threads of history which the first Mother had begun, and guided them into a pattern the future would continue. She added some very fundamental new ones, or at least she permitted God to add them.

Perhaps history is as much letting God work as it is doing His work.

1. Interview with Sister Caroline, July 18, 1962. Sister heard the story from Mother Theresa in her later days.

2. MSS Archives.

3. "I wish to add," says Sister Pauline, "that my mother had no objections but my father waited three months before he gave his consent, although he was never resigned until a few weeks before his death. The treatment and care he was given at St. Margaret's Hospital changed his idea about Sisters. He wrote me he was perfectly satisfied and he was glad that I had embraced the religious life."

4. Laundry was so major an affair because it included convent, academy, and abbey.

5. Sister Felicitas Rudroff also died very young.

6. MSS Archives.

7. Letter, MSS Archives.

8. For a time the Atchison community staffed Annunciation Academy in Nebraska City. But it did not prosper and was ultimately closed in 1903. The convent retained St. Benedict's parish school there until 1909. Lay teachers were employed there until 1913; Sisters of Charity taught there from 1913 until 1927, when Ursuline Sisters took charge.

9. Expenditures for the year 1882, for example, were $8,832.23. Of this amount $1,361.20 was for interest. Total receipts that year were $10,082.43.

10. MSS Archives.

11. MSS Archives. These were the days when the idea of a Congregation was pending approval by Rome.

12. Father Herman, who told the story at Council Bluffs to the Sisters who taught there, was himself something of a legend. When Sister Ludmilla, who contributed the incident, was sent there as a new Scholastic, she recalls that the Abbot giving her his blessing said, "Oh, you poor thing. And to teach for that terrible Father Herman." But on the night of her arrival, Father Herman, traditionally a practical joker without mercy, merely looked at the diminutive young Sister and said, "Poor child. You should be home with your mother."

13. Decree issued from the Bishop's residence, August 11, 1892. Archdiocesan Archives.

14. *Convent Chronicle*, February 24, 1933.

15. *Ibid.*, February 25, 1933, feast of St. Walburga.

MOTHER ALOYSIA

"No convent survives," writes Bishop Ullathorne, "which has not begun in a cellar or garret."

For all its display of cupola and winding stairway, Mount St. Scholastica had lived a great deal of its first thirty-four years in basements and attics when Mother Aloysia Northman was elected, July 12, 1897, as its third Prioress. She brought it out of both. She was a pioneer who lived from real homesteading days in Kansas to the age of skyscrapers and North Central accrediting agencies. She was a heroic human being who asked no sacrifice of others which she was not herself prepared to make. And deep at the bottom of her life, she was a person who had consecrated herself to God and come early to stay at a Benedictine convent, quite in the tradition of St. Gertrude.

Her life had that lack of complication which often surprises us in the great. She was prophet and practitioner, and believed both in faith and in works.

"But Mother, I have had only novitiate Latin," a Sister might protest. "You have time. Get a book and see Sister Natalia," would be her answer. "And so I taught Monsignor Obrist his first Latin," recalled Sister Ambrose Conway. "He says it was pretty good Latin."[1]

In modern educational verbiage this would be called tutoring combined with independent study. For Mother Aloysia it was the possible and the necessary. In all the convent's struggle for certification of its teachers and schools she never advocated pretense of learning, but she believed in mutual help and in hard work.

A Superior who comes down in story as one who walked down the aisle during choir to see that tone and rhythm were kept, she also improvised meditation material to fit the need of the moment, and is said to have inserted the words *Et Verbum caro factum est* when she noticed that the Sisters were drowsy, for the sake of the energetic, profound bow customary at those words. Those whose duties made it necessary for them to go to second Meditation, which was read simply from the book by a Sister, would listen in vain for the words which the first group had heard. These general memories are the property of all who knew her. The specific stories fill in the picture of the tall, dark-eyed Superior of marvelous vision, daily courage, and magnanimous heart.

Helen Northman was born in St. Louis, Missouri, at 1105 Biddle Street, Nov. 25, 1854, across the street from St. Joseph Church. Her father was Frank Northman and her mother Catherine Beckman Northman. She was the youngest of five, and the only girl. Three of her brothers became Fathers Wolfgang, Ulrich, and Bede, at St. John's Abbey, Collegeville. The fourth, George, married.

She attended a school in St. Louis conducted by the School Sisters of Notre Dame. A month before her eleventh birthday, in October, 1865, she came to Atchison on a boat up the Missiouri River with Sister Boniface. Mark Twain knew many things, and suspected more, about the excitement of the Mississippi River and its tributaries, but of this event the then thirty-year-old author would not have known.

She was a reverent, energetic little girl, who took piano lessons. Her mother, a widow, had let her go both because she already loved the Order, to which three sons belonged, and because she wanted the talented child educated. But when in the summer of 1867 she asked to return to Atchison to stay, it was hard for Mrs. Northman. One account of the story says that Helen made a novena to St. Aloysius; another, that the mother made the novena. One account says that the child had a dream of the saint, telling her to enter; the other, that the mother had the dream.[2] At any rate, she did go back to Atchison in the fall of 1867 and was received with the drama previously related on March 19, 1868. Still thirteen years old, she received the habit

August 15 of that year. On February 10, 1870, she made her first vows, when she was a little more than fifteen, and three years later her perpetual vows, on the same day.

Her life was plunged immediately into teaching in the academy. She was a good student in everything, but excelled in music and in mathematics.[3] She was appointed Directress of the Academy in 1884 and kept the position until her election as Mother.

Surely the refrain of sickness and death was not the first or even the dominant note of her early months as Mother. But it stands out in the record.

In the late months of 1897, Sister Cassilda Bourke of Centropolis, Kansas, and Sister Perpetua Kratschmer of Vienna, Austria, twenty-three and twenty-five, died. The chronicle shows the pattern. Sister Cassilda had come home the previous Christmas from Creston, Iowa. There was not much room; double beds were rented and set up in a guest room. She took cold from which she never recovered, and died the following October. She was a beautiful Sister. Her remains rested in the chapel one afternoon during Matins, and when the choir finished praying they commented to one another in their evening walk that the Office of Virgins would have been more appropriate for her than the Office of the Dead.[4] Remembering Sister Cassilda, her biographer says:

She had only one brother, a Christian Brother who taught in St. Joseph and who used always to meet her at the station to visit between trains. He wrote her wonderful letters which, I think, had a great influence for good on her.[5]

Sister Perpetua Kratschmer followed. Then Sister Eulalia Kopp, and Sister Felicitas Rudroff, who had been sixteen when her sister preceded her and who had come to take Sister Anastasia's place. Their deaths meant one thing for Mother Aloysia, one thing she could do.

In early 1900, she wrote to Bishop Fink asking permission to erect a new building which would cost $65,000. The Bishop answered: "Where will you get the $65,000? I will not let you run into debt to get out of it only in Purgatory."[6] Mother answered immediately, perhaps after some hard thinking:

You misunderstood me, we did not think of going into debt for $65,000. This is the cost of the building when completed. We counted on putting it under roof, then finish as much as we absolutely need for the present, so we can vacate the house we are occupying. We are crowded in our Academy and if we don't have more room we will lose the best pupils we have, as our accommodations are not proper. We want to ask your permission to make a debt of $30,000. We can pay the interest on that sum and pay off $1,000 every year. . . .

Now dear Rt. Rev. Bishop, please grant our request. We have considered the matter and feel we can see our way out. Asking your blessing and a reply, I am,

Your humble servant in Christ,
M. Aloysia, O.S.B.[7]

There was a touch of humor in the Bishop's reply. "Well, if you can pay for it honestly without having to go to Purgatory for it, you may go ahead." [8]

On September 14, 1900, ground was broken for the massive convent. Crystal Lake, the small stream which had been the center for many conventual picnics and the water supply for laundry when the cisterns failed, went before the machinery grinding out storage rooms. But this new convent, happily and designedly, had no basement at all for dining room space. This was above the ground, kitchens and refectory surrounded by huge rectangular windows. A long, wide, high corridor led straight to the new chapel and from there to St. Scholastica's Hall and St. Cecilia's Hall, now to be turned completely to academy uses. Dining room, community room, dormitories rose in level fashion one above the other — all characterized by space, windows, and high ceilings. "You will never fill that building," the Bishop warned Mother Aloysia, thinking with her of the 119 Sisters she now had. "You will never fill that chapel either," as the chapel with its possibilities for 300 Sisters took formation.

"Oh I am sure we will," she said bravely aloud. "May God and the community forgive me," she is said to have answered interiorly.

On Pentecost Sunday, May 18, 1901, the community moved into its new quarters. "Not every Sister moved in that day," said Sister Mary Finnegan carefully, in the summer of 1962. "There was one novice who had smallpox and who was left in the other building for two weeks. Oh, I might as well tell you. It was I." [9]

In mid-summer, when everyone was home from the missions, Bishop Fink wrote:

I avail myself of the happy occasion — the blessing of the new convent on the 11th — to offer a small present in token of my good will and best wishes for the community and that God may bless their work, give them health, patience, and piety, so they may do a great deal of good for religion and renew in their midst the work of their holy predecessors, brethren and sisters of the Order of St. Benedict. Remember in your prayers the writer of these lines and his Diocese.[10]

The chapel was blessed on that feast of the Solemnity of St. Benedict, July 11, with Abbot Innocent and many priests assisting the bishop, and in the presence of many lay people The dining room was finished in time for the first meal to be taken there July 16 of that year. Community retreat was a glorious thing that year, in a chapel large enough for all. Prior Oswald Moosmuller himself, now Prior of Cluny, Illinois, a foundation which did not exist long, preached the retreat. He who had so hoped the Sisters would have a self-contained home where clausura would be possible must have rejoiced.

Mother had kept her word to build only what she had to build. Life itself supplied permanent altars, statues, and choir stalls for the beautiful structure. On July 7, 1901, the chapter admitted to the community Sister Paula O'Reilly, who had entered the community at Newark, New Jersey, making profession there in 1867. She had gone from Newark to the foundation at Creston, Iowa, and as Mother Superior there had moved the community to Guthrie, Oklahoma. Upon the election of another Mother Superior at Guthrie, Sister Paula asked to transfer her stability to the Atchison community. She was sixty years old, and would live to be eighty-one, and the memory of the tall Sister who always prayed became part of the tradition of the convent. She asked and received special permission to have her family inheritance used now to help pay for appropriate choir stalls and altars. The stalls were made and installed, and altars of Carrara marble came in a few years from Italy.

They were beautiful altars. The candlesticks chosen for them were beautiful too, and the convent flowers which became traditional for Adoration Sundays became all part of one piece, so that if the biography of the "choir chapel" were written by the girls and Sisters who prayed there it might well throw great light on the perennial question of people and their environment.

The story of the statues had a special beauty. The convent chronicle tells that when Sister Fabiola Black entered the Novitiate the young man who had hoped to be her fiancé told her to sell the engagement ring he had hopefully bought and use the returns to help buy statues for the new chapel.

History moved on outside the growing Chapel.

Three years after he blessed the chapel, March 17, 1904, Bishop Fink died — brother, father, friend, adviser, and bishop. He was succeeded by Thomas Francis Lillis, who was consecrated December 27, 1904. The Academy held a reception for the new bishop at which an excited girl orator said:

Our first Bishop, that holy old pioneer John Baptiste Miege, must look down with complacency on the vineyard he planted in what was then the wilds of Kansas. His arduous labors, his prayers and tears, reclaimed the barren soil. With a joyful heart this good patriarch resigned his charge into younger hands. We were obliged to give up one saintly apostle, but God gave us another, no less good and great, — the Right Reverend Louis M. Fink.

On every side, your Lordship is surrounded by a devoted body of clergy — zealous, active, eager to execute your least command . . . Monastic houses, the glory of every Christian land, sacred houses of sanctity and science, whence flow the refining influences of religion to elevate man's fallen nature, — these grand institutions are not wanting, not only to guard our frontiers and to lead the advance, but also to form a staunch bodyguard for the chief pastor of our diocese . . . We welcome you, our dearly beloved Bishop, with childlike trustful confidence for the Holy Spirit has poured out upon you those wonderful gifts and graces which make you the visible image of the Fatherhood of God.[12]

This seems a flowery speech, and of course it was. But its writer, who must have been Sister Hildegard, had a great sense of the sacredness of history and of heritage. She had lived through all the stages of Kansas diocesan life, and if anyone had the right to speak of them she did.

The new bishop consecrated the chapel June 24, 1908, on the feast of the saint whom St. Benedict had honored with a chapel on Monte Cassino. Life took on a great luster, and the *Illustrated Chronicle* of Chicago said glowingly of Mount St. Scholastica:

At all times the Sisters exercise a maternal solicitude for the weal of those under their guidance. Gently and firmly the childish mind and heart are developed by precept and advice until the tender bud bursts forth into the full bloom of glorious womanhood, going out into the world to disseminate the seed of love and wisdom implanted by those gentle preceptors, who were so instrumental in moulding the beautiful character so worthy of emulation (November, 1902, Vol. V).

These words were ornate, too. But they were really true. Some of the children who came were very small. Clara Peterman was only four. Her father had brought her, indeed, a year earlier, after the death of her mother. But the Sisters asked him to give her one more year in gayer colors. Then at four she did don the little black uniform, the ribbons in her hair, and the protecting love of Sister Thecla, whose "minims" had slates and pencils, crayons and books, teeter-totters and cookies, and prayers at night.

In the winter of 1902 the new convent and the new chapel had a special visitor. Mother Frances Xavier Cabrini, traveling west, stopped over night. Sister Barbara loved to recall: "She was a very nice ordinary Sister. She liked coffee." It became important to remember that it was in the present office of the subprioress that she slept, and in the room next to it that Sister Barbara poured that coffee.

Then in Lent of 1904, Sister Edith, the subprioress, wrote the following letter to the Missions:

Mother has been quite sick. Drs. Gray and Shelley say that it is only a matter of time and that they cannot do much for her. Dear Mother thought this matter over seriously and concluded to have recourse to the Blessed Virgin. She feels that Our Lady of Lourdes will intercede for her. So she made the following promise: She will offer fifty Holy Masses and Holy Communions, one every Saturday for fifty Saturdays in honor of Our Lady of Lourdes.

The Community said a special prayer every Saturday, too, which included the reminder: "Although we are distant from that holy place, yet even from afar we call to thee, O dear Lady of Lourdes, and loving and beloved Mother."

The convent began the building of a special Lourdes grotto and kept up ceaseless prayers. In the spring of 1907 the grotto was complete, five young elm trees were planted near it, and the processions which continued for twenty years, once on February 11 with the total home and student body, and again on August 15 with the total community, began. Besides the prayers it became a community story that Sister Marcella Dignan, a little more than twenty years old, offered her life in exchange. She died January 18, 1908. Mother Aloysia recovered from the erysipelas which had so constantly recurred.

It did seem that she was greatly needed. Illness and crowded conditions in which the sick had been mingled with the well had made steady community observance hard in the pioneer days. Now with a mixture of rigor and gentleness Mother Aloysia tried to pattern her rapidly growing house on a high ideal. She herself saw to it that silence was observed and that the little things which index the big ones were sacredly regarded. Reverence to one another, instant obedience, courage in life's small battles were the things she asked.

Now indeed Mother walked the long dormitory aisles sometimes at night to insure the perfect silence of the best monastic tradition for her Kansas convent. Then began the long years in which the steady whir of cicadas in August and the sound of sifting snow on the evergreens in winter would come through the big windows. There was great beauty for the convent which Mother had planned.

She placed the missions, too, under the protection of a vigilant, supernatural viewpoint. A list in her pencilled handwriting assigns the following "Holy Helpers":

St. Pantaleon .... Academy
St. Dionysius .... Nebraska City town

St. Eustachius .... Higginsville
St. Blasius .... Wild Cat (St. Mary's School, rural Seneca)
St. Achatius .... West Atchison
St. Erasmus .... St. Louis College
St. George .... Our Lady of Sorrows, Kansas City, Mo.
St. Barbara .... St. Anthony's, Kansas City, Kan.
St. Catherine .... Polish Parish, St. Joseph, Kansas City, Kans.
St. Cyriacus .... Seneca
St. Vitus .... Creston
St. Giles .... Hanover
St. Margaret .... Nebraska City Academy
St. Christoph .... Council Bluffs

Not all the events in a convent happen directly in terms of the Superior's life, but all of them ultimately touch her and receive some color from the response she makes to them.

In 1904 a nation came knocking at Atchison's door, a new culture touched the convent. A community of Benedictine nuns at the Abbaye de St. Eustace at Flavigny sur Moselle, France, was faced with exile or the giving up of their life as teaching Sisters. Atchison heard of them and invited them. Between 1904 and 1907, eight French Sisters transferred their stability to Mount St. Scholastica. Sister Mary Mechtildis Schmucher, Sister Mary Agnes Miessler, and Sister St. John Touissaint were skilled in vestment-making, Sister Mary Jane Wecherlin taught music and French; Sister Odelia Schenk was for many years guest-mistress; Sister Franceska Scheinder took care of flowers; Sister Julia Miller taught a fine art of convent living. Sister Walburga Veser made coifs and prayed. Most of them were of German origin, placed in a French setting by the War of 1870. They brought with them the best traditions of both lands.

One book cannot even touch all the names of all the Sisters who made Atchison's first century. But the exiles had left two homes, and in a time of history when that phenomenon was rare, they seemed to leave a special stamp on their third. Sister Mary Jane awed the Atchison house a little by bringing it a hand-written, hand-painted *Lives of the Saints of the Desert* presented to her by its creator, her uncle, at her reception into the French convent. She awed her pupils by being able to tell sharps and flats from a great distance. There was a fineness in

111

her. One day in her old age, when she had begun to walk heavily with a cane, she passed a wastebasket and saw in it a page from a church goods catalogue advertising holy pictures. She hooked her cane to the stairway nearby and, down on her knees, cried out, "Ah, la sainte Face," retrieving a print of the *Ecce Homo*.

Sister St. John tried to teach the small girls. She was a large Sister with a French accent which imperfectly revealed her kind heart, and they were needlessly afraid of her, sometimes fleeing from the volley of French which meant how much she wanted to help them. Sister Franceska brought to perfection the snapdragons which became traditional on Exposition days, and many incoming postulants never told her how the very sight of them on the altars had drawn them to the Atchison convent.

Sister Odelia almost totally formed the convent's tradition of guest-mistress. Sister Mary Agnes and Sister Mechtildis made vestments. Sister Julia, on request, would show her plain gold ring to young Sisters, with its engraved inscription, "Jesus-Julia." She spent her afternoon mending socks for the Abbey monks, and as her eyesight failed seemed to live in the choir chapel where she did not need to see.

There is something special in the French spirituality. It came with the exiles and did not leave. Some of them had been lay Sisters in Europe and they loved the Divine Office now, in a land where all were Choir Sisters. Sister Walburga in her last years was frail and slow. But entering postulants took their cue of the value of Thursday adoration from the bowed old figure who never let the candle stubs go completely out. All but Sister Julia, smiling over her pile of socks, seemed in a way always to remain exiles.

Many avenues of the world in those early years of the twentieth century were leading to the Atchison convent. The young Kansas, Missouri, Nebraska, and Iowa schools were sending postulants. Benedictine Sisters of Tutzing, Germany, were directing vocations there. In Germany and Austria pastors were channeling girls to the Kansas convent. The health of Sister Angela O'Gorman, novice-mistress, was declining. Mother Aloysia set out to select a successor for her. She did it directly, as she did most things, and made a decision which had a great deal to do with the future.

1. Interview with Sister Ambrose, July, 1960. Sister Ambrose died October 5, 1961.
2. Letter from Fred and Adelaide Sanders, cousins of Mother Aloysia, to Sister Mary Salome Northman, also a cousin, January 14, 1938. MSS Archives.
3. To the end of her life she retained her love of music. Sister Geraldine Jacobs recalls her listening while she took piano lessons from Sister Edith. Mother loved singing, and if Sister Geraldine struck a false piano note, Mother would say from her chair in the corner of the room, "Sing a song." Sometimes she came from chapel at the sound of disharmony in a practice room.
4. Sister Pauline, *Biographies of Deceased Sisters.*
5. *Ibid.*
6. Letter of March 5, 1900. MSS Archives.
7. Letter of March 26, 1900. MSS Archives.
8. Quoted in the article, "Mother Aloysia," by Sister Jerome Keeler, O.S.B., *Benedictine Review,*
9. A very young postulant of three months, watching and taking part in it all, was Sister Senorina Dignan. An interested academy girl who did not get to carry anything in the moving was Sister Bertilla Harmel. The only immediate record of the days of gradual moving which followed, for not everything was finished at once, comes from the diary of the foundress. Mother Evangelista wrote: "On June 13, 1901, the feast of St. Anthony, I occupied St. John's Cell in the new convent. Resolution: Son of God, Jesus Christ, who art our example, grant that I may be Thy servant and remain faithful to Thy love. I will serve Thee, only Thee, dear God; help me to ever serve Thee faithfully."
10. July 5, 1901. MSS Archives.
11. All these details come from the diary of Mother Evangelista.
12. MSS Archives, in the handwriting of Sister Hildegard, who took seriously the heritage of her name and always saw every event as part of a big picture.

THE TREE THAT BENDS

Girls seeking entrance to a convent do not usually ask first what are the convent's works. Most of them come, to Benedictine convents at least, not so much to do external works as to find a real answer to their real longing. To call this a search for God is to credit the twentieth century with the same kind of depth St. Benedict had in the fifth.

When the bells rang November 11, 1962, opening the convent centennial year in Atchison, the person who for forty-one of those 100 years had received the newcomer into the convent was an old, old Sister watching the November sunlight on the orchard trees outside her Infirmary window. She was oblivious to most of the excitement, but to one who stopped in she said: "So? And are all of you still teaching for the love of God? And are there many new postulants?"

Scipio, Kansas, was a mission of the community in 1907. There Sister Josephine Weber was teaching. She had entered the convent in 1892, and now in the fifteenth year of her religious life she saw herself observed in the classroom one day by the most penetrating glance in Kansas. "Mother called me when that school day was over and told me she had another piece of work for me," Sister Josephine said. "I cried and told her I could not do it, but I would." [1]

She returned to Atchison with Mother Aloysia and took up the beginning of her long work of reading the newcomer's search and going part way with her. For forty-one years she was novice-mistress, and because she helped stamp so many

114

lives the story of her own which she wrote just before confinement to the Infirmary is important:

I was born October 24, 1867, at Wenns, Tyrol, the fifth child of twelve children of John Joseph Weber and Katherine Anna Haid . . . they had me baptized the same day I was born; they named me Aloysia after my maternal grandmother. . . .

I grew up in a happy Christian home; my parents were both deeply religious, and they guarded us against evil influence; the help they had were always good men and women. So I grew up without knowing even the name of evil. My father taught us the value of the Mass, and impressed on our minds the lessons of the Bible History stories. My mother had a cheerful, kindly disposition. She knew when to punish and when to persuade. When we would come to her with our grievances, she would tell us in her convincing way: "Child, the wiser gives."

The village school was taught by the Sisters of St. Vincent de Paul; the Sisters taught the girls and the small boys. The older boys had a man teacher, and they were in a separate building. We, all of us, loved the Sisters and we never had any difficulties with either the teachers or the school mates.

At the age of ten I received my First Holy Communion. There were no beautiful ceremonies observed, as they have now, to impress the great event on the child's mind. The following year I was confirmed; we had to go to Imst, the largest city near by, where the Bishop of Brixen confirmed an immense crowd of children. Aunt Cleopha was my godmother. On our way home we stopped at an inn to take refreshment; the innkeeper was a friendly man. He spoke to us of the grace and importance of the sacrament. Before I was all taken up with externals: going to the city, new wine-colored dress, apron in changeable colors, kerchief to match, new hat. I began to think about what the man said, and I began to see the difference.

Then came a deep sorrow into our lives. My father met with reverses, and we lost our home. Julia and I were sent to a boarding school in Zams, conducted by the same Sisters that taught our home school. The others went to live with my parents' families. At school it was very nice. The Chaplain, an elderly father, knew how to console. The instructor in religion was very good. The Sisters were kind and sympathetic. Singing and needlework belonged to the curriculum. Julia and I would have been very happy there, but in our heart was the sorrow and grief over the misfortune that had befallen our parents.

115

When everything was settled there were enough funds to take the family to America. So we got ready to go. What a transition for me! Seeing strange people and strange sights! The voyage across the ocean was calm, but on account of funds we traveled third class which was very unpleasant especially for our Mother. She did not complain, but we knew how she felt and we felt for her.

When we reached New York, we stayed at the Leo House to rest. Then we took the train to Plymouth, Indiana, where we had friends from the home place. They received us very kindly and we stayed with them till the family was settled. The children went to the Sisters' school; my brothers, Julia, and I, went to work. I stayed with a good Christian family and I felt at home with them. Grandpa Flashantrager was a landscaper in Germany. He was well read and had Christian ideals. He liked to talk to me; I think it was because I was a good listener. I hope they are by now in heaven.

The family did not like the country there, and they moved to Verona, Missouri, thinking of settling on a farm, but after a few months they moved to Hanover. Here, too, the little ones went to the Sisters' school and we older ones knew it was up to us to work and help. . . .

Nothing had any attraction for me except duty, home, and church. In my heart was a longing for the convent. . . . My first impression of the religious life I had received at the boarding school. They had a large number of novices whom they called Praeparantinnen. I listened to their hymns and prayers to the Sacred Heart in their evening visit. When we met them as they walked along the river Inn, I saw how happy they looked, how quietly they were walking along two and two. I heard them give a message to the setting sun.

I kept this longing hidden in my heart, for I considered it my duty to give my family the little help I could. Then on the eve of the Immaculate Conception in 1889, after confession, Father Neusius told me that I had a religious vocation and that I should go to the Convent. I prayed for courage to take the step. In spring of the following year, Mother Theresa, of happy memory, came to visit the Sisters. I went to see her and asked her to receive me; she kindly welcomed me, so I got ready.

On May 26, 1890, I bade them goodbye. The scene is still vivid in my mind. Sister Adelaide met me at the station in Atchison. Mother Theresa and the older Sisters were sitting in front of the convent. I had nothing to offer except a good will . . . I knew I had no qualification to teach. I loved the spiritual exercises, particularly reading.

I learned many lessons in the religious life as time went on, many of them by mistakes. In looking back I see how good God was in dealing with me and with my family. I am grateful to Him and to the Community which took me in and gave me an opportunity to serve God in ways and means that I would never have had outside the convent.

When, in 1907, she came from classroom to novice-mistress office, Sister Josephine took up the Rule, the study of the vows, the psalms, and the Scriptures with the devotion of all her life. She studied carefully and prayed much, loving all books including the book of nature. When summer winds and rains stormed among the trees, she would look outside with the candidates and novices, observing: "We can learn from nature. The trees that bend do not break."

She had a way of putting the things one liked to do within the framework of obedience. Sisters who knew how to paint made the spiritual bouquets for namedays. Those who loved to write would be summoned from the laundry some golden Monday afternoon and told: "A young priest is going to be ordained. Sit down and write a poem." And the Muses, thus imperiously summoned, would try to come from Parnassus into the wainscoted room called "St. John's," because it held a picture of the Baptist as a boy in the desert. Decorators had flowers and silk to work with to beautify the altar where for many years novices gathered to pray for everything and everyone in the world. Sometimes the box of candy would be opened and would wait invitingly on the checkered table-cloth of the recreation room until the night prayer bell and the regretful words: "We forgot to pass the candy. Well, tomorrow night."

No one ever could be really sure when the tall dark-eyed novice-mistress was deliberately trying the spirit. Some thought they saw through the daily detail to the basic pattern, however.

One morning two candidates spilled the whole Monday supply of starch by neglecting to apply the stopper to the bottom of the machine. On their way up to relate the monstrous deed one said: "We could tell her we spilled just a cup of starch. After all, the rest was water." But the other bravely insisted on telling the whole story of the molten white flood on the laundry floor. "Did you tell Sister Barbara? And did she have some more starch? Well, it's not so tragic then," said the amazingly interested face.

When, in 1914, Agnes Conway entered, the new postulant's only vanity was long radiant red hair. She decided that she should sacrifice the beauty and fastened it tightly to the top of her head. Sister Josephine beheld the monstrosity on a tour through the laundry and she told Miss Agnes that mortification should not extend to the eyes of others. But the postulant who liked too well a nicely fitting blouse and skirt was asked to wear for the feast of Christ the King a well-preserved box-pleated relic from a decade previous.

No convent would be worthy of the name without something of the hermit tradition, for the Scriptures did say, "I will lead her into the wilderness and speak to her heart." Sister Josephine tried to give young girls that for which they had really come. In the midst of it all she developed a deeply understanding and imperturbable calm.

"Sister, I want to go home. Where is my suitcase?" a postulant said one very hot summer afternoon.

Sister Josephine offered the questioner a piece of fresh divinity candy which someone had sent. The postulant accepted. Divinity on a hot afternoon looked good.

"Sister . . . may I go home?"

Again the box.

"Sister, may I get my suitcase?"

Once more the box.

The warm leaves outside the novitiate suddenly looked peaceful. A breeze stirred them. The postulant remembered the trees that bend. She smiled and went back to her work. No word had been spoken.

Classes of girls came from Germany. One of them learned the lesson of obedience more thoroughly and quickly than she learned English. On one of her first missions after vows, she was instructed by the Superior to put a letter in the mailbox. It was winter. "Be sure to put on your overshoes," was the Superior's parting injunction, as she remembered the walk down the snowy lane.

Perplexed, Sister Canisia stood in the middle of the kitchen floor. At last it has come, she thought, that occasion for perfect

118

obedience. She put on her rubbers, took the letter in one hand, opened what in German was the "mehl" box, and dropped the letter in the flour bin.

In the years of Sister Josephine's term as novice-mistress, five groups of German postulants came. They took their places among all the works of the Community. None of those who stayed to make vows, and most of them did, ever returned to her homeland. All brought memories that enriched the new land.

Sister Josephine understood them all, those from the Old World and from the New. One novice recalls going with sewing box in hand and asking mischievously, "Sister, may I have a black eye?" only to see with delight the austere novice-mistress double her fist. Another remembers hurrying downstairs in the middle of the night to knock on Sister's door when someone had become very ill and hearing the calmest of all voices say, "Praised be Jesus Christ, come in, Sister."

There were things she did whose deepest meaning the novices never really did fathom. Why she never seemed to give quite enough time for work, why she summoned a workman to class so often just before the last finishing touch, one often tried to figure out when the day was done and night had come down so quietly over the ancient trees. Did she really know it was possible for a girl to give up the whole outside world and then become attached to rows of dishes set just right or successful piles of work ranged beside an ironing machine?

Did she really know when praise was better than reproach and reproach better than praise? "You smiled your way into the Novitiate and you smile it out," she said to one young Sister on the day of her vows. "Well, you are leaving us," she said to another, also on profession day, "to go out to the Missions. And with all your faults."

And what did she mean by responses like the following? "Don't we sing when we take down the Christmas crib?" a novice with an Irish name asked her. "Why, yes, of course, we should." And the next laundry day from the midst of her work the novice was summoned solemnly to sing German carols with Sister Josephine while they put away shepherd and sheep, angels, and the Holy Family.

She kept a stable house during the changing and developing years. Old age came, and in 1948 the veteran novice-mistress "retired." More than 500 girls had learned the art of being Sisters from her. Somehow she had wonderfully permitted them to be themselves, to find what they had been looking for. One day one of them, on a flying trip home from a mission, slowed her steps and offered to help Sister Josephine up a stairway. "No. Just watch me. Then you will know how to walk when you are eighty-eight."

And during her long wait in the Infirmary, in even older age, she liked to say to the visitor: "You are glad you came and stayed, aren't you? Sisters can do so much good. We must pray. We must pray for souls. The Sacred Heart is so good."

1. Interview, Summer, 1961.

REVOLUTION IN THE SCHOOLS

The early years of the twentieth century at the convent had all the charm of faith, growth, and work to do. At the convent and academy itself there was activity. In 1905, on June 1, the choir sang its first Gregorian chant and Sisters Edith Stein, Petronilla Willems, and Scholastica Kratschmer went to Conception Abbey for a course in Solesmes Plain Chant, recommended, wrote the convent chroniclist, by Pope Pius X.

On June 24, 1908, when the chapel was solemnly consecrated, many friends gathered to reminisce. At the noon banquet, Bishop Lillis was toastmaster with Abbot Frowin Conrad, Monsignor Kuhls, chancellor, and the Very Rev. Boniface Verheyen as guests of honor. Father Peter Kassens of the Abbey, called upon to give a toast, recalled his days as a student in 1863 when he anticipated the Sisters' coming by helping to carry the straw mattresses to the convent. Father L. J. Beck of Argentine, Kansas, spoke on "The Benedictine Sister in the Parochial School." That hardy personality who used to accompany his choir with the violin while it sang the Gloria, said that the Sisters followed their motto of "Pray and Labor" to the letter and spirit, and the grateful table-waiters beamed with pride.

Monsignor Kuhls, the first alumnus of St. Benedict's College, spoke of the poverty with which Benedictine life began in this country. He recalled days at St. Benedict's when the most frequent dish was a mysterious substance called "Charley Come Back." He praised Father Thomas Bartl, the Sisters' first chaplain, saying:

He was often hungry that others might eat, and thirsty that others might drink. Heat and cold, snow and rain, could not discourage him. He traveled by day and night, on foot and on horseback, administering the consolations of religion. He was a saint and I would kneel at his grave and ask for his prayers.[1]

Somewhere in the audience listening, Mother Evangelista remembered. The next year, June 21, brought her death. At her funeral, loyally attended by Atchison people, her pallbearers were William Dolan and George Ostertag, her benefactors from the beginning; John Intfen, and John Reynolds, representatives of the first parochial school opened by the sisters; and Joe Weingard, faithful convent workman. Among Mother's papers was found an old poem she had loved, "Secrets of the Saints," the first stanza of which reads:

> To play through life a noble part,
> Yet humble and unknown;
> To seek no rest in any heart
> Save only God's alone;
> To have no will in little things,
> To have no share in great!
> To shun no burden labor brings,
> And for the crown to wait.

In 1911 two different groups of famous persons visited. Mother Ferdinanda and Sister Xaveria, Missionary Sisters of St. Benedict from Tutzing, Bavaria, visited on their way to the Philippine Islands on July 22.[2] And on September 27, the convent had its only presidential visitor in the century. President William Howard Taft, accompanied by Major Archibald W. Butt, called at the convent and academy. And when on April 12, 1912, the community mourned with the world the sinking of the *Titanic*, it mourned doubly. Major Archibald Butt was one of those who went down with the ship.

The days of the convent and academy were intricately woven and yet importantly separate. The convent's first Constitutions had bravely provided that the Sisters should know what they were teaching. The convent's program of study demanded that Sisters be educated in religion, the science of religious perfection, Latin, music, profane sciences, literary study, as necessary for their lives as Sisters and teachers. And the early catalogues with their detailed spelling out of courses in English, mathematics, Latin, history, German, government, mythology, mental and moral philosophy, geology, botany, astronomy, and physics, suggest that by either remote or immediate preparation the faculty were doing very well.

They were golden days for students. Girls did recreational reading on Sunday mornings only, but they tackled Shakespeare and Dante with a vengeance. "I was a student here in 1914," a visitor said in November of 1962. "All my life I remembered what Sister Hildegard said in Dante classes."

Academy graduations and recitals took place amid many flowers and much dignity. There was music and art, journalism and creative writing. The first efforts at the latter took the form of Annals appended to the catalogue. Pupils loved to scan the new ones and find the old ones, for in them they were able to discover the family names of their teachers, which appeared on reception and profession days and then disappeared forever.

Plain and art needlework were on the curriculum. "Nov. 14, Benedictine All Saints. Who will ask for a free day is a question which has been passed around the Academy for the past few days. Finally R. H. (Sister Dolorosa of later days) summoned all her courage and asked the Venerable Directress. . . . We all took advantage of this favor and plied the needle diligently all day; for we were very anxious to finish some of our numerous Christmas presents," [3] said the faithful Annals. A science laboratory at the head of the stairs on the second floor of St. Scholastica's Hall was used chiefly for demonstration. The equipment was costly, and so greatly loved that pupils kept their hands behind their backs during demonstration, it is said, for fear of breakage.

The educational world was bright with lectures on art, literature, and famous places in the old world, with the community attending along with students as the young Father Martin Veth gave the results of his study in Europe. The young Father Felix Nolte operated the lantern and slides. In his talk on May 1, 1912, Father Martin said:

Art is not recreation; it cannot be learned in spare moments nor pursued when we have nothing else to do. It is a ladder to God, one of the purest and highest elements in human happiness. [4]

His listeners knew what he meant. They had their own struggles to produce the really artistic. In their own assemblies, the audience sat awed at presentations of the elocution classes with Sarah Howe as the "wily Anthony," Gladys Lednicky as the "plain, blunt Brutus," and Lucille Pearl as the "lean and hungry Cassius." "Each," commented the reporter, "revealed the true character of her role and, in doing so, showed wonderful power of endurance." [5] Beatrice Jacobs, later Sister Geraldine, gave a "charming vocal rendition of Weckherlin's Nina."

It was such a program which the Abbot Primate Hildebrande de Hemptienne and his companion, the Rev. Julius Jonckhure of the Abbey of Maredsous, found in operation when they visited Mount St. Scholastica. They came as delegates of Pope Pius X to visit all the Benedictine monasteries and convents in the United States and Canada, on November 18, 1910. When they arrived in the carriage with its black curtains, driven by the convent chauffeur with his prancing horses, says the chronicler, "the students, in uniforms and wearing white veils, formed in long lines at the entrance to the grounds and as His Lordship alighted a glad welcome rose from every heart." [6]

In the program following the Mass, forty little girls in white, bearing yellow and white chrysanthemums, escorted him to the hall where the student body sang a welcome chorus, the rendition of which was considered "heartfelt and faultless." One of the singers, Sarah Howe, made a speech and gave the Abbot Primate a Kansas sunflower. The Abbot responded, the assembly sang *Jubilate Deo*, and then all 161 students, "a bright procession of happy faces," received the Abbot's individual blessing. Then to everyone's delight he asked for a copy of the welcoming address. The convent's cup of happiness was full to the brim, and the chroniclist concludes:

The students stood gracefully grouped upon the stage and down through the body of the hall. The whole scene was symbolic as it was imposing, the West [the students] reverently facing the East [the Abbot and his monk escorts] where the light of true Faith is preserved and whence it is dispensed, Kansas looking back gratefully to Rome and Monte Cassino.[7]

But even more joy was to come. The Abbot Primate said he intended to give the sunflower to Pope Pius X himself. Not to be outdone, and because the occasion really meant so much, Mother Aloysia sent fresh sunflowers to Newark, New Jersey, to be given to the Abbot Primate when his tour was over and he was setting sail for home, so that although the Holy Father would have the original gift the Abbot himself would have his own.

Father Julius, his companion, was so impressed with what he thought was the joy and achievement he saw, that he wrote back from Maredsous on his return. He had been asked to write a booklet on the works of the Order, in connection with a congress of social works to be held at Maredsous, and he wanted a copy of the academy catalogue and an outline of its faculty's preparation. He wondered too before what examiners the Sisters had to appear.[8]

The chief court of examination before which they appeared was Mother Aloysia and Sister Hildegard, but she could hardly say just that, so she relayed the letter to Abbot Innocent who answered her:

Tell him that your Sisters have a regular course which he can see in your catalogue; that they have a special scholastic examination after having made first vows, and having finished that they are examined by the faculty of the Academy.

When they teach in the parochial schools, they must get a certificate of fitness from the Diocesan schoolboard, which expires. Then, after three or five years of teaching, they may get a life certificate. When the Sisters teach in so-called public schools, they must get a state certificate. Such schools are attended by Catholic children and are practically parochial schools, except that the schoolboard pays the teachers and the schools are visited by the school superintendent of the county.[9]

All of this was true and Mother knew it. Perhaps she was like the gentleman in Moliere's play who had been talking prose all his life and did not realize it. Atchison's educational policy looked quite dignified on paper. The letter, in the shaky script of the aging Abbot, bespeaks his whole patient approach. It finished: "This morning is nice, but I am so frozen I fear to go out. I hope the cold is broken."

Slowly the convent was coming of age, codifying its program, spelling out its objectives, even sending back to the Old

World some of its own gift stamped with the energy of the New World which had received and used it. The convent's golden jubilee was approaching. March brought a death which took the memories of everyone back to early roots. The *Annals* announced:

It is a long time since the city of Atchison has been stirred to such a sense of loss as has been awakened by the death of Mr. William F. Dolan, which occurred today at St. Margaret's Hospital, Kansas City, Kans., and especially is he mourned at Mount St. Scholastica where his memory will ever be cherished as that of a staunch and esteemed friend. His life was beautiful in its integrity and devotedness to duty, a life animated by faith and charity and crowned by a holy death. While offering sincerest condolence to the bereaved family, let us hope that the glorious Easter-tide may dispel the gloom his death has caused, and lift all sorrowing hearts to the risen Savior whose triumph over death took therefrom all semblance of sting.[10]

The great benefactor who so long had befriended the convent, who with Mr. Falk, Mr. Jacobs, Mr. Kennedy, and Abbot Innocent had helped to negotiate the purchase of Price Villa, who had for many years given a hundred pounds of coffee to the convent each Christmas, who had not only sent his gifts but had brought them with the air of a man who personally cared, had gone now to the reward of those who build the Church of God.

It was with the memory of him and of many others that the community observed on July 26 of that year its golden jubilee. "It was decided," says one of the convent's early historians, "to put a bell in the convent tower that would send its jubilant tones to the city of Atchison that this year was fifty and we were placing a bell in our tower to ring out morning, noon, and night its glad thanks to the ones who made it possible." The bell was also intended "to call to prayer all those who wished to return thanks to God who is always with us by the great mystery of the Incarnation." [11]

Academy students and alumnae contributed the necessary $600, with Sister Hildegard managing the collection. She herself was a patient in St. Margaret's Hospital when Bishop Ward blessed the bell and Mr. Wright, a workman, hoisted it to its position, but the convent called her by telephone to permit her to hear its first chimes. In a special gesture to the European Sisters who had so missed the sound of bells, Mother Aloysia commissioned Sister Mary Jane Wecherlin to be its first ringer.[12]

But history did not pause for anniversary.

In late December of the Jubilee year a whole new world entered the convent's area of service. A Western bishop, Bishop Matz of Pueblo, arrived suddenly in Atchison. In the shadow of the Spanish Peaks, in a land of coal and silver mines, were people of many nationalities with many untaught children. A school which had hopefully opened in September had suddenly been deprived of teachers by the discovery that the community of Sisters was not canonically erected and was being disbanded.

"I have no Sisters left to send," Mother Aloysia said, even while her eyes were mentally reviewing the list.

"I will pray in the Chapel while you call your Council," the Bishop said.

And on January 3, 1914, to more than 500 children with Italian, Spanish, Greek, Irish, and German names, St. Mary's School in Walsenburg, Colorado, reopened. Mother Aloysia sent Sisters whose names either duplicated or sounded like the names of the previous community. From peaceful Kansas agricultural areas, they stood in the doorways and faced the classrooms packed with students of all ages. Sisters who, in those days, had no formal sociology courses, learned quickly the lives of mine workers and translated into classroom situations the differences between union workers and non-union members. They saw a militia from Fort Leavenworth come out to help settle a strike. And they did their best to settle their own. After a while, though, it was not so hard. "I had in my fifth grade Angelo and Eusebio, both aged eighteen. They helped me with the smaller ones," an early teacher said.

"Sometimes we had no equipment but the word of God," another recalled of the vast crowds in the religious vacation schools that developed in surrounding areas. "Some people say we only herded in those years. But I remember their faces and their dark quiet eyes. For many of them the word of God was enough equipment."

Colorado with its changing Spanish Peaks was a new world.

But life was, at the same time, offering the convent two other new worlds. A few months previous, Father Martin had lectured on "Constantinople and the Turkish Government," and his peaceful listeners became aware that there was crisis across the ocean. Then in July of 1914 the conflict broke out. Episcopal letters asked everyone to pray, Academy students bought Liberty bonds, and in the convent choir the Divine Office was offered for soldiers and people on both sides of the conflict. Some of the German postulants destined for missionary work in the Philippines after education in Atchison found the waiting too long, and Sister Perpetua Kugler and Sister Gonzaga Engelhart entered the Atchison community.

The war years were terrible years, but there was no bitterness in the convent. It sang its *Stille Nacht* after the Divine Office each Christmas that the God of peace would come in peace to all. It prayed and saved for the suffering everywhere, and mourned the brothers and friends of both German and American Sisters.

It went on with its daily work, in which there was indeed no war, but something of a slight revolution at least.

Something was happening to the pattern of American education. High school boys were taking their places in classrooms taught by Sisters, and state accrediting agencies were mingling with diocesan school boards to affect the pattern by which Sisters would forever afterward be prepared.

The first group of high school boys in Atchison history made their appearance appropriately at SS. Peter and Paul, Seneca, Atchison's oldest mission. And there were touches of great beauty in the venture. "Make them learn and behave," said Sister Hilda Booz, the Superior and principal. "Don't you tap the bell for them to go out to recite?" she asked a younger teacher, not too long graduated from a coeducational high school herself. "Well, teach them the way you think you should."

When Forty Hours Devotion approached, Sister Romana Farrell, that younger Sister, asked that the boys be scheduled to keep a noon hour of adoration. "They'll never do it," Sister Hilda warned. "They won't give up their free time."

"May we have a front pew left vacant just in case they do?" Sister Romana petitioned.

The front pew loomed empty at a minute to twelve. But as the noon whistle and the Angelus began simultaneously to sound, into the pew rushed the eight boys. Sister Hilda, speaking to them later in their classroom, commended them and finished: "And an old lady in the back of the Church sat down and cried." One of the grade school teachers, making a visit to the Blessed Sacrament with her docile group, said that the little old lady who wept was Sister Hilda.

The mission list grew quickly in those years. Mother Aloysia took fifty-eight new schools in her twenty-seven years as Superior, and the fourteen Holy Helpers had to multiply their responsibilities. Many missions had coeducational high schools, and Mother expressed her official attitude to the Rev. Francis Orr, chancellor of the diocese:

Realizing that many boys will be debarred from a Catholic High School education unless Sisters offer themselves as teachers, we believe it to be in accord with God's design that we should be willing to accept the care of high schools.[13]

Bishop Ward encouraged the Sisters to meet the growing requirements of the state and to secure proper documentary evidence of their higher education. There had been real education, real learning at St. Scholastica's from the very beginning. But there was not yet a single so-called college degree in the house. Suddenly all the work and all the demand were upon it. And in June of 1917, four Sisters embarked for the national capital armed with the following letter, still preserved in Abbot Innocent's faithful handwriting:

St. Benedict's Abbey
Atchison, Kansas
June 24, 1917

The Venerable Benedictine Sisters Hildegard, Adelaide, Dorothy, and Bernarda, members of St. Scholastica's Convent, this city, are going to the Catholic University of Washington, for the summer school. Any favors shown them will be highly appreciated by the

Rev. Mother Aloysia, OSB
Prioress of Saint Scholastica's Convent,
and by
Innocent, OSB
Abbot

A revolution in the schools was turning the wheels forward in a long trail to the outside world of classified higher learning. It would bring that world back to the hill of Mount St. Scholastica, whose first purchase had been books.

1. MSS *Catalogue*, 1909, p. 39.
2. After many years of service there, Sister Xaveria died, a victim of the bombing of World War II, in 1944.
3. MSS *Catalogue*, 1907, p. 38.
4. *Ibid.*, 1912, p. 54.
5. *Ibid.* Sarah Howe became Mount St. Scholastica's drama teacher, Sister Benedicta Howe.
6. MSS *Catalogue*, 1911.
7. *Ibid.*
8. Letter of January 17, 1912, MSS Archives.
9. Letter of February 4, 1912, MSS Archives.
10. MSS *Catalogue*, 1912, p. 54.
11. Sister Pauline Anderson, *Earliest Memories*, MSS Archives.
12. "On the train coming from New York," reminisced Sister Cleopha in the summer of 1961, "we thought the train bells were church bells and rejoiced we had come to such a religious country." Bell-ringers after Sister Mary Jane were Sister Odelia, Sister Cleopha, and Sister Pia Leithmer, all from Europe.
13. September 13, 1916, Archdiocesan Archives.

MORE ROOM FOR GLORY

From 1917 on there was a steady stream of summer school students to East and West. In 1918 eight Sisters began the long, never to be broken trek to Creighton University.[1] That summer they stayed at Papillion, Nebraska, in the parish school convent. They rose at three o'clock, meditated, went to Mass, had breakfast and caught the interurban to Omaha for eight o'clock classes. The mode of travel was repeated in the evening.

In one of those early summers, when the group of Sisters assembled for instructions before leaving, the convent procurator, Sister Rosalia Krieger, said: "Now you will be studying at Brownell Hall. Be sure to take care of it. It's a nice hall for women students. Don't put any glasses on the windowsills or mar it in any way. The Jesuits will expect you to know how to take care of a building."[2]

The thirty Sisters agreed solemnly to their part. A circular letter from the university had asked them to bring small rugs. Arriving at Creighton they saw Brownell Hall. Little that in their most irregular moments they could have done would have harmed Brownell. Constructed in 1877 as an Episcopalian boarding school for girls, it had been more recently occupied by the army. Now it was being rented by the university which had invited the Sisters to bring rugs not to protect the floor but to protect the Sisters.

By August 4, 1921, after a series of summers, special examinations, and home study, the first four Atchison sisters received Baccalaureate degrees. They were Sister Hildegard,

Litt.B., and Sisters Bernarda, Bonaventure, and Helena, A.B.

Summer schools were set up by St. Benedict's on the convent grounds themselves in 1919. Meticulous and patient, far-seeing and exact, Father Sylvester Schmitz directed the sessions. The convent chronicle records often in winter and spring months: "Father Sylvester was over today to plan the summer courses." Father Bonaventure Schwinn marshalled the community into literature and versification classes, and the same chronicle is rich with the record: "Father Bonaventure gave back our short stories today — 70 papers. The Sisters had done very creditable work, he said." There was genial Father Pius Pretz for mathematics, while Father Felix Nolte brought his boundless zest for geology and his really vast and firsthand knowledge of rocks. The community assembled, hands under scapulars, to hear Sister Flavia Hogan read "The Outcasts of Poker Flat" with the same zeal and objectivity with which she read the morning meditation. Learning was a community project, and one book served when seventy were more expensive than necessary.

Years later Sisters would say: "I wrote a poem once, in Father Bonaventure's class."

From 1919 until 1924 the Sisters took some summer classes at St. Benedict's itself because of inadequate laboratory equipment at the convent. But even as they did so, other plans were being made. Their own new college building was being dreamed and built.

Inspectors from the State Board of Health in 1916 had found the academy quarters in "admirable condition, beautifully clean." But, they reported respectfully, the dormitory in St. Scholastica Hall was "rather crowded, and although it had dormer windows on all of the four sides, the ventilation, according to modern standards, would be considered insufficient." [3]

By the spring of 1921 the convent was ready and received the following letter from the episcopal residence:

March 4, 1921

Dear Mother Aloysia, O.S.B.,

You have my permission and approval in your proposed building. You know of course if you need to borrow a very large amount, the permission of Rome would have to be obtained. Judging from past experience in this matter, I don't think you will have the least difficulty in obtaining this favor from Rome. Wishing yourself and Community every quadragesimal grace and blessing, I am, Yours sincerely and appreciatively,

John Ward, Bishop of Leavenworth

The long blasting, digging, cement-pouring, and bricklaying began. On October 5, 1922, the feast of St. Placid, who had been one of the first pupils at a Benedictine monastic school, ground was broken. On February 28, 1923, the cornerstone of the building was laid, containing, says a manuscript, the following items:

Catalogue of 1910, containing the account of Mother Evangelista's death; catalogue of 1913, containing the story of the Golden Jubilee; short history of Mount St. Scholastica Academy, written by Sister Hildegard; list of officials of the convent and academy and of the academy faculty; list of the spiritual and temporal authorities present at the laying of the cornerstone, list of graduates of 1923, copy of the *Holy Rule*, Constitutions, and customs, the *Atchison Daily Globe,* and the *Catholic Register;* pictures of St. Benedict, St. Placid, and St. Maurus, groups of five great Benedictine saints; picture of St. Joseph, under whose patronage the building was placed; picture of St. Hildegard under whose patronage the college department is placed; picture of the Rev. Father Henrichs, martyr priest of Denver, Colorado; picture of Blessed Brother Konrad; postals of the various buildings, souvenir of American Benedictine convents in the United States; a large medal of St. Benedict, two inches in diameter; silver coins.[4]

Early in the building, four men fell from the second story under construction. The community made a novena to the newly beatified Thérèse of Lisieux for their recovery. When two of them died, the Sisters grieved, and a small statue of St. Joseph was fixed to a pedestal on the wall of St. Cecilia's old building so that the great workman, perhaps more experienced in building than the younger saint, could watch over the rest of the process.

There was great bustle on the grounds during the building. Mother Aloysia and Sister Rosalia followed almost every inch of its progress with anxious joy. Thanksgiving dinner and

133

Christmas dinner were served those of the workmen and over-
seers whose homes were not in Atchison. Every brick mattered
and every day mattered. Atchison itself had not yet really
seen such a structure. In the spring of 1923, Mother wrote the
missions schools to encourage girls to enroll in fall courses.
The rapidly rising shell of brick and glass, with its five acres
of prospective classrooms, was secretly challenging everyone's
faith, and Mother Aloysia had been heard again to say: "May
the community forgive me if I have built too big."

The class of 1923 was the last to graduate from the old
buildings. They made the most of it by rehearsing the early
days of Mount St. Scholastica under the title, "Out of the
Old into the New." Sister Hildegard wrote the verses which
were dramatized by thirty-five girls dressed in the green
dresses and white aprons worn in early days. The verses began:

> Twas late in chill November
> When our Alma Mater came
> To ope her doors of welcome
> In Scholastica's sweet name.

By January 15, 1924, feast of St. Maurus, that other first
pupil of St. Benedict, the building was finished enough to
bless. In five acres of brick, stone, and window, it rose in five
stories, a majestic and wonderful building which had cost
$810,000. Bishop Ward celebrated a pontifical high Mass in
the convent chapel at nine o'clock. The blessing took place at
10:30, followed by a banquet. Memorable toasts were given at
the banquet by Bishop Ward, Bishop Gilfillan, and Sheffield
Ingalls, son of the Senator John Ingalls who, as editor of the
Champion in 1863, had lauded the Sisters when $4,000 was
an impossible sum and they needed laudation so much. There
was an organ recital at two o'clock, and in the evening a recital of both organ and harp with Marie Singleton of Kansas
City as organist and M. S. Russo, also of Kansas City, as
harpist.

The *Atchison Globe* sang the praises of the new administration building with its 150 rooms, saying: "The building is a
monument to the wonderful success of the Benedictine Sisters,

and gives to the city a school for girls which is second to none in pedagogy and equipment. It is by far the largest building in Atchison." Preparatory to the blessing, the Sisters had converged on the terrazo floors with their cleaning and polishing equipment and the acres of stone knew the possibilities of their new proprietors. The *Globe*, commenting on the day of blessing, said: "NEW ACADEMY AMAZES ALL. THOUSANDS BRAVE COLD SUNDAY TO OPEN HOUSE."

That paper which, since the tradition of Ed Howe had touched it, had been sparing of superlatives, opened its linotype keyboard now:

Notwithstanding its great size the lines of the building are of great beauty, and simplicity which makes for grandeur. It is the last word in architectural perfection, and as up-to-date as any building in the entire country for scholastic purposes. Ornamentation has been entirely left out, except in the entrance, lobby and auditorium, where with excellent effect white Tavarenelle and cream-colored Bottocino marble is used.

All roads seemed to lead to the new building yesterday and from eight o'clock in the morning until six o'clock visitors swarmed the rooms and the corridors. The Sisters were tireless in their efforts to entertain the guests.

People sometimes build their own reflections into their work. "My life is done," Mother Aloysia said, regarding the huge majestic structure at the end of the day when the crowds had gone. "I will not see another building erected."

"Neither will I," said young Sister Dolorosa Hoffmans, an academy teacher, standing beside her in awe.

Mother Aloysia turned instantly. "How can you say that, young Sister! Don't you love the work of God and the community more than that? You must dream and plan for the future."

The revolution in the schools which had led to the necessity of this huge building was to her not a breaking away from anything good but a turning of great wheels forward. Atchison's giant building would hear great speakers of the world. It would be the background for the meeting of many people. The revolution in the schools had gone in the same direction that the stagecoach, locomotive, and skipper's wheels had taken when the great idea of Mount St. Scholastica first came to Kansas.

As the new electric light switches turned out the new lights that night, there was just more room now on the Mount for God to be glorified.

1. Sisters Hildegard O'Keefe, Dorothy Dooley, Bernarda Brentano, Helena Brandmeir, Hedwig Heinrichs, Eusebia Rooney, Romana Farrell, and Bonaventure McKenna were the pioneers.
2. Interview with Sister Romana Farrell, Summer, 1960.
3. March 16, 1916. MSS Archives. The report was signed by B. J. Alexander, M.D., and Lydia Allen DeVilbias, M.D.
4. List in the MSS Archives.

THE CONGREGATION

There was an old thread dangling out of the past, a tormenting, important, beautiful piece of work involving both sides of the Atlantic and ultimately, perhaps, the equator. It was the question of a congregation for Benedictine houses which would give each of the growing convents freedom and security.

In the long history of monasticism, the question was important. The relationship of clausura and external works, of the famous and always inseparable active and contemplative ways, was involved. Some grouping and some stable constitutions for it had been seen as needful already in 1864 by Boniface Wimmer, and had occupied Bishop Fink, Mother Evangelista, and Mother Theresa. Mother Aloysia found the unsettled matter on her desk early in her career, and although one never can apply the word "worry" to her, for she seems not to have done that, it did challenge and concern her. Abbot Innocent tells this fact in a letter to Rome, January 9, 1900. The letter is a fragment in the St. Benedict Abbey Archives, and the name of the monk who received it is not known:

. . . The Sisters are anxious to have statutes or constitutions approved by Rome so that they cannot be tampered with by every new superior or superioress. When I asked for the list [of Benedictine convents] and said that it was for the Abbot Primate, the Sisters were happy, because the Sisters were sure that now something would be done at Rome for them. From the circular I received begging to help Benedictine nuns to buy back their old monastery I judge that the list is not wanted to help our Sisters in

137

getting statutes approved by Rome, but to send a begging letter
to them.

I did not tell the Sisters my thoughts, because I would not spoil
their fond hopes. It is cruel to cut off hope. But when they get a
begging circular and no word about statutes, they will be somewhat disappointed. I think the only one who can do something for
our sisters is the Right Rev. Abbot Primate, he could get the holy
See to do something for them . . . our sisters never tried to push
forward to be praised, and will never ask it. What they want is
not praise but protection. You will do a good work, very pleasing
to God, if you represent their need to the Abbot Primate; he has
the statutes of our sisters in Atchison; they are printed in Latin.

But nothing much happened. In 1908, Benedictine prioresses met in Chicago. After the meeting, Mother Aloysia wrote
to Right Rev. Hildebrande de Hemptienne, Abbot Primate,
requesting that he present the Declarations and Constitutions
to the Holy See with a petition for approval.

Instead of writing, Abbot Hildebrande came in person, for
he said: "I have prayed much and considered often the position of our American Sisters . . . but the question is rather a
complicated one and I believe that experience and personal
intercourse are necessary to assure this happy result." [1] The
complication was really a very identifiable difficulty. The
Sisters could not properly be called *moniales* unless they took
solemn vows, and they could not organize into a really centralized congregation and yet maintain their vow of stability.
They wanted to be real American Benedictine nuns, *moniales;*
they wanted to be a congregation for the sake of mutual help
among convents, help which would have some binding force;
and they wanted to keep their vow of stability. But the enclosure attendant on solemn vows would change the kind of
teaching to which they were committed, and to keep their vow
of stability seemed to limit any real kind of congregation.

Abbot Hildebrande came to see for himself how American
Benedictinism was working. The visit was a happy one, but
he was unable to do very much to help his hostesses. He became ill shortly after returning to Europe and died August 13,
1913, at Beuron, saying: "Oh, how lovely it will be to behold
my God and His blessed Mother." [2] The convent wrote a letter

of sympathy, and his faithful secretary, Father Julius, who had accompanied him on the Kansas trip, responded:

It is very rare nowadays to meet real sympathy, but, during his visit at Atchison, Father Primate could secure himself that your magnificent reception, your *sunflowers*, your wreaths were the very expression of a heartfelt welcome. He himself never forgot beloved Mount St. Scholastica, and your meeting was one of the most pleasant topics of his America journey.[3]

But now the Abbot Primate who had really known the interplay of prayer and work, clausura and external activity, in Atchison was dead. And on August 20, 1914, Pope Pius X, to whom he had spoken and who it is hoped received the sunflower, was also dead.

But on September 3, 1914, Pope Benedict XV was elected. A close friend of the new pope was Aidan Cardinal Gasquet, the English Benedictine who had spent hours, days, and weeks in the British museum trying to restore the true picture of the late-medieval monk. He had visited the United States and had liked the American brand of Benedictinism. His aid in pushing forward the approval of the Constitutions is recorded in his faithful correspondence with Abbot Ernest of St. Mary's, Newark. Rome was at last facing the central crux which had, since 1866 when Abbot Boniface had introduced it to Rome verbally and 1878 when Bishop Fink had put it in writing, plagued the permanent establishment of a congregation.

It was still impossible for the Sisters to become real *moniales* (strictly cloistered), and it was entirely undesirable for them to give up their vow of stability. And this dilemma was the knot no one seemed able to untie. Abbot Maurus Serafini, secretary of the Congregation of Religious, put it all quite plainly. Father Philip Langton, an English monk writing Abbot Ernest from Rome, summarizes his attitude:

The Schema of Constitutions and Declarations presented for the Congregation of St. Scholastica, Atchison, is not in accord with the Normae of existing Canon Law regarding religious women. This Law contemplated "Moniales" and "Sorores." Moniales (even with only simple vows) cannot form a Congregation, each Monastery is *sui juris*. The Sorores can form Congregations — but then they

139

must conform to the Normae — and they cannot take special vows, but only the usual ones of chastity, poverty, and obedience. Authority rests with the superior general. Now the proposed Constitutions and Declarations don't fit into either of these classes, and consequently could not be approved *prout jacent*. In view of the object contemplated, in order to form a union, they ought to conform to the class "Sorores" — abolish Stability with accompanying vow, and preserve merely some sort of grouping of houses, though even this will be a little difficult to obtain.[4]

It meant, bluntly, that to form a congregation they would have to give up their profession for any particular house and be movable anywhere by a Superior General.

Abbot Ernest refused to find it so insoluble. He wrote to Abbot Innocent:

It will certainly under the present circumstances be impossible for our sisters to become real moniales, as Abbot Serafini would want. It is also out of question to have them give up the vow of stability. If they would do this, they would give up being Benedictines. From Canon 488, no. 7, it would appear that Rome for reason would look upon our sisters as moniales, if their case were rightly presented to the Congregation of Religious. I will write to Cardinal Gasquet and ask him to try to get this for the sisters. The urgent need of the sisters for teachers in our schools will perhaps be reason sufficient for Rome to make this exception for our country.[5]

The Cardinal's answer was clear: "The difficulty that has been raised isn't imaginary. If they are Benedictine nuns in Solemn vows, then enclosure follows as a necessity. Would Perpetual simple vows satisfy them? I don't see that it makes much difference."[6]

Cardinal Gasquet, with the Abbot Primate, took the matter directly to Pope Benedict XV in December, 1919, and the result of the interview, in the words of the Abbot Primate, was: "His Holiness promised to exert his power to the benefit of the Sisters so that midway between cloistered nuns and ordinary sisters there would be set up a lasting way of life in the spirit of the Holy Rule."[7] In a letter to the missions, Mother Aloysia translated the message with characteristic directness: "It is surely a privilege to have the Holy Father take a personal interest in us."

The knot that could not be untied was cut. Pope Benedict XV took the question out of the *Plenaria* (the larger general body studying religious groups) where it would have failed, said Cardinal Gasquet, as "contrary to the codex (or accepted pattern)" and created a small commission of Cardinals to work directly on it, "a commission of which I am one," Gasquet wrote happily to Abbot Ernest. "The case of the Benedictine nuns is really moving." [8]

Two months later, March 23, 1921, the commission approved the Constitutions and the formation of a Congregation and recommended the acceptance of the Congregation for seven years. Now the Sisters were *moniales* still, but a rather special sort of nuns with perpetual simple vows, saying the Divine Office, making vows of stability, but established in a Congregation with a Mother President and a General Chapter which could help to stabilize, encourage, and advance Benedictine life without taking away the autonomy of each house so long sacred to the Order, so precarious in some ways but so fruitful in others. Each had its own Novitiate.

The date of approbation was set for January 22, 1922, but Pope Benedict XV died that day. So a fifth Pope touched the story of the Constitutions of St. Scholastica. Pope Pius IX had given oral approval to their beginning in an interview with Boniface Wimmer; in Leo XIII's time, Cardinal Simeoni had sent kind words and important direction to Bishop Fink; Abbot Hildebrande had gone to Pope Pius X; Benedict XV had created the commission of Cardinals to work on the Constitutions. Now Pope Pius XI formally granted approval, February 25, 1922. It was the feastday of St. Walburga.

Petitioning charter members were St. Scholastica, Atchison, Kansas; St. Joseph, St. Mary's, Pennsylvania; St. Benedict, Erie, Pennsylvania; St. Scholastica, Chicago, Illinois; Sacred Heart, Lisle, Illinois; St. Walburga, Elizabeth, New Jersey; Blessed Virgin Mary, Pittsburgh, Pennsylvania; St. Joseph, Guthrie, Oklahoma; St. Gertrude, Ridgely, Maryland; Sacred Heart, Cullman, Alabama. [9]

Cardinal Gasquet paused in his busy life to rejoice. The author of so many studies of monasticism, the rescuer of the Middle Ages from many clouds of misunderstanding, the translator of the Bible, the real friend of the American apostolate, was an old man now of nearly eighty, with two years of an endlessly active and zealous life yet to live. "I am glad," he wrote to Abbot Ernest, "that the Benedictine Sisters are on the whole satisfied with the result of their petition to form a congregation. It was not easy to get the principle admitted [that Sisters could be real Benedictines though in simple perpetual vows and that a Congregation need not be so centralized a thing as to rule out the vow of stability] and I do not think we should have had much chance if the Pope had not granted my request that the question should be treated by a special Commission of three Cardinals. Once we met, in three hours all was done." [10]

The first General Chapter of the approved Congregation met August 7, 1923, at Lisle, Illinois, Sacred Heart Convent. Mother Aloysia was elected president; Mother Regina O'Donnell of Elizabeth and Sister Theresa Hueber of Pittsburgh were chosen as Visitators. It was a solemn five days in Benedictine history, so solemn that it is interesting to note in the Convent Chronicle what was happening at home during the deliberations:

Aug. 7: All are busy sewing, mending comforters and blankets, and trying to be good while our Mother is away. . . . We received word from Mother and are happy to know she is feeling well. The principal assembly will take place tomorrow.

Aug. 10: Benediction after Holy Mass. Confession. Father Gerard came in Abbot Martin's place, as the Abbot is in Chicago. We just received word that Mother was re-elected Mother General again at the meeting in Lisle. She has done much . . .

Aug. 11: Rev. Mother Mechtilde and Sister M. Lourdes, OSB, of Guthrie, came this morning. They just left our Mother yesterday in Lisle, and it seemed good to see them because of this. They are much pleased with all that occurred during the Chapter and say that everyone present was permitted to have perfect liberty and freedom in expressing her views and objections or approval of the New Declarations. They say all opinions were given in a very deferential manner and harmony reigned throughout. Abbot Martin explained the Declarations. The next chapter will be held in 1926.

Aug. 12: Sunday: A telephone from the St. Benedict's College kitchen makes us think that Mother came in this morning from

142

Chicago and went to St. Benedict's for Holy Mass. After spiritual reading we all assembled on the lawn in front of the building to greet our dear Mother. She wanted to surprise us and we wanted to surprise her for we felt certain she was coming. Surely enough at 11 o'clock our car came and our Mother was in it. We were very happy to greet her and welcome her home. She looks tired. We have had a Holy Mass every Tuesday the past two years that this be successful.

Sister Genevieve Scanlan's peaceful pen did not always reflect the total community view as she worked at her chronicle in the evening. But she gave something of a valid picture of the way of life in which Rome had been interested and which great people had worked to preserve. The long trip through the years was almost over. In another seven years the Congregation would be accorded final approval. Mother Aloysia and Abbot Innocent had both lived to see the seven-year trial approbation. The correspondence shuttling back and forth between the eternal city and Atchison since the days of Mother Evangelista and Bishop Fink had woven finally a stable way for Benedictine life in the new land, making to the needs of the Church a response which would have gladdened both Abbot Boniface Wimmer and St. Benedict.

There were things different about Benedictinism in this younger country. The distinction between lay sister and choir sister, characteristic in Europe, had long been discontinued. This distinction had never been something to be proud of in old countries, but to be ashamed of in new ones. It had been rather something rooted in the way of life of a people. It had never been Benedictine to distinguish among members of the house except for need or from inspiration given the Abbot by God. But it had always been Benedictine to note the conditions of time and place. One came to the monastery to do what he could do for God. A person was not elevated above others because he could sing, but if he could sing he was supposed to do so. Because the work of the Divine Office was, in itself, the noblest work, people who did it in European convents walked ahead of people who did not. The preference was not to the persons but to the work. Because persons of nobility had more often received the education which made participation in the Office possible, they served with their gifts. Because there was always work to do, others served with their gifts. In convents of good observance this practice was understood for what it was, and Sister Fortunata Viti, an Italian lay Sister who died in 1915, was proudly presented by her convent for the long process leading to beatification.

But St. Benedict had really intended for all his monks to say the Office, and both Rome and Atchison understood his spirit. The New World with its work for everyone and its chance for everyone was good ground.

The importance of the Sisters' coming under Pontifical Jurisdiction needs also to be understood. This did not mean rejection of diocesan responsibility and episcopal guidance. It meant rather placing one's house at the direct service of the Holy See. It insured the drawing of postulants from all parts of the world and the going of Sisters to all parts of the world. Bishops understood this. "I can see the desirability of your taking this school outside the diocese," Archbishop Hunkeler said when his blessing was asked on a new work. "It will extend the work of the church and bring vocations to you."

Actually, a congregation with constitutions approved by Rome did do what Abbot Innocent said it would. It freed convents from changes which new superiors might too quickly make and it placed all convents more securely within the framework of the stable Church.

The Congregation of St. Scholastica helped set a pattern for two other congregations of Benedictines of Pontifical Jurisdiction: St. Gertrude the Great in 1937 and St. Benedict in 1947. All three profited from Rome's first response in 1878 that Benedictine convents traditionally conduct separate novitiates. Because of the specific nature and work of Benedictines of Perpetual Adoration, that Congregation retains only one novitiate at the Motherhouse, Clyde, Missouri.

The Abbot Primate Fidelis, who had succeeded Abbot Hildebrande, rejoiced in the stamp Rome had placed on American Benedictinism, writing from Rome, November 28, 1923:

It was very little that I was able to do for you. What I did do was done with much joy, intensely, for the love of God. Also Benedict XV we must thank for everything, with such energy and such extraordinary means for taking this thing in hand and seeing it through. If I can do anything at all for you, I will always be ready to do it with joy and you will always find in me a heartfelt Benedictine brother. I count strongly on the help of the Sisters in America because the needs and worries concerning our precious order are constantly becoming more numerous, pressing, and heavier.[11]

What the Abbot Primate said was true. The world was not a quiet world. Convents on the new side of the Atlantic owed the whole earth a debt, the debt of those who have received much. Now a network of those convents, united and yet autonomous, had a way on paper and in actuality to strengthen one another for the prayer and work ahead. The best things the Old World had were growing well on new soil. The fruit of the effort for the Congregation would reach in a few years to other parts of the American nation and to the world.

1. Letter from Monte Aventino, Roma, July 18, 1910, MSS Archives.

2. MSS *Catalogue*, 1914, p. 45.

3. Letter of January 13, 1914, MSS Archives.

4. Abbot Serafini's view, summarized in a letter of Philip Langton, O.S.B., to Abbot Ernest. Copy, MSS Archives, February 26, 1919.

5. MSS Archives, copy.

6. Cardinal Gasquet to Abbot Ernest, April 6, 1919. Copy, MSS Archives.

7. Quoted by Abbot Ernest to Mother Aloysia in his letter of December 27, 1919. The Primate wrote it in German: "Seine Heiligkeit versprach mir, sich mit allem Machdrucke zu Gunsten unserer Mitschwestern zu verwenden, auf dass sie im Geiste unserers Ordens ein zwischen den klausurierten Nonnen und den gewechnilichen Schwestern stehendes Institut im Geiste unserer Hl. Regel geschaffen werde." MSS Archives.

8. Gasquet to Abbot Ernest from Rome, January 20, 1921. Newark Archives. Copy, MSS Archives.

9. In the next four decades, eight more convents joined the Congregation: St. Gertrude, Bristow, Va.; St. Walburg, Covington, Ky.; St. Scholastica, Covington, La.; St. Lucy, Glendora, Calif.; St. Scholastica, San Antonio, Tex.; Our Lady of Sorrows, Tinley Park, Ill.; St. Benedict, Mexico City, Mexico; and Holy Family, Benet Lake, Wisconsin. In addition to the Congregation of St. Scholastica, there are thirty-five other Benedictine convents in the United States, Canada, and Mexico making a total of fifty-three. Of these, forty-nine are in the United States.

10. Cardinal Gasquet to Abbot Ernest from the Palazzo San Callisto, June 14, 1921. Newark Archives. Copy, MSS Archives.

11. Letter to Mother Aloysia, from Monte Aventino. MSS Archives.

PORTRAIT FOR A CONVENT

If one turns left down the convent hall from the main entrance, the first significant thing to see is the crucifix outside the refectory door. It was the gift Mother Aloysia left the community to remind it of monastic silence.

And there were other beautiful things which, under the guidance of the Lord Christ, as St. Benedict liked to say, made the real fabric of the years.

The last of the pioneers — Sister Amanda, Sister Gertrude, and Sister Gregoria — died between 1915 and 1923. Mother Theresa, too, died, on June 7, 1918. They were not sad deaths.

In the Community there was vigor everywhere. Everyone went to the lectures Father Martin gave in 1915 on the life of St. Catherine of Siena, "to do away with shallow home-made theology," as he put it.[1] Students learned the *Missa Beatae Mariae Virginis* and alternated in choirs to sing it that same year. And the next year Sisters and students alike sat spellbound for the lectures and dramatizations by the Rev. Ignatius Stein of the Abbey, commemorating the tercentenary of the death of William Shakespeare. Father Ignatius loved every Shakespearean role and knew almost every one. "The ideal of the literary artist," he said, "phoenix-like rises from its ashes in ever fresh and vivid colorings, numerous as are the languages of the civilized world."[2] He had an audience which loved his words. And in its mingling of education and recreation the convent and academy population sat in some awe in 1920 as the delighted Father Felix Nolte manipulated the first motion picture machine to present the first movie, "The Transgressor," presented by the Catholic Art Association.

146

In another sign of progress, the community purchased an electric dishwasher for $600 and life changed a little for postulants. The ejaculation "Blessed be St. Joseph" was inserted in the Divine Praises. In 1916, Abbot Innocent celebrated his golden jubilee in the priesthood, for which occasion the Academy presented a verse-drama, *Written in Gold*, by Sister Hildegard. In October, 1922, the great man, in the words of the convent chroniclist, "quietly passed to eternity, a man according to God's own heart, a noble son of St. Benedict, for more than 40 years a Father to his own and our community." The words were true. He had never made light of the Sisters' efforts for education and religious perfection. Nothing was too small for him to do, nor was he too much afraid either of the great burdens.[3]

Everywhere around her, as she too grew old, Mother Aloysia saw gradual changes and increasing richness of promise. Life was solidifying the combination of simplicity and complexity which somehow became Mount St. Scholastica. There was time to be nice to every stranger who came, and Mother herself seemed everywhere doing the important things, like noticing whether visiting children had cookies and at least a little attention. In the spring of 1923 Sister Hildegard O'Keefe and Sister Scholastica Kratschmer combined their talents to write a Mount St. Scholastica song, "With songs exultant we sing of the blue and the white." In the autumn of 1923, the new college department opened with six girls and three teachers.

In the spring of 1924 the Kansas State Board of Education met with the deans of St. Benedict's College and Creighton University and concluded that baccalaureate degrees could be granted Sisters who had earned sixty hours by examination, correspondence, and home study and sixty additional hours of summer school conducted at St. Benedict's. "There was no prejudice," reports the Chronicle. "Miss Stone, the secretary of the State Board of Education, was only anxious to do right." Father Bonaventure represented St. Benedict's and Father Grace, Creighton, in a meeting which meant so much for the continued staffing of Atchison's schools.

The home study was no myth. Assignments went out in

abundance to all the missions, and faculty at home corrected papers with punctilious fidelity.

That spring, too, Mother Aloysia's feastday greeting for the feast of St. Scholastica spoke of the joy there would one day be on meeting her. And on February 27, she wrote:

Another Lent is about to begin. There is so much for which we have to be thankful. Therefore, let us make use of this penitential season as a thanksgiving for having been given one more Lent in which to gain merit and to do something for God.

She asked for charity, fidelity to religious exercises, faithfulness in teaching, consideration of the children, and the working together of the community in little things.

Summer came and went. One September day she left the dining room early and a student prefect, also leaving early, saw her leaning against the wall outside the refectory. "Mother, can I help you?"

"No, Sister. This is something I must do for myself." That day she dictated some letters, put her files in order, and went to St. Margaret's Hospital. She underwent surgery for a hernia and seemed to be recovering. But early Wednesday morning, October 1, she must have developed a blood clot. The community chronicle, after thirty-nine years, brings back the very tone of the day:

Our telephone rang at 5:45, just as we finished Meditation. It was from St. Margaret's and stated that our Dear Mother had a sinking spell and was very weak. Sister Edith, the subprioress, left on the first train. Father Edmund changed his Holy Mass intention and celebrated for Mother. When we were at the Communion railing the phone rang again. As soon as Father Edmund finished the prayers after Mass, Sister M. Hildegard stepped inside the Sanctuary and whispered a message to him.

He knelt a moment or two in silence and then turned to us: "Mother Aloysia passed away at 6:10. Let us pray for the repose of her soul." He prayed but it was hard to answer him. She was of inestimable worth to the Community, and we cannot see how we will ever do without her. Our great comfort lies in the thought that her reward in heaven will be great, for she was faithful, not over few things but many.

Sister Edith returned at noon and we crowded round her to learn the circumstances of her death . . . Even last night when Sister Rosalia left her to retire she was feeling splendid, and told her to be sure to come to her room and prepare her for Holy Communion. Sister Rosalia awoke at three A.M., and felt uneasy, but hesitated going to her room lest she alarm her.

At the usual 5:15 she entered and at a glance saw a great change from the preceding evening. She said, "O Mother, how are you?" Mother answered, "I just cannot breathe." Sister called the nurse, and then gave the alarm to Sister Pulcheria, who summoned Mother Anaceta and the Franciscan Sisters. The Chaplain arrived in time to give her the last Sacraments . . . She did not speak at all during the death scene, which lasted about forty minutes. Mother Anaceta [of St. Margaret's] said to her, "Mother, bless your children," and she bowed her noble head, but said not a word.[4]

Her body was brought home Thursday morning and met by the Sisters with lighted candles. Surrounded by ferns and lighted candles, the coffin faced the double doors opening on the convent parlors. Clerics from St. Benedict's Abbey helped sing the Office. The hebdomadarian was Sister Edith, a Kansas Sister, the first postulant from the convent's first mission. The acolytes were Sister Genevieve, an academy graduate of Irish descent, and Sister Josephine from the Tyrol. They were all singing the Church's wonderful chant for the little girl who had come up the Missouri River to school at a pioneer convent and stayed to try to bring it to the status of erudition, solidity, courage, and as sturdy a search for sanctity as history presents, the twelve-year-old postulant who had persevered to be builder, dreamer, and lover of the work of God.

At the Mass, Bishop Ward was celebrant, with Fathers Mathias and Liciotti of Walsenburg as honorary deacons. Abbot Martin performed the ceremonies at the grave.

She had been a great Superior. She had given a young convent a timeless picture of what it ought to be.

Her own photograph is on the wall of the convent corridor, and — enlarged almost to life size — also on the west wall, north end, of the college administration building, first floor. The long Rosary she wears was voted out by the General Chapter in 1932 as not characteristic of Sisters who say the Office. The coif is not so smooth as it should be for the centuries to gaze

149

upon, but the face is for the ages. College girls pass the photograph many times a day. It belongs in a college, this college, because Mother Aloysia built the building out of her prayers and dreams and with the trust of her community, and because she had herself an intense and strenuous respect for learning.

But even more it is a portrait for a convent.

And the lines of the face are filled out by the stories of her which accumulate. She asked a great courage, even — perhaps especially — of the young. When a junior Sister's mother died, the young Sister had gone into the chapel after supper to permit herself to cry. But Mother came in and said, "Now you can be braver than that. Go on out with the rest." [5]

It was courage and depth of understanding, not hardness, in her.

She cut at vanity and loquaciousness relentlessly and unforgettably. And she had a high regard for the people and the children whose lives her Sisters touched.

One Sister, returning from one of her early mission years, mentioned some custom practiced by the farmers in Kelly. Mother did not believe in news being brought in from the outside idly. Nor did she believe in discussing the affairs of parishioners among whom the Sisters taught. While the long ranks of Sisters were moving in dignity from dining room to chapel, she stood outside the chapel door, drew the young Sister into the entrance to her office, and said with terrible audibility: "Sister, what do you know about the farmers of Kelly?"

And Sister Mildred Knoebber, the future foundress of the Mexico City convent, answered, "Nothing, Mother. Nothing, really."

Another young Sister, in her first week of table-reading, anxious to do well, quoted our Lord as saying, "Simon Bar-Yona," latinizing the "J" with fervor.

"By what authority," asked Mother Aloysia, meeting the eloquent one in the early afternoon, "do you say Simon Bar-Yona?"

"No authority at all, Mother," submitted Sister Ambrose Conway, who always added when telling the story: "She was one of the greatest women I have ever known. She gave me responsibility and believed I could carry it out."

She loved the community. "Can I help you?" she said when she was Academy Directress to the young stranger standing at the front entrance. "I came to stay," a postulant many miles from home said. "I hope you do. I will help you."

Later as Superior she told the junior Sisters: "You must be good religious. The future of the house depends on you. If you are not what you ought to be, the Superior cannot make you so; but if you are, the Community will hold, even if we get unworthy Superiors." She helped them to be good. If Sisters grew weary at meditation she would say, "If you're tired, come back and sit in front of me." It was not a grim threat or a dire and subtle remark. She really meant it, and somehow sitting near her it was easier, even without fear, to stay awake. She ranked the Divine Office above all other work. "She would have loved the Liturgical Movement if she had lived a little longer," someone said. And she loved poverty. The first draft of the order she compiled for Abbot Innocent's jubilee vestments is in pencil on the back of used paper. There was no icing on cake, there were few desserts in her time — not just because the giant building had to be paid for, but because there was a vow on a formula sheet every Sister had signed.

Perhaps she never really forgot the child she had been and the mother who had let her go. "Never criticize the people or the children," she used to say. "Be loyal to the children."

She saw progress come and was not surprised. In solemn discussion in the convent parlor she agreed with Abbot Innocent that Sisters should ride in automobiles provided they drew the curtains and did not ride outside Atchison.

"She was cold and yet warm," one Sister said. "She was the Superior we needed for those years. She was brave." She responded to people as they needed response.

The Holy Rule of St. Benedict says that a Superior should have a doctrine and should impart it by word and life. The file of letters to the Missions, the earliest in handwritten carbon paper duplication, reveals Mother Aloysia's doctrine — charity, prayer, cheerful work, devotion to the Passion of Christ. "Pray for one another, pray for the conversion of sinners, that many may return to the Church this Lent," she writes. And almost always she signs herself, "in the Sacred Wounds."

On that quiet morning of October 1, when she died, in the half hour given her to know she was dying, she could have thought of many things. She could have realized that during her regime the last of the pioneer Sisters had died, and both previous Mothers. She could have reflected on the long files of Sisters she had made characteristic of Mount St. Scholastica as long as it lived. For not only had the community grown from eighty-five to 387 professed members during her Superiorship. But the very buildings which made long files possible were part of her thinking. For almost two blocks, one could walk down this hall of majesty and beauty beneath the roof of Mount St. Scholastica when Mother Aloysia had finished building.

She could have thought of the fifty-eight missions to which she had just finished sending her Sisters. She could have recalled the missionaries to the Philippines who had stayed at her convent, the French exiles it had received, the stable Congregation which Rome had at last sealed with approval, and the sunflower the Abbot Primate had liked.

But it has come down through oral tradition that she looked ahead instead, and that on that morning before she lapsed into the great forty minutes of silence preceding her death she said to Sister Rosalia: "Take care of Miss Bertha. She is entering the convent today." [6]

A great wave of love followed her into eternity. One of the novices dreamed that Mother had asked her for Masses and Misereres. She took her dream to Sister Josephine who, desirous of keeping things on an even keel, said: "Don't take that dream seriously, Sister. If Mother wanted Masses said, she would give the message to someone who could get them said."

"But I have already offered them," the novice answered. "I have offered all the Masses that have been said in the world for her, ever since Calvary."

The writer of this book, confronted with the great block of community history which was Mother Aloysia's twenty-seven years of superiority, and with the fact and legend she was, really wondered what to do. Then I was sent to a small parish to teach summer vacation school. Reading the convent chronicles there, during the green and rainy hours of one warm evening, I found myself wishing I could have seen her if only once. Then, I thought, I could have integrated the deeds with the words, the awe approximating fear with the love which was often the reaction to the mentioning of her name. That night, like the novice Sister Willibalda, I had my dream. It was after Compline in the dream, when I saw Mother come out of one of the community offices across from the chapel to give an Office-book to a Sister who had lost hers. I knew her, and edged into the meeting. She saw me, said, "You are writing the book," told me to sit down, and spoke to both of us.

I recognized the dark eyes, the face like the one in the pictures, only broken now into fine, strong, and radiant smiles. Then I remembered, "It is the time of nocturnal silence. And Mother Aloysia believed in its strict observance." I knew she was dead now but thought that would make little difference. Nor did it. She smiled and said to my thought, "You are right. It is after Compline, and the Evil One might try to make something of this."

She placed her arm around me for a moment as we rose. And I awoke, knowing her, I thought.

It was just a dream. But she was the kind of person about whom a convent does dream, because she had a great blueprint for it and gave her life to achieve it.

Benedictine life is always referred to as family life, and that is a true reference. But the family life is intended to be strong as well as warm and kind. St. Benedict in the Prologue to his Rule said that his followers had come to do battle for the Lord Christ, the true King.

The picture that looks down on convent and college halls makes a similar summons, calling both to family life and to battle in the words of one of Mother's Lenten letters: "Let us all unite in the Resolution to silence, charity, prayer, and meditation on the Passion, and we will be like to a large and strong army and Almighty God must and will hear us and bless our Community."

1. *Convent Chronicle*, May 28, 1915.
2. *MSS Catalogue*, 1917.
3. Resourceful and humble, humorous and kind, Abbot Innocent was a story too. He shepherded his Abbey to maturity, and many students to manhood. Maurice O'Keefe, of Atchison, remembers the day when stu-

dents listened to table-reading. Often, in the earlier days, it was in German. One day the boys could not decide what language it was. He was delegated to find out, and upon asking the bearded Abbot received the answer: "Ach, Himmel. That was English." In all his dealings with the convent, records leave the impression that he never overestimated himself or underestimated the Lord. He died commanding the love and respect of his whole Atchison world.

4. *Convent Chronicle*, October 1, 1924.

5. Interview with Sister Romana Farrell, Summer, 1960.

6. Miss Bertha did enter that evening of October 1, and received the name Mother had planned to give her, Sister De Chantal.

Section Four

MOTHER LUCY'S YEARS

Eleven days before a new election, on October 14, Sister Winifred Mihm died, the postulant who had once called herself "Bishop Mihm." Sister Pauline wrote of her:

She died shortly after receiving Holy Communion. She was a large Sister, tall and big-boned. She entered on St. Gertrude's day, 1884. She was a pleasing, out-spoken character who had no human respect and was always most prominent where work was to be done. . . . After she made her triennial vows she was sent to St. Benedict's College kitchen and remained there until her heart began to trouble her. She did not have to suffer long. God came and took her to Himself.

The quiet death helped put everything in perspective. On Saturday, October 25, at six o'clock, the community assembled solemnly for a Mass celebrated by Abbot Martin. After Mass and breakfast came the sound of dishes being gathered and washed, the routine of floors and doorsills and picture frames being dusted, the procession of Sisters making the Stations of the Cross, the matter-of-fact ticking of the convent clock.

At 8:15 the chapter bell sounded as if it were the only sound on earth. In solemn concourse, with Abbot Martin representing the Bishop, the Sisters assembled in semi-circles in the community room and on the third ballot chose Sister Lucy Dooley as fourth prioress of Mount St. Scholastica.

"She is a very good Sister and will do everything in her power to keep up the good spirit which the Community has imbibed from Mother Aloysia," wrote the convent chroniclist.

She very humbly acknowledged that she is not capable of the office and wanted to withdraw her name but Father Abbot told her to look upon it as God's Will. It was after 12 o'clock when we left the room as there were so many to vote. . . . We felt greatly relieved when it was over, for it was quite a strain.

The day mercifully slipped back into the normal pattern which convents keep in reserve no matter what cataclysms shake the universe. Abbot Martin heard confessions after dinner for missionaries who would be returning from the election to their schools, open scarcely two months. There was Benediction of the Most Blessed Sacrament. Most of the Sisters returned to their posts to get altars ready for Sunday Mass, choirs and servers ready for performance, and lessons planned for inevitable Mondays.

They left the convent alone with Sister Lucy, and Sister Lucy alone with the convent whose only fear of her was, as people would admit later, that she was too happy, too carefree, too lighthearted. The chronicler tells part of the tale:

After supper we had the Submission Act and poor Sister M. Lucy cried the entire time. We all felt very sorry for her as it is a tremendous burden, but someone must bear it. She has a very good disposition and God will supply whatever she lacks in the line of requisites. Everyone feels she is God's choice, for we all prayed so fervently that we would do His Holy Will. She will be aided in every possible way by the officials. The work will be very new to her, though, for she has been teaching at St. Louis College for 27 years. Children always liked her and so did all who knew her.

The new Mother had been born in Good Intent, Kansas, seven miles from Atchison, in a big white house with green shutters, the fourth child of James and Catherine Hurley Dooley, September 8, 1871. Her parents had come from County Clare, Ireland, the hilly country between the river Shannon and Galway Bay. There were fourteen children, six boys and eight girls.

She attended grade school several miles from her home, and at sixteen enrolled in St. Scholastica Academy as a boarder, where she spent two years. Sister Aloysia was directress then. In 1892, September, she returned to St. Scholastica's to enter the convent. She was twenty-one years old and received the habit the following April 9 from Abbot Innocent. Sister Beatrice Willems was her novice-mistress at first, then Sister Amanda Meier. She belonged to the first candidate class since 1866 to learn the Divine Office, for it had just been resumed. She brought a personality with her, a record of hurrying to the waiting buggy when it was time to go home in her boarding school days. She continued an interesting record. As a young Sister she did some driving and once gave the horse a half piece of bread with sugar on it. Nelson, the horse, needed no second invitation and his long expressive face was daily seen at the kitchen window after that.[1] She was at home in the convent from the start, and her father, Jim Dooley, brought loads of hay and corn from his abundant farm to feed the twenty cows and thousand chickens the convent ultimately accumulated.

On April 15, 1894, Sister Lucy made triennial vows, receiving the black veil from Father Gerard. Her first mission was to the first and second grade pupils of St. Louis College, an imposing name for what evolved into St. Benedict's parish grade school.[2] Father Charles Stoeckle was the pastor.

After making perpetual vows, August 15, 1897, Sister Lucy was sent by the new Mother Aloysia to St. Anthony's parish, Kansas City, Kansas, where she taught the seventh and eighth grades. Sister Hilda Booz was her superior. She returned to the motherhouse, June, 1899, and went back to St. Louis College to teach successively the third, fourth, fifth, sixth, seventh, and eighth grades. In 1901 she was made principal of the school, a position she kept until the day she called the pastor, Father Gerard Heinz, to announce: "Father Gerard, this is Mother Lucy."

Her younger sister, Bertha, entered the community in July, 1897, and was named Sister Dorothy. In 1921, Sister Lucy was appointed treasurer of the community. That same year she learned to drive the community's first automobile. People on Commercial Street enjoyed watching the teacher who had taught them or their children and neighbors. And many years afterwards, at a meeting of the National Catholic Educational Association, a book-company salesman was to call across rows of people to ask a Sister if she were not of Mother Lucy's community. "She taught me."

Now it was Saturday night, October 25, and Sister Lucy Dooley was alone with a community of 387 Sisters. And now began the long years that would make her Mother Lucy.

Abbot Boniface Wimmer and Abbot Innocent Wolf were dead. The last pioneer Sister had died a year ago. Sister Agnes Glancy of the early days was still walking the halls, enlivening the recreation. But for the most part a new era was beginning for the community and for her. Things would not be the same as when she was Sister Lucy and could proclaim lightheartedly that lunch hour with the Sisters of the Abbey kitchen was her favorite course in the St. Benedict's summer sessions. It would all be different.

It became her great gift not to know everything herself, but to see the Sisters grow up around her with their gifts to God and to one another in their hands. Her pattern began and remained simple. She rose before the community — it was the one exception she permitted herself, and whatever first blessing the first prayer in chapel really earns was hers by right. All the day long she sat at her desk. In later years she retired early, saying that a problem which had not settled itself by seven o'clock could wait until morning.

Her touch on life seemed light, but the hold was firm. Laughter came from her office, but there was a dignity in her walk down the convent corridor which she could adapt to any speed. A Sister records the memory from her postulant days of turning into the dining room after a deliberately thoughtful pace only to discover that the person walking so patiently behind her was Mother Lucy.

St. Benedict's College did not have time, in the four summer sessions it conducted before her election, to award her a Bachelor of Arts degree. But in 1925 it gave an honorary Doctor of Laws to this principal of St. Louis College turned so suddenly Prioress, and the certificate in the library attesting to the college president's degree gathered quality and significance with the years. She seldom quoted anything, but when she did her choice was right. And everything came into her life, all manner of joy and pathos, of temporary heartbreak and lasting peace.

One warm summer day a postulant worrying over her vocation asked to go home. Mother let her go reluctantly, knowing something was not right about this choice. The forlorn passenger took her place aboard the Missouri Pacific Eagle across from some other young girl who was harmlessly wearing lipstick. Somehow the sight of the lipstick suddenly made the new passenger realize long and lasting things. The Eagle waits only four minutes in Atchison, but they were enough for the one-time postulant to hurry off the train. Back in Mother Lucy's office, she heard as the kind arms welcomed her: "Now you can pray *Bonum mihi quia humiliasti me, ut discam justificationes tuas.* This has all happened that you may learn God's ways."

It was in a steady, deep manner that while the community expanded its missions, formed its college, and extended its prayer and song, the happy Sister Lucy Dooley became the great Mother Lucy whose name would never require adornment. She did not seem heroic, except that she was always where she was needed; she did not seem overly pious, except that she had believed God heard her every prayer; she did not seem unduly penitential, except that she had an almost stern concept of duty. It was hard to look at her and ask a selfish permission, but it was possible to tell her that one had been selfish.

She made everything that happened to her seem desirable and, near the end, a thin figure with enormous blue eyes sitting in her office while life went past the door, she told her secret: "My faith has been my hope." [3]

But all of this had not happened yet that Saturday night of election when the chronicle summed up the *status quo*:

It will be hard to call another Mother, but love of God makes all things easy, and we do love Him. It all seems so wonderful in Mother's [Aloysia] case, for wherever you look you see everything finished. The new building, the lawn, the furnishing of the Building in a most complete way, the assigning of the Sisters to the various missions — well, just everything! It would take a book to tell all the improvement she has made and another to tell all she has done for the Community, and still another to tell all she has done for the Poor. Then the number of girls she has had educated gratis in the Academy is very great and many of them have become members of the community through her influence.

But Mother Lucy tried. Sunday morning she sent for Sister Dolorosa, young academy teacher and prefect. "I want you to be the procurator, assistant to Sister Rosalia." "But Mother, I know nothing of hay and corn." Sister Dolorosa thought of the cows and chickens accumulating and the hungry horses still plowing the convent gardens.

"Just take your responsibility," Mother said.

Monday morning, October 27, she introduced Sister Claudia, her successor, to St. Louis College and said goodbye to all her pupils and all the children. Tuesday morning she wrote to the missions:

My dear Sisters:

You are, indeed, aware of the heavy burden that our dear departed Mother wants me to take up for a while. God alone knows why such a sacred duty should fall to one so unworthy and incapable. But since it is God's holy Will, and the Community asks me to try to continue the work that dear Mother so zealously performed, in all humility and obedience, I offer all I am capable of doing for you spiritually and temporally.

I only ask, please to have patience with me and give me your prayers and support. Please help to continue dear Mother's self-sacrificing work, for our united community which she held in such high esteem. I beg of you, dear Sisters, to keep to the practice of charity, ever overlooking one another's faults and offering your merit of same for dear Mother that she may help me in some measure to fill the responsible place she has left vacant. May her dear soul rest in peace.

Asking our dear Lord to bless you each and every one, I am

Yours in St. Benedict, M. Lucy, OSB

During the rest of the week she sent a housekeeper to the Guardian Angel mission and three Sisters to St. Joseph to buy thread and silk for vestments. Father Gerard came for Novitiate instructions, someone went to a hospital, Abbot Martin gave the General Absolution on the Vigil of All Saints, the weather was splendid, and on November 1, Saturday, Father Bonaventure sang the festal Mass. Mother Carmelita, Assistant Provincial at Carondolet, St. Louis, visited the new building. And Mother Lucy's first week was over.

On November 19, for the first time in her capacity as Mother, she assisted at the deathbed of a Sister. "Wonderful in all she did as musician, primary teacher, altar decorator and seamstress," Sister Walburga Weber had been the convent's sixth candidate.[4]

The feast of Christmas was coming, the Sisters drew Advent practices, and Mother Lucy announced that there would be no Christmas holy pictures, for the giant building still stood there demanding payment. Mother wrote the missions:

I hope you will not be disappointed in not receiving a Christmas package from home. Dear Mother said last Christmas that this year she thought she would not buy any pictures or medals as we had the new building to pay for. She also said she thought the Sisters would be willing to make this sacrifice. You know the Christmas pictures and medals came to several hundred dollars. It was all right when we did not have any debt, but as it was Mother's own suggestion, we decided not to have anything for a few years at least.

We also all agreed on practising silence in a special manner in the lower hall. That was one of the places that Mother used to remind us so often about. The last purchase she made was a crucifix, to be placed near the dining room to remind us of keeping silence, particularly in that hall. The merit of this little act of mortification we will offer for Mother. I am sure it will please her. I ask you, dear Sisters, to take some time or place in your little community to practice a similar mortification, so when you come home you will be accustomed to the practice here, and all working together in one little thing will help us to keep united in the many, many greater things. You will all recall how dear Mother so often and earnestly begged us to always be as one large family so I also beg you all to try to help keep up the same good spirit.[5]

Sister Dorothy and Sister Jerome came home from Catholic University for Christmas that year. When the feast was over, and St. Scholastica's day drew near, Mother wrote again. She was beginning to find her own ground, to adopt her own style, as the letter shows:

In making our novena in St. Scholastica's honor, let us beg her to help us ever to remain faithful to our vows and promises, never to

161

lose courage if things seem hard and monotonous, or if we often fail through our own poor human weakness.[6]

And her Lenten letter asked everyone to meditate on the Second Station, "Jesus taking up His Cross." "Pray for one another," she asked. "Pray that God may bless our community and send us good members; pray for our sick and infirm."[7]

That spring the months were filled with trips to Topeka and letters to other state departments of education, with Sister Adelaide and Sister Genevieve renewing school certificates for the teachers and applying for new ones. On February 11, the community observed the anniversary of the building of the Lourdes grotto, and February 16, the first lay teacher since Nora Cotter's days in Seneca in 1876 was employed on a mission when Sister Karlene at Cathedral School, St. Joseph, required a substitute. On March 5, Clara Peterman, a student at the academy since she was four years old, gave a piano and violin recital. On April 9, Sister Lioba brought twenty-three dozen carnations from the greenhouse for the altar of repose, Sister Sophia arranged the refectory for Holy Thursday, and Mother Lucy observed the ceremony of the Washing of the Feet, earning the comment from the chroniclist: "Mother tries so earnestly to do everything just as dear Mother did, and that makes us feel happy."

In April, Sister De Sales Wavada, superior at Cathedral School, was discovered to have tuberculosis, and destined for Walsenburg where the community had built an infirmary wing in 1922. Sister Ursula and Sister Bertilla from the Benedictine Convent in Clyde, Missouri, came to show Atchison Sisters how to manipulate their new coif machine, and groups stood around in delight as the blade picked up the linen in fine pieces, cut a forty-five minute task for experts (and an endless task for beginners) into a five-minute work for machinists, and for some still long-distant future sounded the knell of Novitiate recreations sometimes spent in tears over stubborn linen.

Mother Lucy and Sister Rosalia spent part of April in Walsenburg visiting the sick as well as one of the community's largest schools. Judging from the Chronicle, it was as if she were on probation: "We miss them very much at home, but not as we used to miss Mother Aloysia, yet after Mother Lucy is Superior for a few years we shall miss her greatly too."[8] On Ascension Thursday, May 21, the community heard its first sermon on St. Thérèse, canonized the previous Sunday, and on the Sunday within the Octave of the Ascension, the Chronicle loyally recorded, a Benedictine Sister, Marie Rose, was beatified.

There were no medals for distinction in the graduation exercises that year, not only because medal-awarding was not "being done much any more,"[9] but also because the giant still stood there unpaid for and the community purpose to pay for things before Purgatory remained constant.

That summer of 1925 saw novices carrying torches in the Corpus Christi procession for the first time, the community having its largest number of postulants — twenty-six in all. Father Sylvester Schmitz conducted the college's first senior college registration; Ruth Walsh, the first postulant with credit from an American college, entered; Miss Louie Lesslie was appointed as Secretary of the State Board of Education; and there was the march of more Sisters to summer school. They were brave years, the middle twenties, with a vigor all their own. "The doctor didn't extract my brain, just my teeth," smiled Sister Euthalia Skinner on her way to classes.

The summer and autumn were filled with activity. The students had a Columbus Day picnic and Mother Lucy gave recreation at supper saying, "The Sisters must have Columbus Day too." Father Herbers, S.J., dean of St. Mary's College, gave a two-hour lecture with an intermission of classical music; Father Agnew, S.J., of Loyola in Chicago also visited; and Sisters Frances and Agatha of Nevada, Missouri, came to make arrangements for two teachers at their convent the following summer.

All that year statues were arriving for the vacant niches in the great administration building: the Sacred Heart statue, to preside at the north end of the long first floor college hall; St. Rita and St. Thomas Aquinas, wood carvings from Italy, the gift of Dr. Horner and his wife; St. Aloysius, to preside over the south end of the college. One smiles to see the faithful chronicler note: "The statue of St. *Aloysia* arrived from Europe today."

Statues of St. Anthony, St. Anne and the Child Mary, St. Thérèse, found their places in the new building, all donated by friends of the convent. And SS. Benedict and Scholastica in Italian marble, selected in Italy by Abbot Martin and donated by Mr. Nordhus, father of five Benedictines, were placed in the main foyer of the new building.

In January of the new year, 1926, Sister Digna Staab, retired from St. Benedict's College kitchen, was king at the Epiphany gift-giving with Sister Gertrude Winter distributing pictures for her to her many smiling subjects. Mother Lucy gave her New Year exhortation to charity and silence, and Agnes Brentano — the first candidate to enter with a college degree — came to the convent.[10]

Then on January 24, while the community sang *Vexilla Regis*, Abbot Martin blessed the large crucifix ordered by Mother Aloysia before her death and erected it at the entrance to the refectory.

On January 25, some of the Sisters attended the funeral of Father T. J. Downey, one of the oldest priests of the diocese and a member of the first diocesan school board. In February the Stations of the Cross in the Oratory on the convent second floor corridor were blessed so the sick could make their daily call. Father Abbot Martin used up quickly the permissions he had for erecting stations at the Mount.

Death came that spring. Sisters Ernesta Falk died at Horton, of pneumonia. Just before she died, she said to the Superior and to her mother: "I wonder what my father will think of me. It is just three years since his death." Her five brothers and one uncle were pallbearers.

In June Sister Marcelline Sinnott came home with a broken arm and, having asked for a one-armed position, was temporarily named portress. Sister Regina Baska, Sister Eva Halasey, and Sister Immaculata Kramer received bachelor's degrees from Creighton; Mother and Sister Edith went to the national capital to see Sister Dorothy and Sister Jerome receive master's degrees in mathematics and French. On her return, stopping in Chicago for a General Chapter, Mother Lucy was elected Mother General.

On June 21, summer school opened with senior college classes for the first time, St. Benedict's supplementing the Mount's three Masters. Then seven days later Mother Lucy and Sister Edith returned from the General Chapter. The zealous teachers of the college's first senior session unbent a little for the occasion, but Mother Lucy had already begun to establish her way of doing things. The Chronicle paints the picture:

All the arrangements were made how and where we would greet Mother Lucy General. The professors agreed upon giving us a quarter of an hour for the occasion. But at 9:00 Mother came in without anybody seeing her. We were disappointed not to have been able to see her come.[11]

Sister Lucy had lived nearly two years as Mother. She had begun in a unique way to build the days of her regime as if she were a bystander, interested and genuine and intermediary when she could be, but a bystander all the same in each one's effort to reach God, saying to the community that June: "We make our vows to God, not to anyone else, and the keeping of community customs will help us keep the vows."[12] A sample of everything had happened, the days were passing in an exultant low key, and life at Mount St. Scholastica had slipped into the pattern of Mother Lucy's years.

1. Interview with Sister Luitgard, Summer, 1959.
2. This was a grade school "dignified with this name because its ambitious founders hoped that some day it would grow up into a rival of Midland College, a Lutheran institution formerly located in Atchison." Sister Jerome Keeler, "Mother Lucy," *Benedictine Review*, VI (July, 1951), 6.
3. The writer's own interview with Mother, April 22, 1950.
4. Sister Pauline, *Biographies of Deceased Sisters*.
5. Letter, November 26, 1924.
6. Letter, January 25, 1925.
7. Letter, February 19, 1925.
8. *Chronicle*, April 16, 1925.
9. *Ibid.*
10. The degree was from Clarke College, Dubuque. Agnes Brentano became Sister Mary Theresa.
11. *Chronicle*, June 28, 1926.
12. *Ibid.*, June 9, 1926.

THE MAKING OF A COLLEGE

"St. Benedict's true contribution to European civilization is not that his monks were pioneers and builders and scholars and guardians of the classical tradition," writes Thomas Merton. "These were only insignificant by-products of the wonderfully simple and Christian communal life that was led in the early Benedictine monasteries." [1]

In its own way this was all true also of Atchison, Kansas. At Mount St. Scholastica the religious life was so associated with education that to separate the motherhouse convent from the motherhouse school would be a violence. There was always indeed a line between the "North" and the "South" campuses. Anyone can walk down the hall to the center where St. Benedict's statue stands. There, however, begins the clausura with all its mystery both to those who live there and to those who do not. [2]

But the line unites the convent and school as much as it separates them.

A college became doubly needful in the mid-twenties. The young lady of the middle twenties was beginning to need and want college education, and community professional and recreational conversation, reflected by the chronicle keeper, emphasized that more than ever in this "pleasure-seeking age of the twenties," truly Christian young women were needed.

Secondly, the Sisters themselves needed the college not only to teach there but also to learn there.

The Constitutions of 1880 had legislated that the Sisters should receive a "literary education:" [3] They were to be "so

166

well-versed . . . as to be able to teach to the glory and honor of the holy church."

In 1889 Bishop Fink had called the first diocesan teachers meeting, an eight-day institute, July 24–Aug. 1, at Saint Mary's Academy, Leavenworth, obligatory for all religious teachers of the diocese. The bishop had outlined the content to be mastered for third, second, or first grade certificates,[4] and had decreed that only Sisters able to show their certificates to the pastor at the beginning of the year could teach in the parish schools.

In the first two decades of the twentieth century, Nebraska, Kansas, and Missouri began asking further proof of the preparation. In some cases, Kansas had granted state certificates on seeing diocesan certificates. Then the states asked for proof of preparation through college credit. Now, in the middle twenties, the community knew, with the chronicle-writer: "A college will not mean income for us, but we will get great benefit from an accredited college as we can have our Sisters work toward their Degrees right at home."

The first catalogue was issued for 1923 and showed an architect's drawing of the new college. It was simple and clear, grouping its curriculum into English, Ancient Language, Modern Language, Mathematics, Physical Science, Biological Science, History, Philosophy, Religion, Drawing, Music, Home Economics, and Education. For graduation it required 128 hours. It said:

A semester hour is a subject pursued one hour a week for one semester. Each hour of recitation requires two hours of preparation. A selection that will insure a good liberal education and satisfy the requirements for the Bachelor's Degree should include the following: Apologetics, 8 hours; Science, Latin, History, Sociology, Mathematics, 6 hours each; Education, French or German or Spanish, English, Philosophy, Home Economics, 12 hours each.

The catalogue outlined requirements for majors and minors. Fifteen hours of music could be taken for credit; one hour of painting or other special work per semester.

That first year of 1923–1924 had six students and three teachers, and saw the blessing and occupying of the new building. Sisters and novices polished its wonderful halls until so late that Mother Aloysia had sent them to bed after just a thank you to God on their knees beside the buckets.[5] The next two years saw enrollment climb a little. "I was in the Junior College in its second year of operation, 1924–1925," writes Sister Jane Frances. "I was the only member of the Livy class taught by Sister Scholastica Kratschmer, also the only member of the Beginning French class taught by Sister Mary Jane Weckerlin, and one of two students in Sister Romana Farrell's chemistry class. There were several members of the History of English Literature class and of the Major and Minor Philosophy class taught by Sister Hildegard O'Keefe. All ten students of the college were enrolled in Father Gerard Heinz' Scripture course. Those were the days when we rattled around in the college like a couple of peas in a large pod." [6]

Spring of 1926 brought accreditation as a Junior College from the University of Kansas, and autumn opened with great hope and five more students than the law demanded. The massiveness and beauty of the new building and of the whole educational venture engaged everybody's talent. Sister Mechtilde Stenger, portress and custodian, had failing eysight but infallible touch. Young Sisters who cleaned the terrazo, Sister Maurus Wempe recalls, had to pass the test of Sister Mechtilde's finger applied to the floor to see that it was dust free.[7] The convent bakery baked the bread and rolls essential to Mount spirit, the convent laundry did the laundry, the convent Sisters kept laboratories, classrooms, and library spotless.

"Do you like to do that?" a college girl asked Sister Leonharda, at work cleaning in the biology laboratory one Friday afternoon.

"Yes. I came to do whatever God would ask me to do." And the answer powerfully helped draw the girl a few years later across the invisible line between north and south campus.

To one who reads the records now, filling the building with the things it needed is more a story to be watched than a problem to be solved. The first botany laboratory day, February 21, 1924, was so important that a separate account of it was written for the Archives. On that first day Sister Chelidonia brought a fever-fern, a wandering Jew, and a begonia. Evelyn Saylor brought a maiden-hair fern, Sister Lioba an hibiscus

168

plant from the convent greenhouse. The Mangelsdorf Seed House sent seeds, vincas, ferns, and flowers; a sister of Sister Scholastica Kratschmer sent moss and strawberry plants from the Cascade Mountains; students brought flowers from home; a class tour through basement and trunkrooms located tables and stands once considered out of season but now serviceable as plant holders. The kitchen managers — Sisters Juliana and Laurentia — supplied glass jars in which things could grow.[8]

The equipping of each department told a story, but none so rich in human value as that of the library. To tell that story involves something else the convent had been faced with — the recruiting of faculty, through full-time leave of absence for all-year study.

In September, 1924, two weeks before her death, Mother Aloysia had sent the first pilgrims to Catholic University for a full year in search of graduate education. Sister Dorothy Dooley and Sister Jerome Keeler had asked, "Where shall we board?"

"You will have no trouble finding a place," Mother had answered. "You are religious, and the city is full of convents."

To the dismay of Miss Cotter, Catholic University registrar confronted with such faith, the convents were already filled when these two Sisters arrived unheralded. The Benedictines at 9th and Newton, teachers at St. Anthony's School, found a room however and Sisters Dorothy and Jerome had a home. In the summer of 1926 they returned with Master's degrees to join Sister Bernarda and Sister Romana, already equipped with such from Creighton University, first mother of Mount degrees.[9]

Inspectors from the North Central and the University of Kansas, invited to see how the college was doing, looked politely at what was in later years the reading room but then the entire library, with its rather scant book collection distributed against the north and south walls, and several rocking chairs arranged invitingly near the windows. "You have a very nice room," they said.

So during her second semester at the University, Sister Jerome received instructions to "pick up" some library-science credits also, and when she returned that summer of 1926, the room awaited transformation. With Father Colman Farrell, St. Benedict's College librarian, as chief adviser, books by the thousand were ordered. A corps directed by Mr. Flack, librarian at St. Benedict's, and composed of Sisters Hildegard, Jerome, Ambrose, Chelidonia, and Felicia, processed four thousand books that summer, so that the college catalogue in September could proclaim:

The standards adopted by the joint committee of the National Educational Association and the North Central Association of Colleges and Secondary Schools and approved by the American Library Association have been followed closely in every detail. The reference and stack collections are both rapidly growing organisms, and the selection of new books is based directly on the courses taught and the recreational and cultural needs of the students. Accessions are constantly being made by purchase, gift, and exchange . . . No other part of the College equipment has received more careful attention than the library.

Adjoining the library had been a museum. The walls were pierced to make a door; out went the stuffed birds and animals to various quarters. The huge antlers and animated expression of a reindeer went to the wall outside the biology laboratory and the stuffed devil-fish began its career of exciting visiting children who peered through the glass in the same laboratory. The museum became the stack room. An epidemic of ordering books continued, all books came out of glass cases, and rocking chairs disappeared.

Sisters Hildegard, Jerome, Bernarda, and Eva were librarians during the earliest school years until Sister Florence Feeney returned from Rosary College in 1933.[10]

In September, 1926, the college began its first year as state-accredited institution with Mother Lucy, president; Sister Adelaida, directress; Sister Dorothy, dean; Sister Edith, treasurer; and Sister Hildegard O'Keefe, librarian. Father Bonaventure Schwinn, who knew its early days so well, said that its very first dean, while Sister Dorothy was still studying, had been Sister Helena Brandmeier.

It is easy, in the light of the years, to touch too lightly the real achievement and the real earnestness of that year, perhaps because there seemed to be so much happiness about it. Twenty-five students were necessary for accreditation, but a munificent thirty were enrolled — twenty-four girls and six Sisters. The six Sisters were novices who had completed eight months of their canonical year, and for their registration special permission was requested. The Novitiate, regretting the encroachment, made three unavailing novenas to prevent the college attendance, but the saints seemed on the side of the harried college administrators this time. Permission came and Sister Helen Sullivan, Sister Vianney Kaiser, Sister Mary Cyril Busenbarrick, Sister Mary Charles Walsh, Sister Theonilla Stessman, and Sister Teresita Snoddy became the first Sister-students during the year. Sister Dorothy taught algebra; Sister Jerome, Latin and French; Sister Hildegard, ethics; Sister Romana, chemistry; and Sister Bernarda, English. Father Abbot Martin taught ethics and religion.

The college grew in faculty. Sisters Regina Baska and Immaculata Kramer were at the Catholic University, studying history and education. On September 9, the Chronicle importantly records: "Sisters Edith and Dorothy went to St. Louis to see Father Schwitalla concerning the subjects in which three of our Sisters are to specialize," and a week later Sisters Eva, Rosemary, and Anthony had gone to study chemistry, philosophy, and biology. They were the first resident Sisters on the St. Louis University campus, staying at the Queen's Daughters house. Father Schwitalla, dean of St. Louis' Medical School, was a hard task-master and guide, but his contribution was profound and never forgotten. Many years later, when he was retired and as a feeble and aged priest lovingly handling research works in the University library, he was to meet Atchison Sisters studying there and to inquire warmly and instantly about the Mount.

The manner of choice of majors was interesting. That summer, Sister Anthony, an undergraduate English major, had been discussing something with Mother Lucy when a June bug buzzed about the office. Sister calmly took it in her fingers, carried it to a window, and set it free. "How would you like to major in biology?" Mother Lucy asked.

That year of 1926 and 1927 is valuable as an index of how colleges are built. The University of Kansas and the State Board of Education were coming to see if permanent accreditation could take the place of the provisional approval granted in the spring. The community began a novena to the Poor Souls and had a novena of Masses celebrated. Before the visitors could arrive, some good news came which prepared the atmosphere for victory. St. Benedict's College had been admitted to the North Central Association.

"This is a great boon, and we are thankful they have attained it," wrote the chroniclist. "We are indebted to St. Benedict's Faculty for innumerable favors." Two days later, March 25, Father Bonaventure, long the college friend and adviser, came to hear students' confessions only to be besieged by college teachers who wanted to know what the impending examiners would ask. He did not know.

Life was not standing still, waiting. On March 27, the college students debated the question: "Resolved that the United States should cancel the war debt." Judges Father Edmund Pusch, Sister Genevieve, Sister Scholastica, Sister Jerome, and Sister Pauline awarded the decision to the affirmatives Evelyn Payne, Jeannette Anderson, and Cora Schaback. Defeated were Virginia Seybold, Lillian Goodwin, and Cecilia Heli. Two days later, with the examiners still absent, the faculty in solemn Sunday meeting decreed that all noisy talking in the corridors, all unnecessary walking in the corridors, all leaving of places in classrooms between periods must be prohibited, and courtesy made a definite requisite in college life.

With the examiners one day distant, Sister Adelaide Cass, more than seventy years old, and directress of the Academy since 1897 and of the college since its beginning, was taken to St. Margaret's Hospital, very ill. She did not get to see Dr. Engel and Professor Mitchell of Lawrence or Miss Louise Lesslie of the State Board of Education, who came next day. She who was such a lady would have liked them.

Perhaps the University of Kansas and the State Department would be interested to know how a convent regarded their inspection of one of its great dreams. Here is how the community chronicler recorded April 7, of 1927:

April 7, 1927. 6:45 p.m. About 10:05 this forenoon, Dr. Engel, Professor Mitchell, and Miss Louise Lesslie arrived for the purpose of inspecting the conditions of the Junior College which we hope to have accredited by both the Kansas University and the State Board of Education. Shortly after their arrival they repaired to the science laboratory where the class in Chemistry was being taught. From here they went to make an investigation of the library. They went from the library to some of the other parts of the building, the domestic science department, the kitchen, and the dining rooms. Then they went to the auditorium, and Clara Peterman played the pipe organ for them.

Dinner was served for them in the Convent building. Father Bonaventure came with them and we were very grateful that he did as he was acquainted with the KU professors. Sisters M. Juliana and Laurentia had a real banquet prepared and they appreciated it very much. They had a specially nice pudding prepared in the form of a large cake trimmed with roses made of pink paper. When Dr. Engel saw it he said, "Oh, today is my birthday and Sister made me this cake."

He counted the roses and found there were thirty and he laughingly said, "And just thirty roses too." This made his companions laugh, for he has been at the Kansas University for 35 years and was 26 when he came there. He possesses a very amiable and affable manner, and seems ever willing to be kind to everyone. Professor Mitchell is kind, too. After dinner they visited the Contemporary American History class which is taught by Father Flavian Voet of St. Benedict's College, as no Sister had enough credits to qualify her to teach it. From there they went to the Education class which Sister M. Hildegard conducts. After a short visit there, they inspected the Biology department. This has not been furnished as we will not have a qualified Sister till 1929. From this department they went to visit the Trigonometry class and then went to the reception room to talk of various matters and make some suggestions to the Faculty.

They suggested getting another table for the Chemistry Department, more texts and reference books for the Education Department, but in general they seemed quite well pleased. The three Inspectors then held a little meeting of their own, and decided that everything justified accreditment, and this is all we wanted, so we are grateful to our Dear Lord, to Father Bonaventure, and to the three Inspectors.

Miss Louise Lesslie is Secretary of the State Board of Education and it was very providential for us that she came as it makes us accredited by the State Board as well as by the University . . . We cannot express our gratitude to God as so much depended on the visit of these Inspectors. We practically promised the students that entered last September that we would be accredited before the close of this school year, and inexpressible would be their disappointment had we not gained this accreditment. "Commit thy way to the Lord, and trust in Him," was truly verified in this as in every other instance of our life.

Professor Mitchell left on the 3:15 bus for Lawrence, Miss Lesslie intended to depart then, too, but found that she would make better time by leaving here at six o'clock and going on the bus to Topeka. Professor Engel went to visit the class in French, then expressed a desire to see the "Old Price Building" (St. Cecilia's) as he knew of its history. Father Bonaventure then took him and Miss Lesslie to visit St. Benedict's College and Maur Hill. They made but brief stops at each place, then returned as it was decided that they should have supper here at 4:40, for Professor Engel was to leave at 5:15 for Kansas City where he was to spend the evening of his birthday with two of his children that live there. We had a nice little visit with Miss Lesslie after supper, but she too left shortly after six o'clock. Mother announced to the Sisters that our confidence has been rewarded, for the Junior College was approved and will be accredited . . . We must now do our part in regard to thanksgiving.

The hand laboring over the paper that evening was Sister Genevieve's; it would handle community school certificates for eleven more years and come to feel increasingly what the day meant which brought three such friends to the college.

Next morning it was learned that Sister Dorothy, the dean who had conducted the visitors through the building, had all the time carried a temperature of 102 degrees. But it was the week before Holy Week, and she would have time to rest and "take care of the flu which seemed to have stricken her." The remainder of that spring and early summer she continued as dean, attending meetings at Lawrence and presiding at faculty meetings. In late summer, she went to Colorado for a few weeks' rest but returned "not greatly improved." By January 11 she was coughing "distressingly." [11] In January, Mother Lucy went on a visitation of convents in the South and wrote back to the convent that even in Alabama she could hear Sister Dorothy cough.[12]

On January 27, the chronicler wrote: "If Sister Dorothy does not get some help she will soon break down, as she goes around even now in a feeble manner. Sister Eva is to come home at the end of the semester and that will relieve her somewhat, as she

174

will start a class in biology, a five-hour class." Mother, coming home February 4, found a change for the worse. College life went on. Father Edmund saved the college $500 by having St. Benedict's carpenter make the desired chemistry table, and the kitchen was ready with a resplendent Friday dinner when the State Board of Education dropped in for a follow-up visit. Sister Dorothy taught her algebra class from one until two o'clock that day of March 10, and the State Board's visit was a success.

On March 28, Sister was taken to St. Margaret's, Dr. Horner accompanying the ambulance. Mother Lucy, hurrying home from a visitation in the East, reached her younger sister three days later. Sister Dorothy died at 9:15 Easter Tuesday evening, April 10. It was a free day for the college students, since her nameday, February 6, had been added to the Easter holidays.

In the years that followed, Sisters studying for degrees might not always understand why Mother Lucy said so often to them: "Don't work too hard. A 'C' grade will do, if it is earned for God." Sister Dorothy had known she was not strong for at least a decade, and had spent some time in Colorado even before being sent by Mother Aloysia to earn her Master's degree in mathematics. But she had also known that the early college days were important, and had been at her post during the first two crucial visits of the accreditors.

Father Gerard Heinz sang the Solemn Requiem, Friday, April 13. Bishop Gilfillan came from St. Joseph, where Sister had once taught. It misted during the morning hours but the rain came down in torrents during the funeral and only Fathers Gerard, Bonaventure, and Edmund stood at the graveside, other persons staying in their cars. Perhaps those three — the Abbey Prior who had been pastor of St. Benedict's so long while Mother Lucy was principal of his school, the college's great scholarly friend, and the Abbey Procurator — knew best what that funeral meant.

Two other deaths associated with the beginning of the college touched life that year. December 21, feast of St. Thomas, Sister Adelaide Cass died. The great Academy Directress who had seen her empire embrace junior college students also, would now have been called the first "Dean of Students." Never known to "raise her voice," she had wanted to make ladies out of her students. In favor of school standards, she had managed to be wheeled over to the college to teach until she could no longer do so, and she managed also to die during the holidays, people said, so that no school time be lost. And on April 2, Monday in Holy Week, after months of suffering at St. Margaret's Hospital, Sister Teresita Snoddy died, one of the first Sister-students, with those happy words: "Jesus, You love me."

A stream of Sisters was sent away to study. "It seems such a shame to have that nice home economics room and no equipment and no department," Sister Romana Farrell said in Mother Lucy's hearing. And having obtained a master's in English from Creighton she now went to Kansas State College for home economics. Sister Rosemary, in 1928, returned with a master's in philosophy from St. Louis University. She took the place of Dean while Sister Jerome went to Catholic University for a doctorate in French with Sister Immaculata, who was studying education.

In September, 1930, the college took its first juniors. In November, 1931, the University of Kansas and the State Board visited again, this time to grant full accreditation as a four-year college, and to praise the "uniformly advanced and specialized training of the members of the faculty, the new library of 15,000 volumes, and the large and well-equipped library room." [13]

In spring, 1932, the college graduated its first seniors: thirteen Sisters and seven girls. These were Sisters Benedicta, Editha, from Illinois, Ethelburg, Florence, Jane Frances, Joan, Karlene, Marcella, Mary Angela, Mary Cyril, Maxine, Raphaela, Valeria; and Mary Dawe, Bernice Dooley, Florence Dooley, Dorothy Murphy, Clementine Pietrzyk, Lauretta Schrick, and Doris Vermette. On the evening of June 1, Bishop Johannes gave the diplomas, Francis P. Matthews of Omaha an address "touching the problems of our country in this present distress [depression]," and Governor Woodring of Kansas was an honored guest.

The years passed; the enrollment grew. Girls came to college who were charmed by everything: the cleanliness, the order, the joy, the fascination of being served at table by Sisters with white aprons who seemed never in a hurry, yet who five minutes later would be sitting in classrooms with them, knowing the answers quite as well as if they had crammed by night light. The Sisters had some system, the girls concluded. Sister Flavia presided over the main office with her patience in distributing stamps, her imperturbable, kind face, and her characteristic walk close to the wall down the long hall to the convent for spiritual reading.

Everything grew at once. Flowers appeared before the great Sacred Heart Statue on the first floor, for the perpetual intention (said Sister Mildred Knoebber, Prefect), that the girls who came to Mount St. Scholastica would always be protected by the Divine Heart.

There was an orchestra presided over by Sister Scholastica, and a Glee Club directed by Sister Valeria. Sister Geraldine and Sister Gertrude gave music lessons. Girls with a prefect or two walked to Jackson Park in the autumn afternoons and were transported to Sugar Lake for picnics. There were lectures at night and on Sunday afternoons. There was the school paper, decided upon by Sister Mary Theresa Brentano and Sister Gertrude Winter on a trip home from the University of Kansas one summer day. A school contest for a name resulted in Mary Katherine Sheldon's naming the paper, the *Mount Mirror*. On the trip to the Abbey Print Shop to negotiate the printing, Mr. Andrew Baumgartner, head printer, gave the first subscription and began his long recognized but unpublicized career as its genuine but unsung co-editor. That he retired from work in the Centennial Year seemed somehow beautiful.

The college purpose had been stated in its 1932 catalogue, the first catalogue after its recognition as a senior college by the University of Kansas:

Mount St. Scholastica College is the realization of a project begun by the Benedictine Sisters who came to Atchison in 1863. It answers a demand in Kansas and the neighboring states for a college in which standard courses may be pursued under Catholic influences. With the high ideals of scholarship held by the older and larger institutions, it combines the peculiar cultural advantages of schools of its kind, in which the students live on the campus in intimate association with the faculty.

This was true. College life meant classes which gripped and held, participation in Monday afternoon clubs — Spanish,

177

French, English, sodality. It meant walks along the Missouri River bank and participation in praying and singing the Mass. It meant the occasional sight of the flutter of a novice's veil. For six or eight years it meant, in the afternoons at four o'clock, trays containing the convent bakery's best buns with butter or slices of fresh bread with sugared cinnamon. For a long time, really, it also meant syrup instead of preserves at breakfast sometimes, in a kind of participation in tradition – the perpetuation of the very first meal Sisters had taken in Atchison. It meant meditating on the garden with its rows of turnips and its ripening grapevines in the fall and on the western skyline with its peaceful flaming beauty in the evening.

This association with the faculty and the faculty's world did not pass with years. The *Student Handbook*, 1960, still says that it is only courtesy for the college girl to show her prom formal to her prefect.

There were other sharings. One night a strange reverberating noise in the gymnasium, like insistent knockings, sent two freshmen in search of the prefect. "Come with me," Sister Marcella said calmly, "and let anyone stronger than the Holy Ghost hurt us." No one was stronger and the noise proved to be the proximity of the engine room with its necessary noises.

One day, too, a non-Catholic student heard a prefect say: "Come hurry to Mass. Don't keep God waiting."

"Where is God that you must not keep Him waiting?" she asked and stayed to learn, to be baptized, to enter the convent.

Into all this life the North Central accreditors came in 1934. The stress which the convent felt in preparing for them was reflected in Mother Lucy's letters asking the missions for prayer. The day passed excitedly but grandly, and the Association granted provisional regional accreditation.

Entering the college today, one sees St. Benedict and St. Scholastica in the majestic foyer. And framed against a panel of tall curtains against the north window, the Sacred Heart statue stands symbolically larger than the life which finds its strength and inspiration there. Ordinarily donors of gifts to convents remain relatively unknown until a history is written. But it is not insignificant that the statue which protects the students is the gift of the parents of the convent's faithful procurator for so many years and of Sister Karlene, her sister. As a young Sister, Sister Dolorosa had said, "I won't either," to Mother Aloysia's comment that she would not live to see another building. But Sister lived to equip and to know from memory in daylight and nighttime the need of every inch of the giant building. She kept a diary of convent purchases and practices, a diary with almost no touch of the personal except in its subtle revelation of real values and its one-time comment, "Sister Karlene gave a music recital on the organ today. I thought it was very beautiful."

There is no break between that Sacred Heart statue and the farthest end of the convent hall, two blocks distant, where the statue of St. Joseph, first patron of the convent's temporalities, was transplanted from the first chapel Price Villa had; only dignity, majesty, and beauty.

"Where there is no vision, the people perish," wrote Christopher Dawson.[14] The converse is also true. Years after the building and accrediting, a speaker was to say at a graduation:

It is not in the fame and fortune of her daughters that Mount St. Scholastica will find her reward, but in women who have the courage to reflect her spirit and to give to the world what she has given them. There are thousands who have never walked this campus to whom your alma mater is a source of pride and joy. Remember, their hopes are in your keeping.[15]

The college both grew out of the convent life and contributed to it. St. Benedict had legislated on the care the convent should take of the young committed to its care. He had put them in his Rule as a part of the household. They were so integrated into the wonderfully simple and communal Mount St. Scholastica life that Father Arnold Tkacik, speaking on the feast of St. Benedict, March 21, 1962, could say:

"I have tried to find what is distinctive of a Benedictine college. I think it is that graduates here bear the marks of having been loved by their teachers."

1. *Waters of Siloe* (New York: Harcourt, Brace and Co., 1949), p. 5.
2. "It's a mystery to me that all this is here," a visitor making an educational survey once said. "Why do not more people know about it?" And on a trip to the book-bindery, when an inquirer paused to look at the

179

magazines being bound, the book-binder smiled: "We can work a little later because we don't belong to a union." "I think you have a pretty strong union here," the inquirer commented.

3. The course of study for the Scholasticate had been religion, catechism and Bible history; church and profane history; English literature, German, at least for German-speaking Sisters, and such other languages as might be deemed necessary; arithmetic and mathematics; bookkeeping; vocal music; piano, and such other instruments as deemed necessary; in brief, such branches as "are required for Catholic schools and academies." The provision added that not every Sister need be taught all these branches, but besides a good common literary education only those that are "deemed by the respective superiors more or less important."

4. It is hard not to itemize that content for posterity:

(1) For the Third or Primary Grade (issued to assistant teachers only) the examination shall consist of Catechism, Bible History, Orthography, Reading (including the fourth reader), penmanship, arithmetic (fundamental rules, fractions, compound numbers, percentage, simple interest), primary grammar and composition, primary geography, the principal events of United States History, Physiology, Vocal Music, Drawing, and Physical Culture.

(2) For the Second or Intermediate Grade, the examination shall show a thorough knowledge of the above-mentioned branches.

(3) For the First, or Higher Grade, the examination shall be the same as for the Second, together with Ancient and Modern History, Algebra, Bookkeeping, and Physiology.

5. Interview with Sister Willibalda, July 30, 1962.

6. Manuscript, Sister Jane Frances, August, 1960.

7. Interview with Sister Maurus Wempe, July 17, 1961.

8. Manuscript, "The First Laboratory Day in the New Building," February 21, 1924.

9. Sister Bernarda, 1924; Sister Romana, 1925.

10. Joined by Sister Jane Frances McAtee as reference librarian in 1936, in 1958 by Sister Kieran Curry as assistant, and through the years by many librarians such as Sister Vianney Kaiser, Sister Huberta Anderson, Sister Hildegarde Marshall, and Sister Felicia Schilling, Sister Florence linked the library days. She was to be cited by the Catholic Library Association as one of the founders of its Midwest Region at its 25th jubilee meeting, December, 1960.

11. *Chronicle*, January 11, 1928.

12. *Ibid.*, January 20, 1928.

13. *Catholic Daily Tribune*, January 28, 1932.

14. *The Critic*, June–July, 1959. Dawson is quoting Proverbs 29:18.

15. *Benedictine Review*, X (Summer, 1955), 45.

THE MAKERS OF THE COLLEGE

Mount St. Scholastica College grew out of what appears to be almost a light-hearted effort by a convent and its friends. There was an elasticity in the response of everyone to everything; Mother Lucy had such joy in visiting the Sisters away studying; there was a touch of buoyancy in the days, and the growth of the school had a radiance about it.

"Don't blame her. She's only a University student," Sister Rosalia said once when a sister away at school entrusted the precious Missouri Pacific railroad pass to a cab driver for mailing. To the lasting credit of the taxicab industry the envelope arrived safely and promptly.

Educators of older institutions, as has been already amply demonstrated, shared in the growth of this one. St. Benedict's College did not dilute classes either on its own campus or at the convent because of "pioneer difficulties." Father Sylvester Schmitz thundered educational principles which his students were to ponder during the sewing house hours which followed class. Father Edgar Schmiedeler, to crowded classes in the community room assembled on armless chairs, thought sociology the most important subject in the world. Father Felix, Father Pius, Father Adrian, Father Virgil never engaged in long preambles to their subjects but plunged into the matter with zest. "Because of the way they began, we have Sisters today who could conduct a whole college by themselves if a day long enough could be found," Mother Celeste was to comment in the summer of 1962, for many of the young listeners of the early twenties kept up their education for at least four decades, going the whole gamut of the circle of sciences.

Between 1922 and 1933, St. Benedict's College granted sixty degrees to Sisters of Mount St. Scholastica. It provided from the beginning, chaplains, advisers, lecturers, and friends.

Creighton University counted credits wherever they could possibly be validly found. Father Grace came to Atchison to speak to an accrediting committee meeting at St. Benedict's and to give counsel at the convent. "Dean Martin," said Sister Romana of the early days, "strained the letter to recognize the work being done wherever he could do so." Creighton awarded eleven Bachelor's degrees between 1921 and 1933 and several Master's to the energetic Atchison Sisters pioneering in higher education in Omaha. More than that, there was a quality in the teaching which students never forgot.

The University of Kansas gave its first doctorates to women when Sister Anthony Payne and Sister Mary Theresa Brentano earned theirs in 1933. It sent approachable, learned people to evaluate education here, and Dean Lawson, speaking in the early years, left at the new Atchison College a rich view of liberal education. The Catholic University of America educated three deans in the college history, and professors in history, sociology, Latin, mathematics, philosophy, education, French, and English. St. Louis University received its first full-time resident Sister students when Sisters Rosemary, Eva, and Anthony came in 1926. It awarded four doctorates and many master's degrees to Mount St. Scholastica Sisters. On paper the contribution looks quite matter-of-fact. But the Catholic universities cut tuition prices for Sisters so that almost mass education needed in the continuation of a Catholic college could be possible.

Fordham, Notre Dame, Detroit, Laval, Johns Hopkins, Marquette, Loyola of the West, De Paul, Oklahoma, Missouri, Denver, Northwestern, Kansas State, California, Cornell, Columbia, Kansas City University, St. Teresa's, Winona, colleges, Chicago and Kansas City Art Institutes, Washington University Art department made their real gifts through graduate work, special research, and workshops. These were all makers of the college, for a college in a very real sense is its faculty as well as its students. The overwhelming majority of Sisters went to Catholic universities, but they met great teachers and fellow students too on other American campuses, and in the exchange tried to remember Sister Rosalia's original advice that all things be cared for wherever they went and that universities had the right to expect fine things of Sisters.

Pierre de Chaignon la Rose, Prescott Hall, Harvard, designed the college coat of arms. He explained it thus:

The medieval heralds assigned to the Anicci a red shield with two gold lions thereon (deducing them, I believe, from Hector, to whom they assigned a similar shield). They also invented a legend that Saint Benedict, who was, of course, a member of this noble Roman family, used only *one* of the two lions on his shield. As personal heraldry was not invented in Europe till the second half of the twelfth century, we may, as archaeologists, smile at the ingenuous enthusiasm of these medieval heralds with their unconsciously apocryphal ascriptions. Still, as we are using medieval art, we have to use it in the medieval manner, and in default of other heraldic data accept these heraldic legends as viable conventions, traditional uses, of which we may make present use in an art of symbolism which, to the instructed, makes no historical claims.

If, then, Saint Benedict used as his arms only one of his two family lions, Saint Scholastica, as his devoted sister, would do likewise! So I propose: A red shield, thereon a gold lion holding a book in profile (for the college), with a silver dove resting for a moment on the top edge of the book. The dove, of course, represents the spirit of Saint Scholastica, as Saint Benedict saw it ascending, at her death. This, I think, will make as choice a bit of heraldic symbolism as that very restricted art permits, and I think I can make a handsome shield of it.[1]

Students made a contribution. The idea of the *Mount Mirror* was explained to the college assembly, October 4, 1929, by Agnes Huppe, and the first issue appeared October 22 of that year. It was sponsored by Sister Mary Theresa; its editor was Ruth Mattochi with assistants Viola Koppes, Margaret Bergman, and Mary K. Sheldon. Imogene Aaron gave the college national publicity with a heart-breakingly wonderful prize of $500 for an essay on "The Role of Chemistry in the Diffusion of Knowledge."[2] She was followed by young Sister Ethelburg Leuschen, a Scholastic, who won $300, also for a chemistry essay. Success was good for the young college. It spread a pleasing wildfire among Sisters and students and all through the young building itself. Helen Casey, in those early days, performed flawlessly on the organ, the beautiful new Wurlitzer in the auditorium with its assortment of band and orchestra instruments hidden behind the decorative iron grilling. "She matched silent movies perfectly," Sister Rosaria Schafer remembers. "A dog would appear on the screen and she could make it bark from the organ." [3]

Students en masse also gave the college character. Their productions dipped deep into the classical past but were brimful of so much Midwestern youth. They entered a contest translating Horace's Odes to commemorate the two thousandth year of his death. They sang Handel's Oratorio. They organized a chapter of Kappa Gamma Pi, whose first members were Imogene Aaron and Rose Lane of the class of 1934; Clarabelle Mumford, of 1935; Kathleen O'Connor and Dolores Hoffmans, of 1936. They took part in religion contests, explaining theological truths from the stage while Abbot Martin, Father Richard Burns, and a board of judges, along with the whole religious community south of the line, listened with solemn delight. They had a spirit. In the midst of the spiritual, academic, and social luster of their lives when college days at the Mount were young, one boarder, Clarabelle Mumford, helped keep the common touch by darning stockings as people used to do and by appropriating the photographs of other girls' handsome relatives to give a dash of excitement to her own dormitory dresser.

They provided music recitals and college assemblies, drew the convent to the balcony to listen with pride to orchestras and glee clubs, and enlisted the laundry to provide a huge basket as the main prop for the French play, Le Farce du Duvier. With Sister Romana as director, they staged the fantasy Once in a Palace. They met for mission committees and sodality meetings, livened the grounds, walked down to the river in the Indian summer with prefects, and sometimes listened in one's or two's or groups outside the choir chapel windows between five and six to the sound of the Matins chant.

The faculty were makers. Sister Rosemary Hogan and Sister Jerome Keeler were deans after the deaths of Sister Helena

Brandmeier and Sister Dorothy Dooley. Sister Mildred Knoebber became the first Dean of Women. Father Bonaventure,
vice-president, gave the Sunday evening sermons and led the
prayer of Reposition when the altar was rich with snapdragons
from the greenhouse, when girls with white veils knelt in the
pews between postulants in black in the choir stalls on either
side. Certain *Tantum Ergo* chants became part of the very
atmosphere along with the words, "We know O dear Redeemer
that the weight of our iniquities pressed down Thy Face to
the earth in the Garden of Olives." Behind all those young
people praying, the older members of the house to which the
college belonged — the bakers, the infirmarians, the teachers,
the seamstresses, the total family — knelt and loved them all.
"I like Sister Vitalis," one girl said. "She makes you feel so nice
and sick when you go to the infirmary."

On February 13, 1930, at 4:30, death reminded everyone of
who the makers were. Sister Hildegard O'Keefe made the
whole place pause for the death of an ageless person who was
part of its origins and very being. In her last several years, she
lost her strength and could be seen at her desk trying to write
a poem or at her place in choir not quite able to find the page.
But she never lost her real meaning to the convent and the
convent school. Tributes poured in from everywhere, and the
Mount Mirror recognized history by printing some of them.
One from a schoolboy she had taught in her parochial days
sounded a note not so familiar to those who knew her work
at the Academy and College:

If I am anything [wrote Monsignor Robert M. Nolan of Fort Worth,
Texas], I owe it, under God, to Sister Hildegard, for it was her
understanding of my character as a boy that got me to go half right,
and I am sure her constant prayers for me all these years went far
toward keeping me in the straight and narrow.[4]

Signatures and words from others helped make the college —
the following words and signature, for example:

The Vatican
July 30, 1930

Reverend and dear Sister [Jerome]:
I have the honor to acknowledge in the name of the Holy Father
the receipt of your doctor's dissertation "Etude sur la poesie et sur

THE MEANING OF THE MOUNTAIN

le vocabulaire de Loys Papon poete forezien du XVI siecle" which you sent him.

His Holiness has gone through your work and expressed pleasure with it. He is particularly pleased that so many religious women are taking their higher degrees at the Catholic University of America, the work of which University has been so often praised and blessed by Him. The Holy Father graciously deigns to send you the Apostolic Blessing.

May I add my own congratulations to those of His Holiness.

Asking a remembrance in your prayers,

Yours very sincerely in Christ,

E. Cardinal Pacelli

Secretary of State to His Holiness.[5]

Some of the words came from lecturers who stepped between the red velvet curtains of the new stage, beside the seal Pierre de Chaignon la Rose had designed, while the hush of a student body new to college ways waited with real delight. "Neglect rhetoric if you want to be lonesome," said Mr. Brown of the *Atchison Globe* in April, 1930. And, "Education brings the experience of centuries to youth . . . brings forth latent things, the best that lies within, the cultural, highest, noblest in life," said Father Henry Courtney.

The towering Jesuit philosopher of Gregorian University in Rome spoke from the stage. Father Keeler said first that almost the proudest thing of all for him, next to being a priest and a Jesuit, was to be the brother of the Mount St. Scholastica dean, and the audience broke into wild applause.

To the dark red velvet curtains that opened so majestically came the great and varied gifts of many different men: Father Francis LeBuffe, S.J., J. Elliot Ross, Frank Sheed, Dr. Sherry of Lourdes with his message of Mary's love, Chancellor Lindley of the University of Kansas, Maurice O'Keefe of Atchison, Father Marian Kotinek, O.S.B., Dr. Deferrari, Daniel Conway, S.J., Jerome Kerwin of the University of Chicago, Mortimer Adler, Bishop Lillis, Christopher Hollis, Dorothy Day, T. A. Daly, John F. Helm of Kansas State College, and Shane Leslie — "that strange man" as the diary of the Convent Procurator recorded.[6]

To the chapel where for three days of the year the girls sat

quiet with their white veils, came retreat masters such as Father
Robert Sweeney, Redemptorist, and Father Benedict Brosna-
han, O.S.B., whose memory stayed forever. And the early years
went by in peace and solemnity and achievement of all kinds.
Sister Scholastica Kratschmer won a second place among Kansas composers, Father Felix lectured on birds, and seniors on
April 13, 1932, members of the first graduation class, took their
first comprehensive examinations "in accordance with revised
standards of the North Central Association and the custom of
the University of Chicago."

Abbot Martin came every Sunday. After his conference to
the Sisters he spoke to the college girls without diluting the
message. Sometimes the hour might grow long, but they never
forgot the love of the Church on the face of the kind Abbot
or the gentleness and depth with which he spoke. Mother Lucy
moved between convent and college, and a student summed up
the general reaction:

> She is Mother of the convent
> And her sunny, kindly face,
> With its wealth of friendly glances,
> Seems to brighten up the place.
> Are you weary of your studies,
> Are you feeling sort of blue?
> If then graciously she passes,
> Why you feel like smiling, too.
> She is always helping someone
> And a ray of God's own grace
> Shines forth, lighting every feature,
> And dispels gloom's selfish trace.[7]

That was true. Mother had time for both college and academy, and girls came to hope, not without fulfillment, that they
could occasionally meet informally the person whose blue eyes
had a way of seeing the heart without telling all that it saw.

Life moved on. In 1936 the college was hostess to the con-
vention of the Kansas State Sodality Union with Father E. J.
Weisenberg presiding. In preparation for it, the library requested greetings from Catholic authors. When, on May 1, a
thousand students assembled, they found on display in the
library greetings from Father Daniel Lord, S.J., William

O'Rourke, Ronald Knox, Lawrence Patterson, S.J., Ignatius Cox, S.J., Sheila Kaye Smith, E. I. Watkin, Jacques Maritain, Rev. Charles E. Coughlin, Christopher Hollis, Rev. Wilfrid Parsons, S.J., Raphael McCarthy, S.J., Most Rev. Bishop Clement Kelly, Father Earls, Shane Leslie, Thomas F. Coakley, D.D., Arnold Lunn, Enid Dinnis, Frank H. Spearman, James W. Gillis, C.S.P., T. A. Daly, Dorothy Willman, James J. Walsh, Francis Talbot, S.J., Joseph H. Reilly, Michael Kenny, S.J., William Franklin Sands, and Leo J. Latz.

Mr. Latz had written: "If such interest in the writings of Catholic authors were to be shown on a larger scale, it would undoubtedly do much to encourage Catholic literary efforts, which in itself would be productive of much good." [8]

One of the contributors had responded thus:

For KSSU

Dear Sisters:

Out in Atchison,
I write to you in thankful awe;
You give an undeserving one
A place at Saint Scholastica.

I send his face and signature;
His record has few rosy tints;
But for conviction doubly sure
Ask Washington for finger-prints.

Scholastica prayed not in vain
To keep her brother's company.
Scholastica, do pray again
For
Francis Patrick Donnelly. (SJ)

Abbot Martin said the morning Mass, Saturday, May 2. The old hill, once crowned only by Price Villa in its young splendor and its cedar trees, was alive and colorful now with hundreds of young people from all over the state. There were deliberations in the auditorium on the meaning of holiness among young people. There were resolutions. There was lunch in boxes in the gymnasium. The day's events closed with procession to the grotto, Benediction, and entertainment by the Rhythmic Ravens of St. Benedict's College.

It was a great, lighthearted day. Sisters moved with the stu-

St. Joseph's Convent, in the early 1900's. Only the first section existed in 1863.

Price Villa, 1877, as it was pictured in the Atchison Champion, summer, 1877, when the Sisters purchased it.

Early pioneers. Standing — Sisters Hildegard O'Keefe, Hilda Boos, Ebba Kraemer; seated — Sisters Columba Meyer, Boniface Bantle, and Adelgund Stein.

"Minims" of 1915

The convent at the golden jubilee 1913; Convent and choir chapel, built 1900; St. Scholastica Hall, built 1884; St. Cecilia's, purchased 1877.

St. Scholastica Chapel,

built 1938

Administration building

built 1924

Benet Hill Priory,
Colorado Springs, Colo.,
established 1963.

Mother Augusta Parle, O.S.B., St. Lucy's
Priory, Glendora, Calif., receives
departure cross, 1952.

Mother Mildred Knoebber, O.S.B.,
of St. Benedict's Priory,
Mexico City, begun 1944

Children at Tulpetlac, Mexico,
and their Sister-teacher.

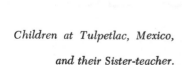

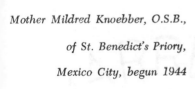

May 1, 1954, day of the renewal of ancient Consecration of Virgins rite.

The meaning of all things on earth. Daily Mass in the St. Scholastica Chapel.

dents, Sisters from schools all over Kansas and from many religious orders and congregations. Priests and high school and college young people from towns large and small were there. The college had become a place where many worlds met in a world that was really one. "It's like a citadel against forces dedicated to tearing down," a visitor said.

That year the college seemed to stand on a peak in its era. That year of 1936, in solemn concourse in Chicago, the North Central Association of Colleges and Universities, said that it was permanently a college granting a worthy liberal education, and worthy of permanent membership with other dedicated colleges. But that fact any student or community member on the campus that Maytime would already have known.

1. Letter to Father Bonaventure, published in the *Mount Mirror*.

2. She went on to major in biology and French and ultimately to head the Romance Languages department as Sister Audrey Aaron.

3. Interview, Summer, 1961.

4. *Mount Mirror*, February 19, 1930.

5. Printed in the *Mount Mirror*, October 7, 1930.

6. Shane Leslie came to give a talk on his book, *Mrs. Fitzherbert*, got involved in dancing an Irish jig, asked to have his socks washed and went solemnly to dinner with the vice-president of the college. "When will they bring my socks?" he asked. "They are in the oven," responded Father Bonaventure with equal solemnity. "They are drying and will come with the dessert."

7. Sarah Dolores Ryan, *The Mount Mirror*, December 20, 1929.

8. *The Mount Mirror*, April 30, 1936.

THE PUREST WISDOM

Sister Sophia Buttenbohmer, dusting the convent corridor, went up and down the halls all through the thirties, keeping Mother Lucy aware of cultural programs in college and academy. If the matter of community attendance was unusually important to her, she would dust the threshold many times, until Mother looked up from her papers to meet the glance of the interested old face. Then a tap of the bell at community supper, to Sister Sophia's delight, would announce that something was happening that night of so educational a nature that prayers would be early.

Much was happening. Interested as they were, neither the North Central nor KSSU could see everything. In 1930, students from Missouri and Kansas universities debated before the Mount St. Scholastica student body and the community, the Pope asked the world to pray for the cessation of cruelties in Russia, the Apostolic Delegate Pietro Fumasoni-Biondi visited, the Rev. F. J. Remler, C.M., spoke on "Imitating the Virtues of Mary," and students of St. Benedict's and St. Mary's Colleges debated: "Resolved that the nations adopt a plan of complete disarmament, except such forces as are needed for police purposes."

On the south campus the new cement drives were completed. Jake Seeger, convent workman, had picked up stones from the grounds and various other places to build with his own faithful hands the backgrounds for the Stations of the Cross. "We saw the pictures of the Stations in a catalogue and wrote the company," Sister Dolorosa said years later. "And the company

190

donated the Stations. Everyone was so good." Someone took a photograph from the air and the towers and white driveways laced among them looked so beautiful.

Sister Valeria Willems passed her examinations for a music degree from the University of Kansas. There was a fire in the furnace room, and Sister Agnes Glancy, from her memory of long ago days, suggested that the community return to the practice of praying daily to Saints Florian, Sebastian, Wendelin, and Patrick for general protection.

In November, Father Bonaventure spoke on "Requirements of Becoming a Saint." He said that a saint is simply someone who says "Yes" to God. In November also, the first *Missa Recitata* with full participation by Sisters and students was celebrated by Abbot Martin. "The attention given the Mass the last two years," commented the Chronicle, "will bring grace. The world is in need." Unemployment stalked the nation.

There was a blizzard in winter, 1931, and Father Bonaventure walked through the snowstorm to say Mass. Holy Thursday, 1931, saw the abolition of the Washing of the Feet ceremony, it being considered appropriate only in an Abbey where the father of the monastery as a priest more actually held the place of Christ. That autumn, Sister Elizabeth, O.S.F., of Conception, Missouri, became the first religious of another Order to register for an entire year's study. That fall, too, the community sang the Divine Praises on the feast of Christ the King in a chant which Sister Gertrude and Sister Scholastica had learned at the Pius X School of Music in New York the summer previous. Judge John Delehant, then a young lawyer, spoke for National Education Week, and the Sisters saw their first talking picture, *The Spirit of Notre Dame.*

There was a Washington Bicentennial program, February 19, 1932, and on April 20, the two colleges staged their first intercollegiate prom. "Father Richard, the Dean of St. Benedict's, has been very earnest in making the boys realize the necessity of being true Catholic men, and we have tried to impress the girls with a like idea as to true womanly qualities," commented the Chronicle.

One June 25, 1932, the General Chapter discontinued the wearing of the large Rosary. And on August 13, Sister Agnes

Glancy died. She was buried in the brilliant beauty of a clear August 15 after a feast day Mass. The Office for the Dead was chanted, but the low Mass of the Assumption was said for the old Sister consecrated by her parents to the Blessed Virgin in the long ago. The Requiem was sung the following morning.

That September of 1932, when all the missions had gone out, the Director of Teacher Accreditation had time to muse:

The day is not very far distant when every teacher will be required to hold a degree even for work in the Elementary School field, and when every principal will be required to hold a Master's degree. With all these added requirements, education is not making any noticeable progress. Would that it were, and that people were really becoming educated, but educated in the right manner, and the true sense of the word.

The convent was trying to do what it could, and it had its own ideas on the right direction. In the fall of 1932, the impossibility of getting 265 boarding students and Sisters into chapel which then accommodated 234 persons threw ahead of Mother Lucy and the community a shadow which might have surprised Bishop Fink — the need for another and larger chapel. The days were depression days, and the only hint to the community that Mother Lucy was measuring the possibility of building or at least of doing something very important was the occasional added and urgent prayer.

The days of the outside world did press on the world within. Everyone prayed for a good president in the November election. Everyone became concerned a little about conditions in Germany. One of the pastors, who over the years had directed vocations to Atchison, simply disappeared in the rising of the regime of a new and strangely militant leader there.

There were the constant things though. On Gaudete Sunday, 1932, the convent had its first set of rose-colored vestments. That fall too the college students staged Sheridan's *Rivals*, and in January of the new year, a convent workman, out of the church for nine years, became sick and asked for a "mild priest." Abbot Martin went to the workman's cottage, and the man died in peace. In the spring a fire broke out in the convent of the Guardian Angel parish during Sunday Mass, and Sisters of Loretto gave the Benedictines teaching there hospitality for several months. The Daughters of Charity shared the giving, receiving the Sisters for their noon meal at the Boys Orphan Home near Guardian Angels. And in the summer, Sister Romana Farrell lectured on the etiquette that a Sister should teach to high school pupils. The venerable convent front porch was the forum; the Sisters sat listening on the green benches that surrounded the circle of brilliant cannas.

The next summer, of 1934, was mercilessly hot. Volunteers taught religious vacation schools for the Negro children of Atchison, soon to be amalgamated in the parish schools. The work raised a question which, it seemed, should have been answered sooner.

Without much excitement, Sister Adelsind came home ill from Maur Hill on July 21. "Now if I can just stay here and rest," she said, as they took her to the infirmary. She died early Sunday and because of the intense heat was buried Monday evening about 6:30, after Office. The cemetery was bright in the evening sun, quiet, and hushed for the faithful workman at rest, and new candidates stood among the 500 Sisters meditating on both the communion and the solitude of every convent story.

In August of that 1934, Joe Weingart, associated with the convent for many years, died at Research hospital. In September the community began staffing the Antonito Public School in Colorado, which was closing because of inability to pay teachers, and the Missouri Pacific Railroad furnished six passes for the first Atchison Sisters going to "the Valley," as Antonito and its surroundings would always be called. There, in a pocket among the mountains of southern Colorado and northern New Mexico, opened that fall one of the convent's most stirring stories.

The shutters in Price Villa (long known now as St. Cecilia's) were exchanged for shades that autumn, teachers went to Atchison High School in October for a meeting on the Unit Method, and on the feast of the great St. Teresa, October 15, the community modernized to the extent of having new breakfast plates.

Returning from a stay at St. Mary's Hospital, Pueblo, Sisters Genevieve and Josephine reported that the Sisters of Charity there could not be surpassed in hospitality. At educational meetings in Kansas City and Topeka, Sister Jerome Keeler and

THE MEANING OF THE MOUNTAIN

Sister Anthony Payne spoke on "Problems and Opportunities of a Woman's College in Kansas," and "What Biology Can Contribute to Character Building." In November, 1934, Mother Lucy resisted an invitation to go to Germany for the 900th anniversary of St. Walburg's convent. It was a bad time, Bishop Johannes had told her on his return, to be going to Germany.

In December, the community sang a new Immaculate Conception novena after forty-five years of the old version. And on December 8, the albs crocheted by Sister Ephrem were first worn at the Solemn Mass. Her companion in sickness, Sister Harlindis, died that December 12 in Walsenburg.

On January 19, 1935, Sister Dolorosa noted from her Procurator's desk, among the other transactions of her notebook, that a redbird sang outside the window. March 1, and the community awakening at five o'clock felt the earthquake which shook the corners of four states — Kansas, Nebraska, Iowa, and Missouri. The Novitiate was delighted, and admitted the fact. Even older Sisters found the variation in Kansas meteorology something which distinguished the day. Dr. Deferrari of Catholic University spoke to the Sisters and students March 11: "approachable and amiable," said the Procurator's notes. That spring the worst dust storm in history struck the convent on the evening of March 20, and after the festive Mass on the following morning, there was a mass invasion of aprons on the dust-covered floors.

Sister Barbara brought in the first radishes, May 1, 1935, Sister John Marie Brazzel received the Winthrop Scholarship in Biochemistry at the Catholic University, and Jerome Kerwin of Chicago University gave the Commencement Address. In June and July, after painstaking practice, the entire community chanted the Mass from the main body of the Choir Chapel, the aisles and hallway packed with those who usually attended the so-called summer chapel. In September, Sister Ephrem died as she had lived, "taking all things as coming from God," said Mother Lucy. Sisters from seven different communities enrolled in the fall session, and the chapel again filled and overflowed.

In 1936, Sister Benedicta Howe opened the Little Theater on the college ground floor with a play. Father Edmund Pusch blessed the dairy herd, a snowstorm buried the city, Dorothy

Day lectured on Friendship House, and the community learned a new *Laudibus Cives* in Gregorian Chant for the St. Benedict's Day novena, a chant it did not at first like as well as the excitable older one. On June 10, 1936, a young priest new to the Mount, Father David Kinish, celebrated Mass at the side altar.

It was a burning hot summer. There were 160 bushels of cucumbers. Mother Lucy told the Sisters to pray for the seventy-five people dying every minute because of the intense heat. A storm of July 20 covered the chapel with dust and dried leaves, and the heat surpassed the memory of even the oldest.

Autumn came. Little Hannah Curtin, an Academy student since her fourth grade, who would have entered the convent in June, died. The little pony that helped in the cutting of the grass died. The community and students saw *David Copperfield*, Arnold Lunn came to speak, and Sister Florentine Bradley, the perfect lady who had so long presided as oldest Sister, slipped quietly into eternity.

So much of convent life sounds like a diary because so much of it is just a diary. Nothing changes violently which is securely anchored. But there do come gigantic events which gather up the fragments and focus them.

Construction on a new chapel began, construction which in the hard years of the thirties would depend, said Mother Lucy, "more on prayer than on planning." On the feast of St. Gertude, November 17, 1936, with a mighty flurry of drills and hammers, the old building started to go down so that a chapel could rise on the site of St. Scholastica hall. Bakehouse, apple cellar ("firm as adamant, defiant to all newly invented machinery," said the Chronicle), and Novitiate walls crumbled before the wreckers until on December 3 only the first floor of St. Scholastica Hall stood, "like a big platform for some performance," said the Chronicle. The college girls cleared a hundred dollars on a bazaar and donated it to the chapel fund. The cisterns were filled up; a large tree west of the Novitiate surrendered its life.

In the course of the tearing down and building, some Sisters attended the consecration of the pastor of Cathedral parish, St. Joseph, Missouri, December 21. Bishop Buddy went to the San Diego diocese from which he would in a few years send the call which would result in a California daughterhouse. In the winter of 1936 and spring of 1937, Dean Lawson of the University of Kansas spoke to the students, Father Anthony and Father John walked from Maur Hill on the January ice to say Mass, Sister Jerome and Sister Immaculata went to Columbia University on sabbatical leave, there was a dust storm on top of the ice, the two colleges staged *The Upper Room*, Bishop Johannes died, and Sister Anatolia Krogman, "always a faithful worker in garden and canning house," took her hands off all stewardships after great suffering at St. Margaret's Hospital.

The cornerstone of the new chapel was blessed,[1] May 12, 1937. All summer Sisters watched and listened with fascination as derricks lifted the heavy stones into the great arch which would support the cross. Music pupils in St. Cecilia's found the sound of machines not unpleasant through the hot days, as the strong and lovely structure became reality, and Sister Valeria Willems counted time and watched simultaneously. In the autumn the gallery of the chapel, with its polished wood and its ample space for invalids, neared completion, and the builders insisted with pride that it would hold 500 persons.

The inner pattern of life went on building, too. Sister Athanasia Koppes, assistant novice- and scholastic-mistress, died on the feast of St. Michael. Forrest Schulz of the Kansas City Music Conservatory, came to conduct the college orchestra. Sister Edith Stein, drawing near to the evening of her life, came to the practices to listen. Mr. Schulz appreciated the great veteran who had always known that music is holy ground. Sister Angela Foley came from Shawnee to review German for her language examination at Creighton. "Don't expect her to read it orally too well," said her professor there to the examiners. "Her mother was a McCarthy and her father's name was Foley." In January, the community paid the grateful tribute of prayer at the death of Dr. Horner, distinguished and faithful Atchison physician. The rose window in the chapel was finished; the wood carved plaques of the medal of St. Benedict and of the Virgin and Child arrived. If all the buildings in the world should be destroyed, and the convent Chronicle should survive, architecture, it seems, could be reconstructed.

A double human drama occurred that February, 1938. While

workmen were hurrying with the building, two Sisters who had done much to build the tone of the place, went peacefully to God. Sister Genevieve became ill and died February 12. Her sister, Sister Aurelia, endeavoring to take over the convent chronicle from her sister's pen without revealing her own personality, must have battled to write: "Sister Aurelia knelt by her side. They had come to the convent together and had been in it together for nearly fifty years." Because of a delay in the arrival of relatives, Sister Genevieve's remains stayed in the chapel a day after the Requiem Mass. "When not at work, she had been in that front pew always," wrote Sister Aurelia with the same effort at anonymity.

Maisie Ward Sheed, friend of Chesterton, lectured in the auditorium on the night of February 18. Sister Scholastica Kratschmer, musician and literature teacher, who would so have loved the lecture, was mildly fighting her own dignified battle with pneumonia. "If my throat would get well, I would be all right," she said. Her death on February 20 left memories for all who knew her. Some kept the memory of the way she read Keats. "Surely the heavenly choirs have an excellent musician now," wrote Father Sylvester of Cullman, Alabama, chant teacher, who remembered how her classic face registered the success or struggle of community practices.

The first green pillar was set up for the new chapel's main altar on March 10, and the Sisters chose amber lanterns for the chapel lights, "about as tall as Sister Elizabeth," they said describing them by letters to the mission. On March 13, Austria surrendered to Hitler and the community listened apprehensively to the radio during recreation. World shadows seemed somehow gathering side by side with the majestic brightness of the wonderful new structure which was almost finished.

In April, the Twin Colleges of Mount St. Scholastica and St. Benedict's, staged *The Upper Room* in Kansas City's Municipal Auditorium. Everything was converging to form the tone which became solemn jubilee, the dedication of the chapel and the observance of the convent's 75th year. Young Sisters straightened the old pictures in the convent hall, the red Numidian marble for the sanctuary crucifix was set up, and the communion railing was built. Convent life revolved around each added step. Abbot Martin blessed the altars on Low Sunday.

Then jubilee bells went up, all over the convent. Nine hundred guests arrived in the downpour of rain which was May 4. Bishop Paul C. Schulte dedicated the chapel.[2] In his sermon he picked up the common things of the convent day and said that they had built the chapel. "This chapel," he said, "is a work of love made up not from the luxury of the great but from the sacrifices of the lovers of Jesus." He looked into the shadows of the future and pierced them with sober hope: "Picture the scenes of joy, consolation, sadness which may take place in it. Let us pray that it may never see desecration as other such chapels in Europe have seen it."

There was a banquet at noon with the Right Rev. Monsignor James Brady of St. Joseph as toastmaster. Loudspeakers carried to the lounge the voices of John W. Delehant, Leo Nusbaum, Very Rev. Daniel Conway, S.J., Very Rev. Eugene Vallely, chancellor of the diocese, Abbot Martin, and Bishop Schulte. The Bishop spoke of the charity of Mother Lucy through the depression years. Abbot Martin looked back over the thirty years in which he had known Mount St. Scholastica and over the glory of the consecrated chapel, which he asked would never be called the "old chapel" and would never be torn down.

A pageant at 2:30, written by Sister Imogene Baker and staged by Sister Benedicta Howe and her helpers, displayed the Benedictine years. Students from the twin colleges were in the cast, with Virginia Minton, sodality prefect, as St. Scholastica.[3] Announcing the event, the *Mount Mirror* had said:

A symbolic dance, "The Dance of the Doves," directed by Mr. Edward Prinz, St. Joseph, Mo., and Miss Mary Jayne Gospodaric, will be presented by the college students; and "The Dance of Progress," directed by Miss Mayme Everhardy will be given by thirty academy students. The choruses are under the direction of Sister Valeria Willems and Sister Geraldine Jacobs, and the chanting will be taught by Sister Gertrude Winter. A grand finale will include a mixed chorus of 200 voices which will sing "Praise to the Holiest," composed by Sister Scholastica Kratschmer.

198

Hundreds of people had made the first seventy-five years of Mount St. Scholastica. Hundreds were making its jubilee.

But the great chapel, seating 720 persons, was the real jubilee. It stood between college and convent, opening to the world. Above its door was the Virgin and Child. On each side of the hall outside it, the Benedictine medal in wood carving and motto *Pax* proclaimed the reasons for being. The great doors swung open to steps leading down a walk beside the old trees, the green grass, the sunlight in spring, summer, fall and winter.

"Mount St. Scholastica has a sacred mission to fulfill, and we must not forget that her work is God's work," Mother Lucy had written in the commemorative edition of the *Mount Mirror Magazine Supplement*. The chapel had a majesty commensurate with the mission. It put the daily deed in the great perspective. It completed the dignity, majesty, and beauty which the Sisters from twenty-seven foreign countries, from cities and towns and rural America needed for the climate of their souls. With an almost great majesty, it received the individual and kept her individual, and yet led her into the fathomless peace of the Communion of Saints. The women saints of the Canon of the Mass would be illumined by sunlight on its varied stages through the day, and by moonlight after dusk. The sanctuary lamp at night could cast light enough for a person to see her whole way through the dark. It was a noble building, before which Kurt von Schuschnigg, former chancellor of Austria, would one day say: "Was this designed in America?"

A college girl had caught the tone of contemplation at the base of the whole Mount life, at the root of the Chronicle amid all its sundry recordings, at the very foundation of all college days themselves. She found it in the new chapel, spacious and quiet, grand and simple (ample to hold 600 students by winter and 720 missionaries by summer), emblem and home, symbol as well as reality. Josephine Ege, later Sister Mary Paul, wrote for the college magazine in January, 1940:

> Here we have drunk from living years
> The thought of men,
>> Have learned to love the sweep of brush
>> Of chord and pen.

Yet we have searched beyond Truth's great
Terrestrial glow
And glimpsed deep mysteries we've yearned
To see, to know.

These days that make us thus so wise
Here too reveal
That purest wisdom comes to us
The hours we kneel.

The deepest lesson the convent had wanted to learn and to give had been written in stone and window and human life. It was sweet to hear it from the voice of a student. And not even the shadow of an oncoming war could dim the peace attendant on the lesson.

1. It contained copies of the Holy Rule, the Constitutions, the Customs; medals of St. Benedict; sketches of the lives of the Superiors; statues of the Sacred Heart, the Blessed Virgin Mary, and St. Joseph; a copy of Sister Regina Baska's history of the Congregation.

2. The Rev. Matthias Stein, O.S.B., former chaplain, and the Rev. L. B. Liciotti of Walsenburg were deacon and subdeacon. Father Bonaventure Schwinn was archpriest; Father Marian Kotinek, master of ceremonies.

3. Virginia Minton, as Sister Terrance Minton, would be Mother Celeste's companion in the trip to Brazil, March, 1963, to explore the hope of a foundation there.

Section Five

THE CONVENT AND THE WAR

A convent has its own way of living through a war. It fights every battle, but in its own way. Its version might be perhaps as valid as anyone's version, its interpretation even more valid than some.

World War II came, not like a celebration for which preparations had been made, but gradually and terribly like a drought in summer. The Rev. William Cunningham of Notre Dame, in June of 1938, told the Mount St. Scholastica graduates that the outlook was dark for college graduates, and that they must continue to build on the intellectual and the moral rather than on the vocational.[1]

By the fall of 1938, the shadow of Europe's unrest and fear had reached the convent and its every school. With hope that gradually dimmed and anxiety that increased, it watched the names of men like Neville Chamberlain and Kurt von Schuschnigg in an unequal battle against something that seemed uncontrollable. Under the shadow, Mother Lucy wrote to the missions, reminding the Sisters to keep the vow of poverty, to think of the actual need of so many people in the world, to be aware of the convent's own situation. Schools could not pay well in these years of depression and omen, the new chapel had not been donated, and it was by the mercy of God alone that the community existed and went forward. It was a time when martyrs were being made. "Let us consider the hardships and sufferings of religious in foreign countries," she wrote, and the sorrows of those "who have no comfort and very little to eat."[2]

201

The real war came. Sisters on the missions in the late summer of 1939 heard the voices of newsboys announcing: "EXTRA! ENGLAND DECLARES WAR ON GERMANY OVER POLAND." Listeners in community rooms in 1940 heard commentators tell the world that the flower of the British Armed Forces was bottled up in Dunkirk. Soldiers may not have fully realized that schoolteachers and choir directors, ushering children into May Devotions that evening, sang the *O Salutaris Hostia* with new reason, for the millions now involved in the bitterness of war.

Soon the conflict made its real impact. The Sisters from Germany who had not yet been naturalized were interviewed, photographed, and examined for their knowledge of the American Constitution. Civic authorities treated them with fine courtesy, and they received their "papers" with real pride.

America itself was not long peaceful. Father Brooks Hale called the Lillis High School convent on the morning of December 7, 1941, to say: "Turn on your radio. The world will never be the same again." Sisters scanned headlines on their hurried way into classrooms. Mother Lucy wrote in her Gaudete Sunday letter: "The condition of the world at present is sufficient to make us understand that time is fleeting and that this world is not our home." There were brothers and nephews and cousins giving their lives on many fronts. There were families going hungry within war zones. The assembly room near the Superior's office was lined daily with boxes going to many parts of the world through the Red Cross. College girls saved shoes and dresses and gave away new ones that their gifts might be channeled to the more needy. The community gave up desserts at all noon meals except Sundays and laundry days. A great deal of suffering and praying went on for relatives and pupils, manning the big planes over desperate waters or waiting in the desperate cities below the humming bombers.

"This is the grave of my sister-in-law, killed in the bombing," Sister Alexia Steimer would say years later, showing the photograph of a German cemetery. "The people of this village keep flowers on the grave of your son," a pastor wrote from France to the parents of a high school graduate in one of the community's schools. Teachers in a community room would grow quiet to hear of Raymond Woltkamp of Seneca, who had named his plane the "Guardian Angel" and had gone down with it. The student who last year had been shown how to analyze a poem or work a chemistry experiment would next year show his teachers how to live and how to die. College composition teachers would grade papers from students who described how relatives in Europe had lost their lives in the strafing of an old and beautiful city; in the same class they would read what it had been like at home when the telegram came that a brother had gone down with his ship.

For Private First Class Andrew A. Pflumm of Shawnee, age nineteen, killed in action in Italy, 1944, the teacher who had taught him in fourth grade wrote:

> Gold Star for Andrew
> You, who were but the merest child —
> This notice, which last night I read
> Incredulous, says you are dead.
> Today, a yellow jonquil smiled
> Up bravely from beneath late snow
> For you, who went as strong men go.[3]

"How can you bear knowing that your country is being strafed and your people daily facing death?" young Sisters asked a German-born Sister-housekeeper on one of the missions.

"God. And the good people who really are everywhere. I remember the first War. I remember how I scrubbed and cleaned our attic room, the only place we had to keep the French prisoner of war assigned to us. My mother said he was just a boy away from home. We must give him our best. When he received some coffee from his mother through the Red Cross, my mother said he must have all of it himself. But he said that if we, who were drinking barley water, did not share it, he would pour it out on the ground."

Enrollment at men's colleges was cut, but women's colleges flourished. Building material was hard to get because of wartime restrictions, but Mount St. Scholastica bought the adjoining Woodhouse home, which had also been a Price Villa built by the same John Price, naming it Marywood, and built a small residence called St. Catherine's to honor Mrs. Catherine Greiner, the benefactor who made it possible. To those at home and on the missions, Mother Lucy appealed, asking that all the efforts be offered for peace. "We have so little to offer when we think of the sufferings of those in our wartorn nations and of the soldiers in the fighting lines," she wrote.[4]

A new dimension entered the convent's life so gradually that it was hardly realized. An occasional soldier on a train, remembering his school days, would tell a Sister what life was like in India, or in Guadalcanal. A train conductor would step up to the group in black habits to explain that a sick man in uniform whose voice rose raucously above the crowded train had seen terrible things and they must not mind his refrain. The map grew larger and humanity more interlaced. Life seemed deeper, small things mattered more, and evidences of the fact accumulated everywhere. The sufferings of the world were the background in reality for the thinking and working of the community. "Let us pray for those who were killed or wounded in war and for the parents and relatives left to mourn their loss," Mother wrote in Advent of 1944. Assistant pastors teaching in schools had to replace other priests gone to chaplaincies, and the convent stretched its resources to help keep the chaplain with the soldiers who so needed him.

Teachers coached students in the writing of speeches on war effort, helped sell victory badges, tried to keep up morale, and saw deeds of bravery. "Aren't you going to eat dessert?" one of them asked a freshman boy in the cafeteria. "Not until my father comes home. He's a prisoner on Bataan." Sometimes children wearied of the war speeches and bought victory badges only because the room with 100% purchase would be dismissed fifteen minutes early. Once an audience of Lillis High School teen-agers groaned audibly at the announcement of another speech on war bonds, until the youthful speaker said: "Wait! I'm not going to say what you think I'll say." And while the astonished teacher of his speech class held the script behind the scenes, the sophomore speaker threw the whole speech away and, stepping to the edge of the stage, just talked to his 700 listeners of what it must mean to be thousands of miles away, trying to live and die as a man should, for the honor and freedom of casual Kansas City. The war imperceptibly brought high school underclassmen to greater stature. It widened the world forever for most people.

The whole pattern of life went on at the convent at home. Inserted among feasts and ferials, mission-going and returning, receptions and professions, retreats, adoration days, general absolutions, gardening and baking and daily teaching, the headlines which spoke of the Solomon Islands, North Africa, and D-day were poignant incidents made bearable only because of life's total pattern. When one looks at the convent chronicle and the school newspapers, some realization of that total plan comes through — the rise and fall of life, like a recurring theme, the story of Father David or Francis or Felix or Anthony anointing the sick and, in the name of Christ, closing a life on earth.

One of these events was perhaps more exteriorly significant than the rest. On the first Sunday of Lent, in 1941, Sister Sophia died. She had always feared death, and had asked others who had come close to its door and returned what it was like. On that ferial day of purple, between the Office of None and the beginning of Mass, the familiar old figure out in the kitchen preparing her work of table-serving slipped quietly to the linoleum-patterned floor, and while the Sisters knelt around her received Extreme Unction. "The Mass will be for Sister Sophia who has just died," Mother Lucy announced, and when all stood for the Gospel a tremor went through the chapel. It was the Gospel which rises to the climax, "Come ye blessed of my Father, accept the kingdom." For Sister Sophia there had been neither time nor occasion for the fear she thought she would have — nor, in the community's opinion, any reason for it. Sister Sophia with her companion Sister Digna attending concerts, Sister Sophia thanking postulants for dusting her mop, would always be in the fabric of the convent's life. With a great sense of the depth and drama of life, Sisters held their Missals through the Mass that morning while sunlight grew to brightness through the windows.

Nor was everything of equal sweetness and solemnity during the war years. On May 8, 1940, Mother Lucy had announced to the community that Bishop Edwin V. O'Hara of Kansas

City, Missouri, had asked them to consider taking Lillis High School, soon to be built. The Bishop had asked her not to speak much of the plans until he was able to publish them and she had responded: "We will show you that 500 women can keep a secret when the Bishop requests them to do so."

That fall four Sisters had gone to Kansas City to open the new school on the second floor of a business office at 39th and Main, with ninety-seven freshmen. They moved in the spring of 1941 to a permanent site at 3740 Forest Avenue.

Many things were to happen at Lillis, the community's first participation in a large central diocesan high school. It would help develop patterns of cooperative effort in education. Literary efforts, speech, drama, debate, and sports would flourish there. Christian families would be strengthened by it, vocations would come from it, real intellectual growth among young people would be furthered by it. The faces of great friends, like the infectiously friendly Father Bernard (Brooks) Hale, CYC Director, would enter community history.

It would be through Lillis too that some Atchison Sisters would receive their first real knowledge of sports. Its first principal, Sister Jerome Keeler, had determined that this would be a school with all study and no nonsense. But when her freshman team went bloody and bowed through a year of football failure, she announced a spring football banquet, with Bishop O'Hara as speaker and presenter of the trophy.

"What trophy?" he asked. "I did not know that they had won any."

"Oh, they didn't," she answered. "But they tried so hard that I bought them a trophy."

"Sister, you don't buy trophies. You win them."

Somewhere the principal had an unassailable set of ideas on the meaning of trophies, however. And although the subsequent years filled the Lillis case with Greek runners and orators and newspaper citations, no trophy stood more proudly or was referred to more frequently at school ceremonies than the small gold cup the school's first principal had bought.

Something else of prime importance had happened in the days of anxiety. The new chapel had made it possible for the community to be together in the summer for the Office and for Mass. The practice of an annual Pontifical High Mass on the Immaculate Conception with the Abbot of St. Benedict's as celebrant was inaugurated. And Father Sylvester Fangman came the first winter after the chapel was finished. The Sisters spent Christmas vacation preparing for the first sung Vespers in their history.

Atchison Sisters had plunged into a full teaching schedule before they could all speak English, within three weeks of their arrival from Minnesota. Their first purchase had been not Antiphonals, but textbooks. It was what seemed necessary in response to the need which had drawn them down the river. Musical prayer had always been loved, and Sister Rosalia, Sister Beatrice Willems, and Sister Flavia Hogan had been among the memorable singers. Gregorian Chant Masses had begun in the early 1900's. In the summer of 1926, Father Gregory Huegle of Conception had taught chant. He had been followed by Father Sylvester whose love of music and of prayer seemed equal only to his absolute serenity in Atchison heat. Now at last it was time to sing Gregorian Vespers. Father Sylvester took the community relentlessly through the snowy December days and evenings of practice. He was aided by Sister Edith, who worked at it all so earnestly; Sister Valeria, always available with her book and golden voice; Sister Gertrude, always seeing the chant first as prayer and then as art.

The first sung Vespers were to occur January 1, 1939, with Sister Chrysostom Koppes as organist. On the last day of the old year, in the last ten minutes of the last practice, almost when it was time to begin anticipated Matins, Father Sylvester said: "And now one more thing. We must practice the *Alma Redemptoris.*"

"Which do I intone?" asked Sister Valeria. "The simple or the solemn?"

The solemn *Alma* stretched ahead of the community in long rows of square notes arranged in crescendoes. Father Sylvester restrained his amazement with difficulty. "Always the solemn *Alma* on the Circumcision," he said. "We always sing the solemn *Alma*." The tones soared out and the community bravely followed. When the next day arrived and profession ceremonies were over,[5] Sisters were everywhere in groups practicing, counting the syllables before the last accent, carrying with them the big books with red edges and many ribbons. Vespers that day took an hour, and the mastery of every cadence was a victory for which each person felt individually responsible. Father Sylvester, Sister Valeria, Sister Gertrude and Sister Celine shaped history that day with their confident faces. Sister Benedicta sang an *Alleluia* to Mother Lucy in the hall, so sacredly otherwise reserved for silence; Sister Edith was the mirror on whose countenance the community saw its history and its present joy. And that evening the Procurator included in her diary of convent events: "Today I intoned the *Ecce Maria*, fourth antiphon."

Was it ever that way at St. Gall, at Helfta, at Solesmes? When we speak of chant that is beautiful do we mean that it has been worked for with love, that a convent's life has been partly expended in it, that like all prayer it is beautiful if ordinary people work hard at it, with love?

There were other fine events in the war years. The college received its first Chinese student, Lillian Chow, who spoke at an assembly October 20, 1939, on Chinese customs. Sisters published books and encouraged writing among one another. Sister Mildred Knoebber and Sister Anthony Payne published books on sociology and biology; Sister Mary Theresa Brentano edited the first Catholic series of literature texts in the United States [6]; Sister Hildalita Carl and Sister Tharsilla Carl wrote on Kansas fiction and Kansas poetry; Sister Alfred Schroll's study *Benedictine Monasticism as Reflected in the Warnefrid-Hildemar Commentaries on the Holy Rule* was published by Columbia University.

In those years Sister Imogene Baker was sponsoring the *Mount Mirror* and the *Mirror Magazine*. She continued the spirit of the *Mirror* room and had a steady yardstick for measuring things truly good, and for promoting literary effort: "That's an authentic poem, or story, or essay."

And somewhere there was always the unexpected. Sister John Marie Brazzel had earned her doctorate in biochemistry, affording the community one of its more famous anecdotes when her companion at the Catholic University telegraphed the convent, "Sister passed beautifully — Doctor very proud of her," only to have Western Union edge the message in black and deliver it with sympathy.

Those were good days for academy, college, and convent. With Sister Theophila Tangney as principal, the academy conducted a self-study and underwent an evaluating visit from North Central, which had originally accredited it in 1927. A snowstorm the weekend of December 16–17, 1940, almost landlocked the visitors, but the visitation ended in glowing hope and left an encouraged academy. The college was staging *Murder in the Cathedral, Our Town, King Nutcracker,* and *Maryland, My Maryland.* Speakers Theodore Maynard, John Tracy Ellis, Seumas MacManus, George N. Shuster, Count Edmund Czernin, and Maurice Lavanoux came to lecture.

The convent had its constant adventures, and each one was particular. In 1944, the Hiawatha Hatchery donated 1400 baby roosters, which became a minor problem. Daylight saving time was in progress, and Sister Cunnigund, their keeper, reported, "They will not go to roost till it is dark; and now in war time it is not dark till after our bedtime."

In the summer of 1944, Sister Immaculata Kramer, named school supervisor, made an acceptance speech to the community, saying: "Let us first study the religious instructions, for the spread of the love of God in the hearts of the children we are teaching. Let us learn the advantages and disadvantages of such things as maps, charts, and globes." In the spring of 1945, the community agreed to take a high school in Kansas City, Kansas, for Negro girls. But before it could open, Bishop Schulte and other leaders and educators had agreed it would be much better to incorporate Negro students into schools already operating. Kansas schools began that fall.

The community took San Ysidro, California, as a mission in the fall of 1943. It was something new for Atchison to have a convent with a large banana tree in its yard.

Death marched across life like a wonderful procession in the war years: Pope Pius XI, Cardinal Mundelein, Father Alphonse of St. Benedict's Abbey, Abbot Lambert Burton who had given an unforgettable retreat, Father Damien, pastor in Seneca, and many Sisters. In the midst of all the years with all their awesome events something happened, a small cloud began

209

to rise "no bigger than a man's hand," as people like to say of the momentous. It was prepared for, but few realized how. The April 22, 1938, issue of the *Mount Mirror*, the issue dedicated to the diamond jubilee, had carried a carefully written but minor story on an inside page. It began:

The renowned picture of Our Lady of Guadalupe, the first colored replica made of the original, has recently been hung in the main hall on the second floor. It is the gift of Dr. A. J. Rettenmaier, of Kansas City, Kans., who purchased it on a trip to Mexico.

With the picture, which is 25 by 39 inches in length, is a short note, written in Spanish, by the curate of the famous shrine in the little town of Guadalupe, which is situated about three miles northeast of Mexico City. When translated, the notation reads: "This is the first reproduction in colors taken directly from the original image of Our Lady of Guadalupe, undertaken by the Basilica as a remembrance of the four-hundredth anniversary of the apparitions (1531–1931)."

Representing the Immaculate Conception, the picture is that of a figure with the sun, moon and star accompaniment of the great apocalyptic sign, and in addition a boy-like supporting angel under the crescent. Artists find the proportions perfect for a maiden of fifteen. The chief colors are deep gold in the rays and stars, bluegreen in the mantle of the figure, and rose in the flowered tunic.

Although several Popes have recognized the authenticity of the story of Guadalupe, it has remained a distinctive Spanish-American possession, and is comparatively little known even in North America. Tradition, four centuries old, tells us that the Blessed Virgin appeared to a poor Mexican peasant, Juan Diego, asking that a temple be built by the local bishop on the spot where she stood. Three more times she appeared and, by curing Juan's uncle of a fever, granted the bishop's request for a sign. She also bade Juan find roses nearby (it was in December) to take to the bishop in his wrapper.

As Juan unfolded his cloak and the roses fell out, the life-size figure of the Virgin Mother, just as he described her, was glowing on the poor *tilma*.

The 1963 reader finds the detailed story of Guadalupe refreshingly unnecessary, like publicity on the meaning of October 12 or July 4. It was not that way in 1938. The picture of Our Lady remained on the wall of the second-floor college hall, a distinctively Spanish-American item, something like a distinguished visitor in the convent until suddenly, on Washington's Birthday, 1944, it took on new significance. Bishop O'Hara and Abbot Cuthbert visited. They asked Mother Lucy to take a girls' school in Mexico City. The situation, in the words of the Procurator's diary, became "something to think about," when it was learned that religious teaching in Mexico must wear inconspicuous dresses, coats, and no veil.

The chapter voted unanimously, March 27, 1944, to take the Mexico mission for a trial period of three years. Sister Mildred, Sister Anthony, and Sister Chelidonia were appointed its first staff, on March 28. And the picture of Our Lady of Guadalupe, no longer comparatively little known, was moved from the college to the convent on April 1.

"Let the clothing and footgear of the brethren be such as is suited to the place," St. Benedict had written, "and let the brother not bother about the color and texture of these." An interesting application of this ruling sent Sister Mildred, Sister Anthony, and Sister Chelidonia to Ramsay's in Atchison, Kline's and Jones', Emery Bird's and John Taylor's in Kansas City. "Why, you don't look so bad," Mother Lucy would say, giving the effect of a private screening when the shoppers returned.

Excitement ran high at the motherhouse on the night of April 30, 1944, when the prayers for those who are sent on a journey were said in chapel. Abbot Cuthbert gave the blessing and the mission cross, the community assembled, and the missionaries stepped into the station-bound car. As the automobile swung away from the canna bed, just rich black earth in the April evening, Sister Gertrude intoned the *Salve Regina*, and amid tears and joy the first mission to Our Lady's special country swung down the cement drive. Sixty college girls made a pilgrimage to the station, singing the college song to their Dean of Women, their biology teacher, and the Sister who so long ago had helped to equip the botany laboratory:

> With hearts exultant we sing of the blue and the white
> Of Alma Mater's march to victory.
> Let's have some pep, fall in line, get in step
> And cheer for MSSC.
> No matter where we may roam in the world or at home

Our Love for you is true,
So let's pledge Mount St. Scholastica
We are strong for you.

The college girls went on to chant "We're from Kansas, dear old Kansas, where the skies are blue," as they walked beside the slowly moving car. Then the Sisters boarded the train and the Missouri-Pacific swept down the tracks to become a speck against the evening sky.

The first line of the college song's second stanza read, "A day of glory and triumph shall crown the Mount," but that day was still far away for the mission to Mexico. Its strenuous beginnings took their place among the other occurrences of the late war years. They are part of the reason why Mother Lucy rose early to pray, and why both for the missionaries to Mexico and the Sisters at home who were aware of the convent's total responsibilities, there could be no slackening of prayer and work even though the tired world was nearing at least a temporary cessation of conflict.

At 5:30, April 12, 1945, at the close of Matins, Mother Lucy led special prayers for a world figure who had just died, and for his successor in these troubled times. And on Saturday, April 14, at four o'clock, the community assembled in the chapel for three minutes of prayer, at the request of the government, for the powerful personality who after thirteen years of strenuous life at the nation's helm in climactic days had died at Warm Springs, Georgia. Mother Lucy prayed for the soul of President Roosevelt with warmth in her voice. She knew something of the burden of office. But the peace of her philosophy of life was in her voice. "What I have not solved by seven o'clock at night, I leave to God," she was beginning to say in those years of her last term.

The war ended that summer. The community, sitting at table at noon on August 15, heard all the bells and sirens of Atchison sound and joined its own convent chimes in the rejoicing. The convent, with the world, had weathered the conflict, had taken its first foreign mission and its first California mission, and was better prepared than it knew to understand the organizing of the United Nations and to be ready for the call of the future.

But something else had happened during the war years. The drama of peace had held its own anguish, and its own beauty.

1. Robert Maynard Hutchins' statement at an educational meeting in Chicago that Catholic colleges were failing to translate their philosophy of education into action had already stirred the Mount to greater emphasis on its heritage, to the introduction of world literature courses as a "great book and great idea" approach to education.

2. Lenten Letter, 1940.

3. Written by Sister Lillian Muell, O.S.B. "He was in the very first class I ever taught, fourth grade," Sister said.

4. Letter, January 12, 1943.

5. On that January 1, 1939, too, the *Suscipe, Venite Filii*, and Profession Preface were also sung for the first time. See Manuscript History of the Chant at Mount St. Scholastica, MSS Archives.

6. Sponsored by the Catholic University of America, *Joy in Reading, Appreciation in Reading, American Profile*, and *English Voices*, published by Sadlier.

THE VICTORIES OF PEACE

Abbot Martin Veth had been part of Mount St. Scholastica's daily life for sixty of his seventy years. He had come to Atchison in 1884, when he was ten years old, and had sat at a desk under the ministrations of Sister Adelgund Stein when she was a brave sixteen-year-old teacher. He had narrated with a mixture of pride and humor, in the community room during a conference, that she had once rapped his knuckles, and she had wept afterwards saying, "I was only sixteen. I would not have struck the Abbot if I had known better how to keep attention." He had tossed the world's news on the convent porch as paperboy, and Sister Amelberga Schuhmacher recalled in the summer of 1962 how the older Sisters said his pitch always reached the mark.

Returning from studies in Rome in the early 1900's, Father Martin taught and lectured in the academy, and when the college came into being, he remained counselor, lecturer, and friend although already Abbot of St. Benedict's.

From 1906 to November 12, 1921, when he was elected Abbot, he was the community's chaplain, and then until December 12, 1944, its official spiritual director. He liked to walk from the Abbey to the convent on Sundays to give his 9:30 exhortation, when his practice was usually to penetrate the Missal. Only a great loyalty on Sister Genevieve's part in recording the convent chronicle would make her protest that his conferences never seemed long, for they sometimes really did. But he taught the real meaning of the liturgy, and although unable to sing unerringly himself, he encouraged and watched the

214

convent with joy as it sang. Everyone knew he loved Mount St. Scholastica. He gave the holy habit to hundreds of young Sisters, and the green leather chair in the convent parlor became an intermediary for many a student pondering the step between the world and the cloister, the north and the south campus. He loved the whole college, though, not just the students privileged to have religious vocations.

He had a real appreciation of doctrine, liturgy, art, and literature, and he poured it into the spirit of education at academy and college. He did not always approve of everything people did, but he stretched forward toward perfection himself and tried to help others. He took a patient and humble approach to the matter of serving God, loving to quote Dom Marmion's famous saying: "We ought not try to dazzle God by our sanctity, but we ought to try to love Him." He loved the spirit of St. Benedict's Rule. "I really knew nothing about St. Benedict," a Sister recalled, speaking of postulant days. "When he referred to our Holy Father, I thought the Abbot meant the Pope, but I soon learned I had another Father."

He came to programs at academy and college, judged religion contests, awarded prizes and diplomas — patient in the minutiae which to the life of a school are so important.

At Midnight Mass, 1940, Abbot Martin realized he was not well, and on December 27 of that year began a long siege with pneumonia. Its aftereffects blended into the discovery and realization that he was suffering from cancer. He resigned from the active direction of the Abbey community in 1943, and Abbot Cuthbert was elected his coadjutor. Between visits to his doctor, and in addition to some chaplaincy at St. Mary's Convent, Xavier, Kansas, Abbot Martin kept to his schedule of conferences and confessions at Mount St. Scholastica until July 22, 1944, when he sent word he could no longer come. The chapel was too large, the effort to make himself heard too great. In the fall he became a patient at the Atchison hospital on a hill within sight of the great Abbey on the river. In October, Mother wrote the missions:

Abbot Martin grows weaker day by day. He was given a transfusion on Saturday, but his strength has not increased. He longs to say Mass again. Since he cannot do so, I am sure each of the Sisters will

215

make a spiritual remembrance of him during the Holy Sacrifice at which she assists daily.

On October 6, the Procurator recorded in her diary: "Father Abbot had a letter from his doctor at Mayo's telling him that nothing can be done for him."

In December, Abbot Cuthbert McDonald, the young black-haired monk elected to succeed Abbot Martin, pontificated on the feast of the Immaculate Conception in the Mount St. Scholastica chapel. The college girls were practicing Claudel's *Tidings Brought to Mary*, and the days were filled with frequent and heavy snow. The second Abbot of St. Benedict's was still at the city hospital, where from his windows he could see the bare trees and the monastery crowning the icy Missouri. Because he had liked to see flowers grow, Sisters who visited him took roses, so that he could follow their progress in opening through the day. On the night of December 11, an unusually heavy snow blanketed Atchison, the Twin Colleges staged *The Tidings Brought to Mary*, and Abbot Martin who had loved brisk weather, real art, and real religion died at 2:30 in the early hours of December 12. It was the feast of Our Lady of Guadalupe, Mary of the Americas. His two sisters and Abbot Cuthbert were with him and were praying to the Blessed Virgin.

A very small cross marks his grave in the Abbey cemetery on the ridge of the hill overlooking the Missouri.

One of the first reactions at Mount St. Scholastica was to collect his conferences carefully. They remain on file in the Novitiate which he so loved and where, in his direction, he had never "given up" on a true vocation. The conferences share a tone and spirit with the writings of Abbot Marmion, under whom Abbot Martin once made a retreat, and the spirit of whose Abbey he loved. They remain Abbot Martin's own particular doctrine, however, or rather his share in and response to the doctrine of the Church. To look at some of his words brings back the dignified, sometimes vigorous stride up the chapel aisle year after year when the hall clock chimed 9:30 and Sisters in Sunday splendor awaited the splendor of the Sunday message.

For a while, Sisters probably secretly hoped that the Abbot's beatification cause would one day be introduced in Rome. Paying tribute to him, Father Peter Beckman wrote in his book, *Kansas Monks*: "Abbot Martin will grow in stature with the passage of time, for the spiritual difference between the community whose direction he accepted in 1921 and the one he relinquished in 1943 is subtle but nonetheless real."[1] He made a difference in the Atchison convent, too. And not all the saints have to be canonized. Nor would the Abbot need to be canonized, in order to speak an abiding message to the convent he loved and served. His picture looks down from the first-floor corridor on the daily work, prayer, and general personal thought of the community while days turn into years and years into eternity.

His correspondence and retreats speak of the steadiness of his faith in God. Any of the conferences recalls the man, the monk, the priest he was.

"His was a full and rich life; there was no waste," he said of Christ, when the end of his own life was near.[2] "I am glad you have St. Benedict and St. Scholastica to smile upon you as you go through the halls . . . St. Benedict looked a little severe at first but he gradually assumed a look of approval," he said of the mural which a Brother was painting in the chapel corridor. And, "Prayer is the great secret of holiness; a saint is a man of prayer."[3]

Of all he taught — and he taught much — this last was his primary theme. It was to be the first thing people would remember about him, and the last.

1. *Kansas Monks*, p. 309.
2. Conference, February 20, 1944.
3. Conference, May 14, 1944.

THE FINISHING OF AN ERA

Convent life, like all of life, can go on in the regular pattern from day to day. There is enough excitement in the Mass and in the day's duty to sustain anyone.

But in a convent one really never has time to enjoy the everyday excitements only. The additional is always occurring. In 1945 the something additional was the coming of Father Anselm Llewellyn of St. Benedict's Abbey, who tempered the Matins choir speed by ten minutes so that words could have their full majesty and rhythm. When people assemble for the seven times a day and the Matins hour to pray, such an incident is significant to them.[1]

Father Anselm's face felt every tone of beauty which came from the choir. He did not believe in making a false peace but kept asking for better things.

On December 24, 1946, the Sisters sang Christmas Matins and Lauds instead of the traditional chanting, and on February 9 of the following spring, on the First Vespers of the feast of St. Scholastica, Abbot Cuthbert McDonald was celebrant of the first Pontifical Vespers at the convent.

There were changes, too, in the works of Mount St. Scholastica. Slowly its touch on literary and educational history became lighter and surer.

The convent and college entered the magazine world in the winter of 1945 and 1946 with the *Benedictine Review*, edited by Sister Imogene Baker. Sister Jerome Keeler, who had been its chief inaugurator, Sister Alfred Schroll, Sister Gertrude

218

Winter, and the Rev. Bonaventure Schwinn were associate editors. The *Review* opened with a letter of approval from Bishop Paul C. Schulte. Editorially, it stated as its aims: "to make known to an ever-widening circle the ideals and spirit of the Order . . . to preserve the tradition of our community, and to maintain a record of its activities."[2] The Rev. H. A. Reinhold, an Oblate of Maria Laach, also writing in the first issue, hoped the magazine would help people to be "indulgent, charitable, and tolerant to difference," and said:

As a by-product of this spirit, I see a generation of Christians formed with a deeper sense of quality for true values than is now common . . . It will give us an organ, so far lacking in English-speaking countries, which will help us to fathom our own treasure, and the world to see a glorious, lovable expression of Christ not too common among our contemporaries.[3]

The first issue contained a biography of Mother Evangelista; notes on a visit to Benedictine houses in South America; an article on Montserrat, and essays on the liberal arts, the Virgin of Guadalupe, the teaching of religion, and the life of St. Scholastica. The magazine continued under Sister Imogene's editorship for three years. In January, 1949, Sister Teresa Ann Doyle became editor.

Aware that missionary days in education were beginning to become days of maturity, American Benedictines formed an "Academy" in 1947 to encourage one another in scholarship, creativity, and good teaching. The Academy was made up of eight sections — sacred studies, philosophy, language and literature, fine arts, social sciences, natural sciences, psychology and education, and library science. Each was to meet every two years at a host abbey or convent for several days of discussion stimulated by the reading of scholarly papers. A journal, *The American Benedictine Review*, with Father Bonaventure Schwinn as its editor, was to encourage the Academy's aims.

Mount St. Scholastica joined the Academy. Members spoke hopefully of a "golden age," spiritually and intellectually. The focus in membership and effort was on Benedictines, but the Academy hoped as it grew in maturity to welcome increasing numbers of non-Benedictines. In 1959, the Rev. Colman Barry of St. John's Abbey succeeded Father Bonaventure as editor of the *Review.*

In early 1949, a new kind of educational opportunity came to the Sisters of Mount St. Scholastica.

Bishop George J. Donnelly had succeeded Bishop Schulte in the see of Leavenworth, soon to be named the see of Kansas City in Kansas. There was in Kansas City a building formerly used as the Catholic High School, and then for CYC activities. Bishop Donnelly offered it to a religious community for a convalescent home. When it did not seem suited for that, he offered it to Mother Lucy of Atchison for something she might want to do, perhaps a home for invalid Sisters.

The President Truman report on higher education had come out a year or so previously, with its plea that community colleges be set up. Kansas City, Kansas, had no Catholic college and there were many young people there desirous of college, but wishing to earn a Catholic college education without leaving home. Sister Jerome Keeler, then the dean of Mount St. Scholastica, had read the Truman Report.

"Could we have the building for a Catholic junior community college?" she asked the bishop.

"What would that mean? Something like Loretto Academy?" he responded.

It was agreed to try a college and to name it Donnelly.[4]

St. Margaret's Hospital in Kansas City, Kansas, and St. Mary's Hospital in Kansas City, Missouri, arranged to send their student nurses to the not yet established college. In the summer of 1949 the building was readied and books by the thousand were bought and processed. On the first registration day, both Bishop Donnelly and the *Kansas City Star* photographer sensed the anxiety of the faculty as to whether anyone would come at all. But some forty students, in addition to the nurses, registered for the newly opened classrooms. Sister Anthony Payne, Sister Hildalita Carl, Sister Elaine Cranford, Sister Scholastica Schuster, and Sister Ancilla Pfisterer as housekeeper were the first Sisters on the faculty of the community's second college. Priests and lay teachers completed the staff.

The decision to make the college coeducational reaped

crowds of young men and young women as Donnelly College grew. A morning schedule of classes from 8:30 to 1:00, evening programs both credit and non-credit, and the afternoon program for nurses seemed so to serve the Kansas City community that the North Central Association granted regional membership in the spring of 1958. The honor was sweet to those who had worked so hard, but not sweeter than the words of the young man who had sought out the examiners to say: "Don't you want the opinion of a non-Catholic? I'm not of their faith here, but I love this college. It has taught me wonderful things."

Great Books discussions, Cana conferences, Papal Volunteer Preparatory Programs, Glee Club, Confraternity of Christian Doctrine classes, lectures on Scripture and theology and on cultural and timely topics in general clustered around the liberal arts curriculum to make the small brick building something of a dynamo. Even the North Central examiners had been challenged by its size and had looked for ways to put typewriters on shelves somewhere so that room could be re-used.

Archbishop Hunkeler gave the majestic episcopal residence to the college and the home of Bishops Ward, Johannes, Schulte, and Donnelly and of Archbishop Hunkeler himself now became the Donnelly Faculty House. Then donations and a private fund drive brought bulldozers to the campus for a new building which would more than double the possibility of admissions. The addition, dedicated in April, 1963, the centennial year, was named Bennett Auditorium to honor George Bennett who gave a gift which made the fund drive substantial, and St. Jerome Library to honor the Dean.

Stories accumulate around Donnelly College as they do around all undertakings.

"May I speak to the Dean?" asked a young priest one summer afternoon of the busy Sister in checked apron who was dusting every available object in the college hall preparatory to registration.

"Yes. What do you want?" And Sister Jerome momentarily halted her dust cloth.

While Donnelly was being inaugurated in hope, events had happened at the convent home, too.

Sister Edith Stein, convent subprioress, died February 27,.

1947. Young Sisters who carried a drink of water to her at night loved the spotlessness of her frugal room. "All she did in her sixty-six years as a Benedictine by example is worthy of imitation," Mother Lucy wrote of her. The clerics of St. Benedict's Abbey sang the *Ultima in mortis hora* at her grave, and the singing of that hymn at the burial of a Sister became from that time traditional.

On December 1 of the same year, Sister Pauline Anderson died. In her last years she had written historical sketches of days gone by and biographies of the deceased Sisters in which she unwittingly canonized herself by seeing the best in everyone else.[5] Prudent and kind, less solemn than she at first appeared to be, she had as Scholastic Mistress left a stamp on many. Once a young Sister, haunted by the need for a penance during Lent, in the days when coffee was served both sweet and unsweetened, had asked: "I don't like coffee with sugar in it, Sister. Should I resolve to drink it during Lent?"

Sister Pauline had studied the face a minute and then answered, "I don't think we should undertake penances which are expensive to the community." All her life she had an almost solemn awareness of the reality of eternity, which seemed to make her unusually human.

Sister Anacleta Peine, college portress, died five days later, one of those people with whom no one ever associated the thought of dying. There had been an inconspicuousness about her, a solidity. Suddenly her work was over.

But not only the old die in convents. On December 1 of that year, Sister Agatha Doyle had asked to return to Lillis High School where she had spent years teaching. Unable to teach now because of a heart ailment, she had been helping in the Lillis office for a week, when death came suddenly at noon on an Adoration Sunday. She had spent an hour before the Blessed Sacrament that morning, left the dinner table ill, and died in the kitchen. She was thirty-eight years old. Students came to her funeral, paying tribute to the prom sponsor and home-room adviser, who in the classrooms of Shawnee, Lillis, and the convent academy had always transformed the ordinary into something better. There had been a pluck about her which, combined with her ladylikeness and Sisterly character, had put a certain joy in life wherever she was. Even her mistakes took on the aura of her character.

"Take your gum out of your mouth and put your feet in," a remonstrance to a Shawnee sophomore sitting sidewise in his desk, would always be associated with her name in convent stories.

It was a year to remember. On April 30 of the next springtime, Sister Gertrude Winter left her class in musical harmony and after thirteen hours of hemorrhaging whispered to the Sister nearest her among the watchers: "Who would have thought the old man to have so much blood in him?" The room wept and smiled, as Sister Helen answered, "Oh stop quoting Shakespeare at a time like this." Then Sister Gertrude said the wonderful words: "Why don't they come? . . . I don't mean my niece. I mean Jesus and Mary."

She died at four o'clock just at the moment when dawn seems to break through the dark. The face that had never scolded in the delicate work of making singers out of everyone in a convent choir, that had brightened so at the Hosanna of Mass IX and wanted the "k" clear in "excelsis," the voice that had come into literature classes to read the *Iliad* in Greek to sophomores, was gone. Sister Gertrude was one of those persons who never grow old, and on her funeral day the spirea was in bloom all the way to the cemetery.

That year Sister Clarita McGarrity had been appointed no vice-mistress. Perhaps some indication of what convent life is really like might be furnished by recounting an experience occurring in the first days of her new role. The novices, aware in their own way that a mantle of the forty-one years of Sister Josephine's wearing could rest somberly on young shoulders, saw their new mistress devoid of much appetite. They held their own conference and then went to her to say: "We don't want to be presumptuous, but don't worry, Sister. We'll try to be good novices."

The last years of Mother Lucy's superiorship came as simply as the first had come. The convent sold its dairy herd in 1948, and the pastures took on a lonely look. Father Florian Demmer gave a series of conferences on the Holy Rule, and Abbot Primate Bernard Kaelin of San Anselmo spent December 8 at the convent. In the winter and spring there were days of prayer for the Italian elections and for Cardinal Mindzenty. There was a visit from newly consecrated Bishop Vincent Arkfeld, a former student of one of the convent's schools, St. Mary's, in Panama, Iowa. And on February 21, few people at the busy Mount saw Mr. and Mrs. Meduna of Wahoo, Nebraska, visit the grave of their daughter, Sister Ladislaus, who had died twenty years earlier as a novice.

In the summer of 1949, the community picnic booths for July 4 were named for the California schools the community staffed. That year a new convent chauffeur, Vincent Snodgrass, made his appearance, requesting that he have some kind of uniform so that the Sisters would know him at the station.

"Are you a good driver?" Mother Lucy asked him, and before her keen glance he answered, "Pretty good."

"Oh, Mother, he's fine," Sister Dolorosa broke in. "Everyone in Atchison speaks well of him."

"Do you drink?" she asked.

Searching his soul, Mr. Snodgrass remembered an occasional glass of beer and answered, "A little."

"Well, we will take you because you tell the truth," Mother Lucy said, and Vincent taking the old and sick to doctors, Vincent shepherding Sisters and suitcases to trains, Vincent doing a hundred large and small deeds for the convent, entered its history.

In May Abbot Raphael of Wandville, France, in the process of establishing an Abbey in Africa, visited the convent. No one could know that *Benedictine and Moor* would be read in the refectory a decade later. Governor Carlson spoke at the college commencement. June 6, the day of the election of a Superior, drew near.

The illness of Mother Lucy during the last two and one-half years had been a whole way of life, and the very occasion for some of the most lasting things she said and did. She had become seriously ill in January, 1947, writing the missions in Lent: "If your resolution has not been sent yet, just keep the one you intend writing." [6] But she weathered the winter, writing typically on March 4:

Thank God if it were not for the doctors, I think I would be well. They think I should rest, do very little, and think about myself, I suppose, most of the time. They mean it well enough, but this does not work in all cases.

And in Lent of 1948, she wrote:

I am very changeable, that is from my neck down. Thank God from the neck up, it is 100% or as high as it ever registered. Please put more stress in your prayers for me on the spiritual side. The physical will pass, but the spiritual will live on.

On April 12, 1950, she wrote her last general letter as Mother. She spoke of the community's financial condition, saying:

When one stops to think of the cost of clothing, dentists, oculists, hospitals, kitchens, repairing, education which costs many thousands of dollars every vacation — besides paying off first for the administration building, then the cement pavement around the grounds, the chapel and the Novitiate, the remodeling of the choir chapel, the three new dormitory buildings, and many other expenses, it would be sufficient to make one worry if we did not know it was all done for God's honor and glory. For your satisfaction I am telling you we do not owe a penny to anyone.

She told the community there was money saved for one or two buildings yet needed, adding: "It is money that has been carefully saved at home and on mission for the good of education and the spread of religion." And surveying the twenty-five years which had elapsed since she became Superior, she said:

We should bear in mind that the Abbots and priests of St. Benedict's Abbey have been and should always remain our helpers and guides. They have been with us since our beginning, though many don't know or realize all the advantages we have received from them.

There had been such a grace about her years, a great largeness of spirit. College and academy girls knew she could be relied upon to make short speeches in assemblies, and to say things with warmth and light and a kind of hidden strength. She liked excitement and surprises, as when she sat in the green wicker chair one late July evening and, without benefit of a list, said: "Anyone who wants a mission may get it this evening."

She had had no panacea for suffering. "I think Heaven is the only place where all goes smoothly. It is by meeting and accepting crosses that Heaven is gained — not by running away from them," she had written once.[7] She had loved books, telling Sisters that a good book helps to form the soul. But she had been able to say No.

"Mother, may I attend the movie tonight in the college? It's historical, the story of Marie Antoinette."

She had looked into the face of the junior Sister and said, "I think it would be better for you to pray for Marie Antoinette."

She had given the impression of being a person who became her whole role, who gave everything within herself totally to being what she was called, and who tasted the full joy entailed. No one knew better than she, no one ever knew half as well as she, what the morning of June 6, 1950, meant when she left her office for the chapel.

The community chose Sister Alfred Schroll as its fifth Superior. Mother Lucy Dooley moved into the next office, a thin and delicate figure now with one kind of life behind her and another ahead. After supper that evening, the nurse wheeled her chair into the gallery of the chapel. The mosaic of Christ with St. Benedict and St. Scholastica above the altar was majestic and gentle in the evening light. No one would ever call a thing old which was now so timeless. Abbot Martin had hoped no one would call the choir chapel the "old chapel."

Outside the chapel, after the prayer was over, a young Sister waited to hand Mother Lucy a poem. "Read me the poem," Mother said to the nurse. "It was written for me today."

Sister John Marie began, but Mother took it from her and read it herself. "You do not read it right," she said. The words were typed on the back of a sheet of used paper. They did not seem to break the after Compline silence:

> Down the long quiet aisle
> We carry past your door the sign we are your daughters.

It was a fortunate word. The first floor corridor was an aisle in the house of God. Mother Lucy knew that she had always known that.

The poem continued:

Your trust within our hearts,
Your faith keeping our souls brave and uplifted,
Your laughter — that seal you left upon our memory
Reminding us that God is strong and faithful.
O guide the feet that hurry to their work,
And follow with your prayer the hearts that,
    striving with imperfection,
Seek still to set the perfect stamp of Christ upon the world.

The second floor hall clock ticked now. The summer sky darkened and lights went out.

1. Some of the hours of Office are very short. In the convent's order of the day Lauds begins the day at 5:55. It is followed by fifteen minutes of meditation, Prime, and High Mass. Mass is followed by the hour of Tierce. Breakfast is at approximately 7:30. The community assembles again at 11:50 for Sext and None. Dinner is followed by Vespers. Spiritual reading, at 4:50, is followed by Matins at 5:10. A fifteen-minute meditation period followed by Compline completes the day. The total time that the community spends as a community at mental and vocal prayer is approximately four hours.

2. Editorial, *Benedictine Review*, I (Winter, 1946), 3.

3. *Ibid.*, p. 39.

4. Letter from Sister Jerome, October 15, 1963.

5. Sister Pauline as student and as Sister had personally known every Sister who ever lived at Mount St. Scholastica except Sister Dominica Massoth.

6. In accordance with St. Benedict's injunction that all special Lenten effort be made with the blessing of the Superior, Sisters send their resolutions to the Mother Superior for approval.

7. Letter to the community, January 12, 1945.

THE LONG QUIET AISLE

Morning broke over the level ocean. In the chapel of the *Mauretania*, the Rev. Hugh Farrington told the pilgrimage of American Benedictine Mother Superiors:

Today we are starting, as it were, a return trip. We shall retrace the lines drawn out from Monte Cassino during the past 1400 years. Step by step we shall visit some of the many places which received the light of the Gospel from St. Benedict centuries ago.

For the first time in the history of the house Sisters had left Atchison to sail east on the Atlantic. Mother Alfred and Sister Augusta Parle, on a tour honoring the Jubilee year and sponsored by the Abbot Primate, visited Benedictine houses in France, Belgium, Switzerland, Germany, Italy, and the British Isles and were received in audience by Pope Pius XII.

From the *Mauretania*, Mother Alfred wrote the community, describing Mass and Vespers at sea, the practicing of *O Roma Nobilis* to be sung in the churches of Rome, and the evening singing of *Ave Maris Stella* in its full setting. The tour included New Ulm, Bavaria, Mother Evangelista's birthplace; Mass in the chapel of Our Lady of Einsiedeln, Switzerland; Maria Rickenbach, the cradle of the house of Clyde, Missouri, and Yankton, South Dakota, Benedictines; Eichstätt; and Engelberg, ancient Benedictine site "high in the mountains, yet surrounded by high mountains, snowcapped with glaciers beneath the peaks." [1]

The climax of the trip came late in October when Mother Alfred wrote:

The visit to Monte Cassino was most impressive. We entered the temporary chapel which contains the relics of St. Benedict and St.

228

Scholastica singing "Sancte Pater Benedicte!" the four Congregation presidents and the Abbot Primate . . . leading with lighted
candles.[2]

On the day after Monte Cassino, they saw Pope Pius XII,
who asked about their schools, their convents, their trip across
the ocean and gave his blessing. "He looked just like his pictures," wrote Mother, "and was all kindness." On the following
day the Abbot Primate Bernard Kaelin sang Pontifical High
Mass in the Catacombs of St. Priscilla, of which Benedictine
nuns have the care.

The trip was more than sight-seeing, more even than a pilgrimage. The restoration of the ancient ceremony of Consecration of Virgins and the hope of a converted plan for furthering
spiritual and intellectual growth among American Benedictine
Sisters were discussed with the Abbot Primate and by the
Mother Superiors among themselves in the beautiful settings of
the Old World. After Italy, the pilgrimage went to England
where a canon at Canterbury was as conscious of history as
they. "Pray for us heretics," he said, after guiding the tour
through the abbey and cathedral so sacred to St. Augustine of
England and his forty monks. "We do. We will," they answered
him.[3]

At home, Mother Lucy had been left in charge. The spark
of her old letters was rekindled. "Thank you for your remembrance of my birthday," she wrote of September 8. "It is a
custom which ought to be stopped except for the prayers."
And, "All day long I have wanted to write to you but I can't
find anyone free enough to take dictation," another said. The
community rejoiced with the pilgrims when, on November 1,
the dogma of the Assumption of the Blessed Virgin was solemnly proclaimed in Rome.[4]

On November 18, the pilgrimage was over. To words and
music by Sister Scholastica Schuster and Sister Celine Goodwin, the convent received back again the footsteps from the
Old World. Welcoming Mother Alfred and Sister Augusta at
the convent entrance, everyone went to the chapel for the
Te Deum and a Mass of Thanksgiving.

That winter two events of moment to everyone occurred.

The choir chapel windows were installed. Their design had been the combined efforts of convent artists, carried out by the Emil Frei studios of St. Louis. Illustrations of statements from the Rule, done in modern art, seemed to show living monks doing the work of God. In blues and reds, grays and gold, the windows came to life in the mornings during Office and Mass. "Their feet seem large," Mother Lucy said, studying them, "but I suppose they must be strong to do the work of God."

And early in the morning of her own nameday, December 13, Bishop George J. Donnelly died at St. Margaret's Hospital, saying: "This day thou shalt be with me in Paradise," and, "No more worry about war . . . God alone . . . nothing else matters." [5]

His death touched the convent deeply. Several years previous it had supplied housekeepers for the bishop, with Mother Lucy warning him that Sister Mary Louis Miller and Sister Lorene Judge were teachers and that he might turn out to be another thin bishop. He had loved her, and visitors to the episcopal house sometimes heard him say as he sat down to the rice and milk his declining health permitted: "Dear Mother Lucy . . . if you only knew how your Sisters treat me!" In the days of his illness at St. Margaret's, he would return to his residence for Sundays and would ask that the Donnelly College conveyance, an olive-green army jeep, take him to and from home. Now on December 13, Kansas and the world had lost a great man, the convent thought, and at her nameday greeting when Mother Alfred wished her many more feasts of St. Lucy, Mother Lucy had murmured, "Not too many! Not too many!"

Christmas had a double solemnity, the community being greeted by Mother Alfred Schroll who had just seen the Old World and by Mother Lucy Dooley, whose parents had been born in County Clare, but who had kept faithfully to the traditional *Stille Nacht* and to enough of the old customs that the convent still knew its Bavarian ties. Early months of 1951 brought the breaking of old bonds and the beginning of new ones. It brought the deaths of Sister Adelgund Stein, a link with the very oldest days, and of Father Mark Merwick, who had been for a while chaplain of the convent. On April 5, Mother Lucy saw the Aeolian-Skinner Pipe Organ installed in the choir chapel with its two manuals and 602 pipes. It had the advantage of being in front of the chapel where Sisters could see a postulant or novice play her first *Salve Regina* or Mass accompaniment. Its gleaming pipes beautified the gallery where the sick worshipped. The renovation of the choir chapel was finished.

Spring came slowly that year and everyone knew that crisis was coming again to Mount St. Scholastica. One early April day, Mother Lucy sent word to Sisters away studying at universities not to work too hard. On April 10, state examiners paid their first visit to Donnelly College, and Mother was eager to learn that all had gone well. On the morning of April 11, she ate breakfast with the community, her last meal in the dining room. On April 12, Abbot Cuthbert came quickly at five in the morning to anoint Mother Lucy and give her Viaticum. In the week that followed he offered Mass in her room several times. Every morning Dr. Wulff came before office hours. Dr. Brady and Dr. Rettenmaier came too. Mother Lucy loved them for their devotion, enough to murmur whimsically but with some real regret on April 18, for she had loved life: "I have been affected by so many shots and so much medicine that it is little wonder I don't know anybody or anything." But they understood her gratitude for their efforts. It was beneath the words, as most of her real meanings had always been.

April 19 came. Father David gave her his blessing after Mass. Through the morning she greeted all who stopped to see her but after dinner, although she recognized visitors, she could no longer speak. Father Francis Broderick, vice-president and chaplain of the college, came to say the prayers for the dying. Abbot Cuthbert and Father David, on their way from the Abbey, were delayed by a freight train at a crossing and arrived just when her life was over. At 3:30 in the afternoon, she died like a child going to sleep, after saying: "Jesus, I love You. Come and get me." The next morning, Abbot Cuthbert sang a Pontifical High Mass for her in the choir chapel. She had asked for an immediate Mass in the consecrated chapel.

All telephone and telegraph wires, mail routes and trains,

seemed to lead to Atchison now, for the great Superior of twenty-five years who on her election had asked the Sisters to pray that she could carry on for a while the work Mother Aloysia was requesting her to do. Bishop Buddy of San Diego pontificated at the Requiem, April 24. The new bishop of Kansas City, Kansas, had not yet been installed, and Bishop Buddy had been the instrument of beginning the daughterhouse soon to be named for her in California. Monsignor Vallely gave the sermon, Bishop Edwin V. O'Hara, the absolution. Abbot Cuthbert presided in the cemetery and the Abbey Choir sang there. The Office for the Dead, preceding the Mass, was alternated by the Abbey and convent choirs, and at the grave the monks sang:

> Ultima in mortis
> Filium pro nobis ora
> Bonam mortem impetra
> Virgo Mater Domina.

The coffin was lowered beneath the crucifix crowning the West hill, just as the Angelus rang over Mount St. Scholastica. All the way down the hill and through the long corridors, people were remembering: "A 'C' will do if it is earned for God . . . How is your mother? . . . : Let us be sure that all our higher education is really higher education . . . Sister Sophia assures me the program is educational. . . . I am convinced that Heaven is the only place where all goes smoothly. On earth the way is to accept sorrows and trials, not to go around them."

The tribute of the world lay on the convent officials' desks in telegrams, cards, and letters. "Even those of us who knew Mother only through the college held her in great esteem, for we felt her wise and motherly ways in the spirit of the Mount itself," wrote an alumna.[6] From the White House, the President's secretary, Rose Conway, said: "When I lost my parents, her many acts of kindness brought me immeasurable consolation."

"There is a void at the Mount," wrote Sister Mary Pius of the Oblate Sisters of Providence. "To her the Oblate Sisters owe a great debt of gratitude for the opportunity of higher

education given us at a time when it could be procured nowhere else. Thus Mother Aloysia and Rev. Mother Lucy were
pioneers in the interracial movement also, as along many other
lines . . . God was with her and worked through her."

"She governed with wisdom and kindness," said Father Cas-
per, Dean of the Creighton Graduate School. "We at Creighton
are thoroughly aware of the great vacuum left in the Atchison
Benedictines through the death of Reverend Mother Lucy,"
wrote Father William Kelley, Dean of the Creighton College.
Dr. Roy J. Defarrari wrote his sympathy. Many other friends
spoke out.

"I do not think I have ever met a more capable superior,
possessing the many wonderful qualities of a truly solicitous
and charitable spirit joined to an extraordinary executive ability," wrote Archbishop Schulte of Indianapolis, who had been
Bishop of Leavenworth for ten years. "We in Colorado have
every reason to be grateful to Mother Lucy and her Sisters,
who have given such valiant service over the years in our
State to the cause of Catholic education. She was an outstand-
ing, noble soul," said Bishop Vehr of Denver. Bishop Willging
of the Pueblo diocese added, "Mother Lucy has contributed
much to the firmer establishment and development of the
Benedictine Order in Atchison." "What a rich legacy she leaves
to the Congregation over which she ruled with such wisdom
and prudence," said Bishop Marling of the Kansas City, Missouri, diocese.

And from Grand Island, Nebraska, came a wire from Bishop-
elect Edward J. Hunkeler of her own Kansas City, Kansas,
diocese: "My sympathy to the Sisters of St. Benedict in the
death of Mother Lucy Dooley. The diocese suffers a great loss.
High Mass on Monday for the repose of her soul." The Apostolic Delegate, Archbishop Cicognani, sent his sympathy.

The test of a great life probably is what it has meant to the
people to whom, under God, it is responsible.

Pastors from Atchison to California sent sympathy and
prayers. Abbeys and convents prayed for her. Mother Presidents of the Benedictine Congregations attended the funeral
along with hundreds of other Sisters who filled the convent

with a hush and solemnity the cheerful Mother Lucy had loved on right occasions.

"Her work for the congregation of St. Scholastica was monumental," said Mother Vincent of Elizabeth, New Jersey, who had served with her as visitor. "It was her deep and simple humility which gave her that discernment of spirits, for which all remember her," wrote Fathers Godfrey and Pascal of St. John's Abbey. "Her goodness will remain with us always," wired Father Bonaventure Schwinn. And the many Atchison priests who had stopped in her office during the year of her retirement, where she sat all day facing the door and being there for all who came, prayed for the Mother whose title had been so correct.

Father Thomas O'Connor, S.J., of St. Mary's College, St. Mary's, Kansas, who had been diocesan visitor, wrote: "Mother Lucy was a grand religious superior, and has left a monumental example."

Food and construction companies, business firms of all kinds, remembered the woman who had combined good business sense with great human qualities. Louie Lesslie, Secretary of the Kansas State Department of Education for so many years of the college's early efforts, said simply: "She was one of my loved friends."

Sociologists make a good deal of the term "social role." The daughter of Jim Dooley had taken hers, and in doing so had not buried herself in a convent, nor had she buried her community. By becoming what she was called, she had given its history a flavor and its daily life a combination of vibrancy and sacrifice, and had demonstrated that Thomas Carlyle is at least partly correct in saying all history is essentially biography.

To live her own life through the lives of others and yet so to keep it was somehow her special gift. She touched all the convent's enterprises, sent the missions to Mexico and California and, in a particular way that the Archives would reveal after her death, left a memory even for the daughterhouse to be established facing Pike's Peak, in the convent's centennial year long after her death. For when she was a carefree summer school student, on a July 4, 1921, she submitted an essay entitled: "A Cup of Coffee on Pike's Peak." It read:

234

THE LONG QUIET AISLE

In the summer of 1905, I accompanied Sister Directress [then Sister Adelaide] on a little business trip to Colorado. We were told to drink in all the pleasure and knowledge the trip could afford us and not to return without going to the top of Pike's Peak.

On a very warm afternoon we made the ascent. When we were about halfway up the Peak a great snowstorm arose. No one in the company was prepared for the sudden change, but judging from the supply of overcoats in store, they must have had midsummer and winter blizzards quite frequently on the same day.

The train salesman, who at the beginning of our journey had been serving ice cream cones, was now peddling overcoats. He showed Sister and me a preference by offering us the first choice. We declined, saying our garbs would be sufficiently warm.

By the time everyone was fitted the blizzard was at its best. We tried to imagine we were warm enough, while on the contrary we were nearly frozen. As we knew no one in the company and no one knew us, we finally decided to rent overcoats, for we could stand the cold no longer. Being last, we had to take what was left, and these two coats looked as if they had been in Noah's Ark, but what did we care. The blizzard continued, and finally we reached the top. Entering the waiting room, we sat beside a small stove, not at all embarrassed about our attire, believing ourselves to be strangers in a strange land.

Before we were half-thawed out, we noticed a stately gentleman making his way toward us. Not caring to make any acquaintance in such a lofty place, we looked in the opposite direction. But our visitor was not to be thwarted. He came up to us and said, "Well, did I ever expect to meet two Benedictines from Atchison up here! Come take a cup of coffee with me. I have it ordered."

When we recognized the gentleman to be no other than Rt. Rev. Bishop Lillis, we needed neither coffee nor coats to heat us.

The fact that Mother Lucy had been on snow-capped Pike's Peak would make the view from Benet Hill Priory, Colorado Springs, forever more familiar.

One letter, preserved in the convent archives, gives another view of the person who was Mother Lucy. An academy graduate, who entered the church while a student, and whom Mother had prayed for and loved, wrote in the last days of Mother's illness:

Here is a check for $5.00 — first for $2.00 will you have a Mass said in your Chapel for Mother Lucy's recovery? Then with the balance

235

will you have purchased any special things she would like, fruits or jams, or anything at all that the doctors say she could and should have. If I were there, I would like to make her some rice puddings and rice custards. Those were the things I made for my husband when he, too, was so ill with his heart, and the doctors said rice is very good for hearts.

Sister Augusta, faithful subprioress, wrote that Mother would have the best rice pudding the convent could make. Then the girl, whose husband had recently died, wrote again:

I am glad you are praying for me, precious Mother, for sometimes longing and nostalgia makes me so very ill and even yet I have not been able to cry, or eat very much. Is grieving selfish? . . . If you do recover by June or late May . . . may I come even for one day? Just to sit at your feet and listen to you for a little while will be such consolation.

The letter would be too personal to quote if it were not that St. Benedict had prescribed in his Rule that the young be loved and that care be taken of them. Mother had loved the young whom the convent received to educate. She had touched many lives and now, said her brothers and sisters who wrote to thank the convent for the beauty of her funeral, "it is going to be so lonely without her."

The convent, too, felt that this would be true. But it would not really be so. The world was not to be without her. There is more mystery to the union of eternity and time than anyone has ever quite spelled out. Past the crucifix Mother Aloysia had ordered and Mother Lucy had erected, past the choir chapel where she had prayed under the window that marked her place, past the office door where her laughter had sometimes really rung out, even the Sisters who had never known her would forever carry the sign that they are her daughters. Children who have never known their mother still resemble her, for real motherhood leaves a legacy.

What Mother Lucy's legacy is may escape full definition, but it is tangible to the spirit. Perhaps it is a simplicity, perhaps a joy, perhaps an acceptance, perhaps a lightheartedness which stems from duty done and overflows back into the depth of life. But on a June day when the community returns from the missions, the legacy is here. It looks down from her face on the long lines of Sisters coming home, that face forever an enigma of almost stern duty and of great gladness, of durable strength and of great sweetness. Early in the morning it is here in Chapel where she knelt before the day riveted her to her desk. It seems part of the sunlight on the colored tile, and the quiet of the afternoon after the two o'clock silence bell. It is part of the day and the night, of all the spirit that becomes common in a house, by which a house lives. Its name is probably best expressed as faith, hope, and charity, presented to the community in the person of a great human being who, as well as she knew how, made the great exchange and, in accepting the gifts of Divinity, did wonderful things with her own humanity and the humanity of others.

1. Letter written from Engelberg, October 10, 1950. MSS Archives.

2. The chapel was temporary because the rebuilding of Monte Cassino after the bombing of World War II was still in progress. The four Congregation presidents were Mother Carmelita of Clyde, Missouri; Mother Rosamund, St. Joseph, Minnesota; Mother Jerome, Yankton, South Dakota; and Mother Alfred.

3. Interview with Sister Augusta Parle, Christmas, 1950.

4. Simultaneous with the great profession of faith in Rome came a small drama of faith in a nearby mission. A Halloween prankster, setting fire to a stack of newspapers held for paper sale near the Sisters' convent in Maryville, Missouri, gave the first grade teacher an opportunity to tell the children the seriousness of using matches carelessly. One of them, listening to the story of how the fire climbed high to the windows, said wistfully: "Oh, Sister. You would have seen Jesus!" (Paper sales as a means of remuneration were discontinued.)

5. Sister Jerome Keeler, "The Most Rev. George J. Donnelly," *Benedictine Review*, VI (Winter, 1951), 8.

6. Sister Mary David Scott, Benedictine Convent, Clyde, Missouri, at that time Valerie Scott.

THAT THEY MAY LOVE CHRIST

A religious community grows up in a given world. Although the world of Mount St. Scholastica is the whole world, the diocese which received it in 1863 had much to do with the shaping of its spirit.

The pioneer bishops Miege and Fink had gone to their just reward and the pioneer age seemed over when Thomas Francis Lillis was named to the see of Leavenworth in March, 1904. He was at Sheridan, Wyoming, on a short vacation when he picked up the *Catholic Register* and read of his appointment. His chief influence on the Atchison community, in addition to his cordial friendship, was to be the climate of education which he furthered. He was a man honored by the state as well as the Church, and his administration from September 14, 1904, until March 14, 1910, marked significant advancement in education and charity. Under his regime, St. Margaret's Hospital was begun, 1909, the Catholic High School of Kansas City, Kansas, was opened, September 18, 1908, and education everywhere was bolstered from within and from without.

The bishop was appointed to the state textbook commission by Governor Stubbs in 1909. Some opposition to his appointment led him to write the *Topeka Guardian*, commenting that there were 11,000 children in the parochial schools of Kansas at that time, and adding:

The schools were not built to oppose or to compete with the public schools . . . I make no apology for the standard of education in these schools. By its results let the parish school system be judged. They are private institutions working for God and country.[1]

Voices came in defense of the bishop. Editorializing, the Topeka paper wrote: "Bishop Lillis of the Catholic Church is one of the foremost citizens of the state and I will honor any job the governor gives him." The bishop accepted the appointment, and Governor Stubbs thanked him in a letter dated April 15, 1909, saying, "I am firmly convinced that your service on this commission will be of great value to the state. While it is true . . . there has been some little opposition to your appointment, I sincerely hope it will not annoy you any more than it has me."[2]

Besides promoting a climate of respect in which teachers might work, the Bishop issued important directives. He urged the carrying out of Pius X's *Motu proprio*, and suggested the adoption of a music book carrying four Gregorian Masses and hymns suitable for Church singing. He encouraged congregational participation. He raised the salary of teaching Sisters. And he kept teachers and all people aware of world needs by petitioning help for San Francisco earthquake sufferers. One senses in the regime of Bishop Lillis a beginning of the post-missionary era, a diocese and school system beginning to come of age and moving now as an arm of the Church and the nation toward greater service.

Bishop Lillis was assigned to Kansas City, Missouri, diocese as coadjutor, March 14, 1910. He became bishop there and died at the end of a long episcopate, December 29, 1938. His successor at Leavenworth was John Ward, a native Kansan. Bishop Ward's directives and correspondence show a singular understanding of his diocese and a great desire that it share in the world's betterment. His pastorals commemorated the sixteenth centenary of Constantine's edict freeing Catholicity from the catacombs; they called for special service and prayer for world peace[3]; they pleaded for deep interior life for his people. An undated pastoral refers to the "hurry and bustle of the present age," saying:

Our life is such a round of work and worry if we are poor, and of pleasure and dissipation if we are rich, that it often happens no sufficient margin is reserved for the necessary exercise of devotion.

He joined with Pope Benedict XV in praying November 1, 1914, for the end of the war, and with President Wilson in praying for our nation's needs in 1918. A letter dated May 20 of that year asked for exposition of the Blessed Sacrament, prayer, and the effort to prove true Catholics and loyal citizens, reading:

With Christian sentiments, our chief magistrate, the President of the United States, has designated the 30th of May as a day on which the citizens of our beloved country should assemble in their respective places of religious worship to beg God's blessing on our Nation. Let us by our love of country and generous sacrifices for its welfare proclaim the loyalty and fidelity that Our Holy Religion teaches us as a Catholic duty. By liberal loans to the government and generous donations to the Red Cross, Knights of Columbus, and other war activities we must uphold the hands of those guiding the destinies of our nation and alleviating the horrors of war. Let no one be justly able to challenge our patriotism or convict us of lack of interest in our country's welfare in this hour of trial.[4]

After the war he asked help for Belgian orphans, the German people, and the Mexican missions. Reading those letters, anyone inclined to think of earlier days as days of quiet classrooms secluded from world problems would soon learn that the city on the mountain has been anchored from the beginning in a world much like the present one, in the ills from which it suffers and in the spirit with which the Church traditionally answers those ills.

Two educational movements characterized Bishop Ward's administration — the spread of Catholic secondary schools and the stepping up of state accrediting measures. Early in his regime, February 2, 1912, as one who knew and loved his responsibilities, the Bishop commended schools where a child is taught "the precepts of Holy Church, and his entire duty to God."

"Speak words of appreciation and encouragement," he said, "to those who are giving their hearts' richest devotion to the true education of the child," adding:

We are glad to see that Secondary Schools are being established in several parishes, and hope to see them wherever needed . . . We should be willing to spend and be spent in the cause of Catholic education, whether it be primary, secondary, academic or collegiate.[5]

A second major development was the establishment of a Kansas School Commission to "codify all existing laws and to recommend such legislation two years hence as may be judged necessary and advisable." Monsignor Francis Orr, Vicar-General of the Diocese, explaining the Commission, urged that religious communities not only maintain high standards but even "set the pace in improvement and efficiency." So far, Monsignor Orr wrote, "we have been treated with kindness, courtesy, and consideration and our present mutual relations with the Commission are eminently satisfactory." He said:

Regarding the important subject of the Certification, it will be more than advantageous for us to show the Professional standing of our teachers, in order, either to preserve our present autonomy of certification, or if necessary, to gain the best possible compromise in any state merger.

Education is not only the highest exponent of the Church but it has long since become the eager and keen ambition of the State, and we must now realize that, to give and take whenever possible, is the secret of future harmony and the preservation of self-sufficiency in our schools.

Bishop Ward led his diocese to all proper works and spirit. He "confided in the grace of the Holy Ghost to direct all things well," [6] as his letters characteristically put it, and helped put the teaching Sisters of his diocese on a path guided by good administrative help. He died April 20, 1929, leaving the diocese to his coadjutor, Bishop Francis Johannes.

The motto of the new bishop, "To serve God is to reign," was designed by the same artist who contrived the seal of Mount St. Scholastica. This artist, Pierre de Chaignon la Rose, wrote that the beams of the cross would be made "in colour, a good American patriotic red, white and blue." [7] The bishop indeed took an active leadership in caring for his country. His pastorals recommended that the faithful read the late Encyclical on the Charity of Christ and join, June 3–10, 1932, in a week of prayer and penance in the "present distress of the human race," part of which was manifested in the economic crisis. He wrote, August 21, 1933:

Of late, thanks to God! some progress toward national recovery has been made in the cities and rural districts . . . May our people not fail to pray fervently for our nation's chief executive that his wise administration may usher in an era of social justice.

He urged prayers too for the cessation of persecution in Russia, collections for the Missions, observance — in 1934 — of the nineteenth centenary of mankind's redemption. He pleaded for a diffusion of truth, writing on May 1, 1933: "Much of the opposition to the Catholic Church is due to ignorance of her Divine foundation, her doctrine, and her God-given rights." He urged the support of schools. A tall, commanding personality, he visited religious communities to give spiritual directives and to tell of his trip to Rome and of the general cultural climate of Europe. He conferred diplomas and degrees, going through the sometimes lengthy ceremonies with an unwearied dignity.

With the death of Bishop Johannes, Bishop Schulte came to Leavenworth, May 29, 1937, and was consecrated the following September 21. The World War II bishop was distinguished and kind, and the children of the parishes where he confirmed we heard to say: "It isn't hard to see that he is a prince of the Church." He devoted his attention to the prayer life of the diocese, authorizing the preparation of a hymn book and writing with approval when the *Laudate* was ready for use, having time for youth gatherings, speaking to children and people with a warmth for the things of God, looking into the future even during the war with faith and hope. He blessed the work of Mount St. Scholastica and when its Sisters left for far missions in California and Mexico he gave warm approval. He dedicated its new chapel and placed its meaning, spirit, and hope in appropriate words.

On July 20, 1946, he was named Archbishop of Indianapolis. And on November 9, Pope Pius XII named as his successor Bishop George J. Donnelly, former auxiliary in St. Louis. Bishop Donnelly took possession of his see on January 8 and 9, 1947, and was formally installed May 22, 1947. At the same time the diocese became officially the diocese of Kansas City in Kansas with St. Peter's Church the Cathedral.

The new bishop had a way of putting great truths in exceedingly simple language. "As no one is saved without prayer, we are urged to be more prayerful in Lent," he wrote in his Lenten pastoral, February 8, 1948. Almost as if he sensed how brief would be his episcopacy, he clothed everything in unforgettably human words that had a way of reminding men of their proper destiny. When he appealed for the Peter's Pence to be used for the needy of the world in post-war days, he asked the diocese to "help gladden the heart and fill the hand of the poor." [8] He made his pastoral letter an occasion of instruction. His motto, *Domine, ut videam,* seemed to include the idea, "Lord, that my people may see too." He wrote, June 27, 1950:

The Pope is the most universally respected person in the wolrd today. By millions in and out of the True Fold he is reverently looked to for guidance, and for a solution of the many, vexing problems that harass mankind. Statesmen and philosophers, moralists and economists who unwittingly or wilfully have put their trust in the fickleness and darkness of the finite human intellect — to the exclusion of the Infinite — have found, and so have their followers — that "If the blind lead the blind, both fall into the pit." (Matthew 15.14).

Like his great predecessors, Bishop Donnelly helped create the climate in which the community really lived. For Sisters do pray, read, listen and teach within the thought climate of the Church. It colors much of how they think and feel. From the prayers against *locusta et bruchus* recommended by Bishop Fink in the years of the grasshopper plagues, through San Francisco earthquakes, two World Wars and a national depression, the episcopal pens kept the eyes of the diocese and certainly of the convents aware, among the changing things of this world, of where the true joys lie.

Bishop Donnelly's pen had humor and unction in something of a sublime mixture. His Confirmation trips made him well known and never forgotten. He always preached fittingly at profession ceremonies, and presided with dignity. But he appreciated the ceremonial marches most when they were brief. To the Donnelly College Sisters who attended Mass in his chapel he gave Sunday homilies. And in the last years of his life, he watched from his house across the way their going and coming to and from school. One morning, he commented: "There's still one more to come. I have kept count."

He had a deep concern for the Sisters of his diocese, manifested not only by raising the salary to $500 annually, but also by the following letter of August 18, 1947, to the president of the diocesan school board.

My dear Father Boland:

Unless you can give some very good reason for their continuance, I think you may safely discontinue those annual diocesan grade school examinations we were recently speaking about . . . If you decide on discontinuing them (and we give you the authority to make the decision herewith) you may so notify the interested parties. Perhaps these examinations serve some really good purpose which I am not aware of. If they are discontinued — the grateful prayers of the good Sisters will bring you many blessings, I am sure. Sincerely yours in Christ, GJD

A legend, found in the Bishop's handwriting among his papers after his death, indicates some of his ideas on education. It is interesting not so much as a blueprint for administration as it is for an indication of his thinking:

THE BEATIFIC VISION
A Legend

Once upon a time a zealous young Sister, molded by modern pedagogical methods, was appointed by her Mother Superior to the parish school of a genial old pastor allergic to fads, frills and foolishness in general. He came from a family of teachers; and for years he had watched with regret the vagaries parading under the name of education. They reminded him of some of the crimes committed under the name of patriotism and charity. The good Nun at first was much surprised, and even somewhat scandalized at the pastor's lack of conformity with the canons of education, which — from her truncated training and consequent bias — she believed to be as sacred and inviolable as the laws of the Medes and Persians. But soon, she grew to like her new assignment and its pleasant atmosphere . . .

The pastor permitted no children to be admitted until the age usual for the beginning of the so-called second grade — the younger ones were allowed to stay home and finish their sleep; no "problem" pupils were accepted — to harass the teacher and disturb the other pupils. There were only six newly arranged grades instead of the former eight grades. School time in all the grades was devoted solely to school work . . . No interruptions were allowed during school hours for: visits of parents; fire-prevention week lectures; clean-up campaigns; sale-of-seals week; contests with other schools; quiz programs; training for periodic plays; Valentine boxes; tests and examinations for physical defects; sports or physical culture exercises, and countless other distractions. There was no guidance, intrusion, or interference in any form by the Mothers' Club, the Fathers' Club, or the Parent-Teachers' Association.

To spare the teachers, and to eliminate many unwholesome re-percussions from the parents and children, no report cards were distributed, no "corrected" papers were given back to the pupils. When a child began to fail he and his parents were duly warned. The Sisters went home each day at the same time as their pupils; they never spent more than a total of forty hours a week on school work, as such; no room had more than 35–40 pupils in it.

The most important thing was that the school during school hours was strictly a school — not a place for even the best-intentioned to display their wares; not a civic or neighborhood activity center, gymnasium or theatre; not a doctor's, dentist's, nurse's, or social worker's office; not a clinic for the study or training of abnormal children. The pastor said that however good some of the projects now a part of the school program might be in themselves, they should not be included among the duties of the Sisters teaching in the parish school, but cared for in some other way.

There was no long-prepared-for graduation program; the pastor — without party, play, or pomp — came over to school quietly after the Graduation Communion Mass in the church, and handed the graduates their certificates.

At the end of a happy year of teaching in this old-fashioned school, the good Sister in June returned jubilant to the Motherhouse for the summer. There a cordial greeting awaited her. Later in the day the Mother Superior told her the doctor had decided she did not need the proposed appendectomy; and that she might retain all her other organs too — vital and non-vital; the latest "graph" of her tonsils was "negative"; her teeth were not pyorrheatic as was previously "indicated." Reverend Mother also advised her that the Council at its last meeting had decided to discontinue all summer school courses for the Community members.

By this time the returning Religious felt she had ascended the Mountain of Thabor and witnessed the Transfiguration of the Divine Teacher. Seeing her cup of earthly joy full, she forthwith leaned on the bosom of Reverend Mother; fell into an ecstasy, and — too happy for this life, she entered into eternal life, and the enjoyment of THE BEATIFIC VISION

These were Bishop Donnelly's ruminations in quiet moments. He was wary of the too-technical word, but he knew the value of education.

Finally, he campaigned endlessly for vocations. One of his pastoral letters, dated April 7, 1949, said: "It is urged by some that the struggle of the pioneer and post-pioneer days did not permit spiritual fruit to ripen more plentifully. This contention is not sound. Spirituality is born of hardship — not of softness."

One of his letters to clergy, religious, and laity, traced a little of history, and made a genuine plea:

One hundred years ago and more the native dwellers of these Western valleys and plains and forests sent messengers to the East, beseeching, "Give us priests!" Though they are not wholly conscious of the full content of their cry — messengers from a spiritually distant world still come down the troubled rivers of life repeating to Holy Mother Church the same distressful plea: "Give us priests." Catholic young men — will you heed that echoing call of Christ, or will you also hurry selfishly away? "He went away sadly, for he had great possessions."

And when we speak to our Catholic young men of vocations, we are not unmindful of our Catholic young women. The world holds out to you much that is attractive . . . but where will you find a more glorious career than in embracing the religious life — where with one of your holy hands in the loving clasp of Christ, the other, like Mary's, is extended to your neighbor, performing for him and for her the spiritual and corporal works of mercy with their pledge of eternal life . . . What a pity, my dear young women, if in all the beauty and promise of your youthful years you sit listlessly within and leave your Divine Caller knocking at your door in vain.

And you parents, will you permit the cares of your farm, your yoke of oxen or your marriage to keep you from fostering religious vocations in the preparatory seminary and novitiate of your Catholic homes? Yours too is a glorious privilege. Will you reject it or will you grasp it?

The Bishop had grasped his own privilege. When he died December 13, 1950, he left the heritage of his reverence, his seriousness, his joy, his whimsy. He had found the spirit of his diocese strong, and in his few years, at least for many people who knew him, he had adorned it with a deep gaiety. He had made St. Peter's Church his Cathedral and he is buried there in a crypt in a side chapel. He was a great man who pondered deeply the meaning of things temporal in the light of things eternal.

On May 22, 1951, Bishop Edward J. Hunkeler of Grand Island, Nebraska, was installed as the new ordinary of the diocese of Kansas City in Kansas. He sent word that the community might expect him for a visit, and everything was in readiness the morning of June 28. The convent front doors were open and the portress listening for the bell. The pre-dieu was ready in the sanctuary, the long aisle waiting, the communion doors open. It was a sunny day. Then the college front door bell rang, and Sister Amabilia admitted a clerical guest. It took her a moment to see the gold chain and then she said simply: "Your Excellency?"

The guest smiled. "Yes, I am your bishop." He went to the chapel, celebrated Mass for the community, and came to the altar railing when the Mass was over to give "not a sermon, but an expression of gratitude and greeting."[9] He told the intent Sisters that it would be through their prayers and the grace of God that he would in any way do the great work before him. He expressed his own wishes for them with the words: "He who has left father and mother for Christ's sake will receive hundredfold and life eternal."

Archbishop Hunkeler, for he would be named archbishop in two years, had sounded the note of his own episcopacy. His motto was to be *Ut Diligant Christum*, "That they may love Christ," and he had begun the program of ceaseless prayer, energy, and encouragement which would characterize the ensuing years, and be woven into the 1950's and the decade now in progress at Mount St. Scholastica.

1. *The Topeka Guardian*, Archdiocesan Archives.

2. Letter, Archdiocesan Archives.

3. The letter commemorating the centenary of Constantine's edict is dated July 15, 1913. The plea for peace prayers is made especially for March 21, 1915, the date which Pope Benedict XV had named.

4. Archdiocesan Archives.

5. Letter of February 2, 1912. Archdiocesan Archives.

6. Letter to the Apostolic Delegate, April 27, 1927.

7. Letter from Prescott Hall, Cambridge, May 16, 1929. Archdiocesan Archives.

8. June 25, 1947.

9. Community Chronicle, June 28, 1951.

DIVINE GUIDANCE AND COURAGE

"To you, who are to take the mantle that falls from the shoulders of Mother Lucy, I wish divine guidance and courage," wrote Bishop Louis B. Kucera of Lincoln, Nebraska, with fine insight in a letter to Mother Alfred.

Community life has stages on the road of its growth. Mother Evangelista was the foundress of Mount St. Scholastica. Her virtues were an almost blind courage, a great abandonment to and dependence upon Divine Providence, out of which grew the habits of frugality and sacrifice which became sacred to the house. She felt the need of every individual she had in order to promote God's work, and it was as if she could not afford to let people die. She had a kind of heroic and simple endurance, a nearness to God which was crowned by a success of which she seems never to have been aware. Her characteristic was, "Not to us, O Lord, not to us, but to thy name give glory." She illustrates how well God can use weak instruments to attain great ends, for there was a fragility in her strength. Her dependence on God was like the dependence of a child, yet her abandonment was not blind but an intelligent abandonment, not opposed to reason but beyond reason.

Mother Theresa, with a gracious unimportance and capacity for working through necessary difficulties, carried on the work already done by others. She shared with other convents in this country and in the Old World. She knew work and sickness and struggle, the pain of the convent's young years when its childhood was over and it was not quite ready to be mature Even the building, St. Scholastica Hall, for which she was

248

primarily responsible in that, because of Mother Evangelista's illness, she did the major planning, would later be torn down to make room for the chapel. She seems to have carried on, doing the best she knew how to do, until the time was right for another to bring the place to maturity.

And Mother Aloysia did that, carrying her ideals beyond the horizons of her day to unknown goals of days she would not live to see. She died at the peak of her own possible insight into future needs. The very building she built, a great, massive, almost empty building at her death, would be symbolic. Again and again it would lend itself to education needs, always seeming to add a grace and beauty with each visit of contractors and carpenters to turn its huge, durable rooms into some new use. She had a keen intuitive judgment, which came quickly and seemed always right.

Then came Mother Lucy, unassuming, lovable, strong as steel and just as keen, with a discretion which seemed innate, and so prayerful that "Thanks, my God, thanks," came as her response to almost everything — fortunate and unfortunate. Sincere, with a keen sense of wit, her main hope was to build and beautify the house of God. She placed the St. Scholastica Chapel where it belonged — a link between convent and school. She built with economy. She was both generous and frugal. "Pay when you can, Father," was her refrain to pastors during the depression. She saved money, not that the convent would ever know luxury, for even its appearance she kept down to its traditional bareness. But she saved money that future educational needs could be met with prepared teachers, train fare, classroom equipment.

Under her the convent could function with some assuredness in the era of maturity to which Mother Aloysia had raised it.

The election of June, 1950, brought Mother Alfred to the superiorship. With her knowledge of the Holy Rule and of Benedictine history, with her preparation in history and economics, with her experience as teacher on large and small missions and in the college, she took the community through a really tremendous period of development. Grants from the Ford Foundation and the Rascob Foundation coincided with her careful management. Marian Hall, Kremmeter, Riccardi, and the Feeney Memorial Library dedicated to Our Lady of Wisdom rose during the twelve years of her office. New infirmary rooms and college faculty offices were provided. The California daughterhouse was permanently established and the site and buildings for the Colorado Priory selected and bought.

Born in Greenleaf, Kansas, the daughter of Mr. and Mrs. Albert Schroll, Mother Alfred had attended the academy before entering the community. She had earned her degree from St. Benedict's College in 1930, before Mount St. Scholastica was a four-year institution. Her master's work in economics had been done at de Paul and Catholic Universities, and her doctorate in history at Columbia.

It did not all happen at once, although there must have been times when it seemed to do so. Mother Alfred's superiorship began on a warm day in June, 1950. "Do you accept the election as Prioress of Mount St. Scholastica?" Bishop Donnelly had asked. "With the help of God and the prayers of the Sisters," she had answered. Between the drama of election and the opening of summer school were the merciful days of Abbot Aidan's retreat, which stressed the place of the supernatural in human life. The Corpus Christi procession was unusually beautiful that year, with long lines of Sisters singing from altar to altar in the early morning.[1]

Mother Alfred named Sister Imogene Baker as dean of studies in her place. On her council were Mother Lucy for the year of her life that remained, Sister Augusta Parle, Sister Rosemary Hogan, Sister Dolorosa Hoffmans. Later, when Sister Augusta was sent out to found the California Priory, Sister Maurus Wempe became subprioress and Sister Mary Austin Schirmer, secretary. Sister Evangeline Green became her personal secretary in 1951, taking up much of the secretarial work which the increasingly complicated world of a college president, Mother Prioress, and Mother General of the Congregation of St. Scholastica made necessary.

She went to Rome and to the sacred places of Europe that first autumn, the first Atchison Superior to go East and across the ocean.

Home in time to send her Advent letter, Mother wrote:

Christ comes in silence, and to show us His great love for men. Let us prepare by carefully observing our rule of silence and by practicing greater Charity towards one another. When we think of the many people who know not God, of the Christians who now are suffering for their Faith, and of the serious threat now facing the world for the third time, we should be spurred on to greater generosity and love in God's service.

It was still a stormy world, a world that would not wait for anyone to get organized. The convent had to proceed through it on its accustomed basic principles, trying to meet new crises with an old and durable peace and an adventurous willingness to do whatever new things were worthy. The coming years would need both.

The most obvious threat facing the world was the Korean War which seemed on the verge of becoming even a greater conflict. Atomic bombs had grown to hydrogen bombs. Yet Sisters on a train that year of 1950 found small things still proving effective. A young girl on her way to Fort Knox, Kentucky, said to them: "I do not really worry about my brother and my fiancé. Every day the Sisters in our school gather the children together at the noon hour to pray for the Servicemen."

"Where is your school?"

"Bahner, Missouri." Bahner, so small it had no post-office, so large that Sister Tharsilla and Sister Opportuna, gathering their few students, touched the world.

In February, 1951, Mother paid her first visit to the California missions and began to plan for the independent daughterhouse. There were so many things to plan. Summer brought the retreat by Father Vincent Martin, a Belgian Benedictine now a member of a new foundation in California. His theme was the significance for eternity of all good things. He spoke of the symnificance for eternity of all good things. He spoke of the symbols enmeshed in human life, all of them eloquent of the meaning of reality. With his French accent on the second syllable of the word "symbol," he became what he talked about, giving the convent permanently a new look at the real dimensions of life.

It was a summer of great realities. It was the summer of the flood, when the Missouri and Kaw Rivers in Kansas City became angry, destroying forces impoverishing people and calling for humanity's finest qualities. It was the summer of the deaths of three Sisters. On July 5, Sister Elizabeth Overton, ninety-six, died. She had been mission superior, college periodical librarian, stamp collector. For many years, paralyzed and blind, she had also been a very gentle voice in the night, saying to the amateur nurses who relieved the real nurses and who did not always know how to help her: "I'm all right. I'm comfortable enough." On July 17, Sister Mary Agnes, vestment-maker from France, died. She had been one of those who brought a taste for beauty from an old, old convent in Europe. And on August 9, Sister Anthony Payne, after working all summer in spare moments on a paper to be given at the American Benedictine Academy science meeting, died of embolism after surgery at St. Margaret's Hospital.

It seemed too soon for Sister Anthony to die. She was a really great biology teacher, who in just two years at Donnelly College had established a tradition in her department there for zest in learning, ambition for service, and reverence for life.

Sister Anthony loved community life and could lubricate it with stories of her early teaching days which could reduce any over-fearsome difficulty to its proper size. She remembered one very early day in her own career, coming across an inscrutable mathematical term which she called "peri-meter." In her textbook the word was unfortunately divided at the end of the line after the second syllable. She pronounced it to a bewildered Superior without showing her the book and was put on the afternoon train to ride over Iowa's golden country to the neighboring mission six miles away where there was a mathematics expert. The senior teacher looked at the word, and by putting the accent on the second syllable and calling it perimeter enabled Sister Anthony to capture her mathematics kingdom without striking a blow. Sister Anthony could tell the story as if she saw still the word division which had frightened her and the golden harvest country which had delighted her from the train window.

In that summer of 1951, July 29 to August 4, the workshop for all novice-mistresses of Benedictine convents in the United

States was held at Atchison. Father Florian Demmer of the Abbey struck the keynote in his opening speech. The purpose, he said, was "to make Benedictine saints." Fifty-one Sisters came from many communities. Father David Kinish and Father Sebastian Weisenberger of St. Benedict's Abbey, Father Conrad Louis of St. Meinrad's, and Father Pascal Botz of St. John's, together with Father Florian, conducted the sessions. The occasion was one of the important events of the early 1950's, one of the things which would last. By 1962, the workshop had become more than eighty postulant, novice, and scholastic mistresses meeting at Sacred Heart Convent, Yankton, South Dakota, to discuss how best to teach the meaning of the vows, how to develop more fully the contemplative and apostolic endowment of the Sister. The answers would not wait. The world was, in a sense, already asking battle of its Christians, even its Sisters, as one of the convent's mission corners was learning in the summer of 1953. In the San Luis valley of Colorado, where the Sisters had gone in answer to a great need in 1934 and where the flourishing schools of Antonito, Capulin, and Conejos were now producing energetic graduates, a crisis arose. In May, 1953, the Colorado Board of Education banned the payment of funds to the Valley schools taught by Sisters on what the *Denver Post* called "the unproved allegation that religion had been taught" in public schools.[2]

The board action, said the *Rocky Mountain News*, "touched off mass meetings and angry protests from residents of every religious faith in the communities."[3]

Students of the valley's past twenty years and their parents rose to the defense of the Sisters who had come to the land of blue skies and adobe huts. The action brought a review of the educational, artistic, and athletic efforts of the two decades, and within two months the Colorado board reversed its decision, its chairman paying tribute to the competency of the Sisters in the schools and praising their scholastic records. Citizens of the area, like State Representative S. T. Parsons of La Jara, echoed the praise. "Above all we must be brave," wrote Frank McCuniff, the great Antonito man who had championed the schools from the beginning, in a letter to Mother Alfred. He warned her that the battle would come up again.

A Denver lawyer, Joseph A. Craven, who had helped in the battle, wrote:

The whole controversy has now been soaked, washed, rinsed, and dried; the State officials are cognizant of a most unusual and highly persuasive local sentiment, expressed with a force and effect I have not seen before in any comparable situation; the people of the State of Colorado would not welcome a reconsideration of the question at an early date; and no doubt the declaration of the State Board of July 13 and the solidity of public sentiment has given a new understanding not only to the principles involved but to the judiciary of the State. Any suit hereafter to be instituted would have to be maintained in the area of these schools, and I may say, with complete legitimacy, that any court considering such a complaint would necessarily and fairly be affected in its final judgment by the circumstances peculiarly favorable to the Sisters because of the tradition and history of their fine efforts in creating and establishing a highly representative school system.[4]

He added, with some humor,

Through the good co-operation of the Mother General of their order, the Sisters of Mercy in the San Luis schools will no longer wear the rosary or the cross. Happily I find your Sisters legally irreligious in the absence of those objectionable insignia, and, I must say again, I have found them most co-operative, intelligent and cordial in their plans and hopes for the continuance of the new order.

The trouble would, in Mr. McCuniff's words, rear its ugly head again in the name of freedom, but for a time it had quieted. So far the San Luis valley people had defended their own house well in the battle of words and slogans against those who would have considered them underprivileged and incompetent; they had recognized principles, and with their own just kind of anger turned the principles into words and actions with which their education had provided them.

The centennial of the dogma of the Immaculate Conception was drawing near. In preparation for it, the old grotto went down in 1953 and was replaced by a new one. The first had been donated by the father of two of the Sisters; the second was given by the brother of another, in memory of their mother.[5] The five elm trees, planted when the first was built in 1908, still stood, stately and green. The grotto would always be something sacred to family life, a place where Sisters would go in groups every evening during summer recreation to pray and sing to the Mother of mankind. The new grotto harmonized with a new joy, and the Scholastics built their Fourth of July picnic booths to honor the Choirs of the blessed: patriarchs, prophets, virgins, and martyrs. These things seemed the deeds of real moment, the building of the ordinary day over and over again upon its cornerstone.

In 1954 the community undertook special penitential practices to honor the Virgin, the Immaculate Conception of the human race. There was special joy too: High Masses on every Saturday and on the eighth of each month, adoration of the Blessed Sacrament on the eighth of each month. The Holy Thursday repository that spring carried the prayer, "All for Jesus through Mary." Archbishop Hunkeler celebrated a field Mass honoring the Blessed Virgin at the Amelia Earhart stadium in Atchison; and on August 4, the day before Our Lady of the Snows, he dedicated Marian Hall, the new novitiate building. What had been the novitiate wing of the convent became now additional rooms for the Infirmary and for older Sisters.

By the dawning of the Marian Year, another event of great moment was happening. Mother Alfred announced it to Abbot Primate Bernard Kaelin in these words:

We are making preparations for the "Consecration of Virgins," hoping that all the Sisters who wish to avail themselves of the privilege may have opportunity to do so during the Marian Year. The date for the first "consecration" ceremony has been set for May 1, feast of Saints Philip and James, with the second to follow soon after, Sunday, May 9. It is with grateful remembrance that we review the never-to-be-forgotten occasion when, largely through your instrumentality, Right Reverend Father Abbot, this unique privilege was obtained and announced to us Pilgrims assembled in the Basilica of St. Sylvester, in October, 1950.[6]

The chapel was filled with awareness that first day of May, 1954 — of awareness that what had been given to Edith and Ethelreda, Gertrude and Mechtilde in the old convents of England and Germany was being given now to Midwestern American Sisters. Abbot Cuthbert was the officiating Prelate.

There was a particular sweetness in seeing the convent's oldest Sisters in the new cucullas, in the solemn words of the Church giving each, as it were, the seal of her affiance with God, in the carrying of candles, the singing of *Mel et lac ex ejus ore suscepi, et sanguis ornavit genas meas* . . . "I have tasted the honey and milk of His lips and His blood glows in my cheeks." Out in the kitchen, feast day dinners were prepared on each consecration day. "Seven for the Seven Gifts of the Holy Ghost," one of the Sisters said, putting rose petals on dishes; then "Five for the Five Wounds," and as the supply dwindled and undecorated dishes still remained, "The Holy Trinity is nice too."

That year the entire community, singing and praying, went on pilgrimage in busloads to the Immaculate Conception Cathedral, Leavenworth. And when the year had closed, it was decided to establish and continue daily sung Masses as a tradition.

It was in the summer of 1954, when the community was preparing for the consecration ceremony, that Father Anselm's face became a study in joy as the *Sanctus* of Mass IX poured out from all the voices with such clarity that he stopped to say, "This is . . . this is wonderful." Encouraged by his words, the Schola practiced *Prudentes Virgines* so well that evening that the night watchman rang the front doorbell to ask, "Who is the contralto in the choir?" The watchman with his flashlight, his raincoat dripping water while the flood of music came from the partly opened windows, was going out into the night interpreting what the ancient ceremony meant in a modern world.

Death came in those years like an old and faithful friend. Sister Mechtildis Schmucker, embroideress and last French exile, died February 7, 1952, after years of illness, a tall Sister who had suffered much and who had in her days of health made beautiful things. Sister Eleanor McNally, a great lady from very early days, died in June. It was said that her grandmother was once a waiting maid in the house of Benjamin Franklin. It would be pleasant to think of a relative of Sister Eleanor lighting a lamp in the house of the man who made lightning more interesting, and who negotiated with France. For Sister Eleanor was herself a fund of stories, of prayer, of a certain indestructible and unpredictable vivacity even as her eyes failed and she cleaned second floor hall from memory. She had for some years made Mother Lucy's Stations of the Cross for her, when Mother was too busy or too ill. She had permission to rise at four o'clock each morning to pray when the chapel was so quiet and no one else in it was seeing either. The slightly bent figure, always ready for the unusual, seemed as if it would always be around, and her memory did not die when she did, although Sister Sennorina took the cleaning of the hall when Sister Eleanor's hands relinquished the task suddenly, that June 18. Few would ever say her name without smiling, thinking, remembering, and pondering.

In July, Sister Mary Grace Sheppard died unexpectedly, leaving a great gap on the mission list and a record which everyone suddenly began realizing. And on February 10 of the next year, young Sister Benno Jermain died at Del Norte, far out in the mountains of Colorado. That September, 1953, when the autumn was beginning to come, Sister Ruperta Puhler, who had put holy water on so many loaves of bread before they went into the oven, died also. Others followed, in what seemed quick succession in quick years. Sister Irmengard Beedo had whispered one night to the Infirmarian, while locusts hummed outside the screens and summer trees were laced in the orchard sky: "Do we go to Purgatory?" "Oh, Sister, no. Aim for Heaven." "All right, that's all I wanted to know."

It was said of Sister Cajetan Kroth that in her last hours she asked: "Are the monks over here? I hear singing."

"No, Sister. You are remembering when you cooked in the Abbey kitchen and used to attend Abbey Vespers in the College Church."

"But this isn't Vespers. It's Psalms 148, 149 and 150."

And it was said of Sister Armella Wirth, that when she died as housekeeper at Christ the King parish convent in the middle of the night, she said to the young Sisters who clustered around her, "Let me die, He is coming for me."

Sister Louise Schneider, faithful teacher of many classes; Sister Ursula Stern who so long survived her sister, Sister Brigitta, to be a tiny lady in the community room and infirmary;

Sister Euphemia Welp, who after many years of living in the past at last found the present — all of their deaths made a difference.

Everywhere there were significances. On July 16, 1952, Sister Augusta Parle and Sister Dolorosa Hoffmans had gone out to Glendora, California to make permanent provision for the new St. Lucy Priory there. And in the autumn of 1954, Atchison Sisters would help a little to begin a new convent in their own archdiocese. The blue and white checked aprons of Benedictines and of Sisters of Providence Hospital mingled with the blue denim aprons of Carmelites, as a renovated house at 3535 Wood Avenue in Kansas City readied itself to be St. Michael's Carmelite Monastery. It was an experience to share the work, the laughter, the joy. St. Michael's was ready for occupancy on September 29. It was an experience to hear *Laudate Dominum omnes gentes* as the five Carmelites in brown habits and white cloaks left the nations to go behind the enclosure and to join the singing. Sisters who attended would often, when crowded nights closed over crowded days, recall that the Carmelites were praying with and for them. That winter, Sisters from Atchison sang the Mass of the Immaculate Conception on December 8, joining their voices with the first cloistered community in Kansas City, Kansas, in their small chapel. Glee clubs from Kansas City schools would go every year after that to carol for St. Michael's at Christmas time, for the people they could not see but whose hearts seemed to be listening so hard.

In the summer of 1956, the rose garden was blooming as usual, moss roses were brightening the ground between St. Scholastica chapel and the laundry, the peonies were unusually beautiful, the tall white snowball flowers were radiant, and the election of a Superior was set for June 5. The community assembled in the chapel and Archbishop Hunkeler led the opening prayer. On the first ballot, Mother Alfred was reelected. Sister Mary Peter left her place, with the wonderful quiet and purpose she always had in the chapel, and went to the sacristy. She lit the tall candles for Benediction. Then she climbed the small stairway to the altar, spread an extra white cloth, and knelt to remove the red curtain honoring St. Boniface, martyr, to replace it with the gold for Benediction.

"One of the candles is crooked," someone from a pew in chapel was meditating. "But Sister Mary Peter will straighten it."

She left the altar to get the incense and did not return. Archbishop Hunkeler stepped out into the sanctuary and looked with puzzlement at the community. Something was wrong. Everything was usually ready on the moment. A Sister went from the front pew into the north sacristy. Sister Mary Peter sat on a bench near the window. The whole story was finished now, like a masterpiece any good author would write. In the room where for eighteen years she had prepared for Pontificals, processions of Corpus Christi, profession and reception days and daily ferial Masses, the sacristan of St. Scholastica chapel was anointed. It was Archbishop Hunkeler's first administration of the Sacrament to a Sister.

"Sister Mary Peter has just died," Mother Alfred told the community, which somehow already knew. The Archbishop intoned the *Te Deum*, traditional for the closing of an election, and the community sang with giant gaps in volume, as the meaning of the words flowed over the polished pews, between the great windows, down from the tall tabernacle in its gold beneath the wonderful crucifix. "I have found Christ among the doctors in my Seneca classroom," a Sister had told Sister Mary a few days previous.

"Yes, I know. I have all that in the Sanctuary," she had answered.

The Archbishop gave Benediction of the Most Blessed Sacrament. Sister Sidonia, who had left her Western Kansas home as a very young girl, knelt to receive the Benediction in the sacristy beside Sister Mary Peter, who had stayed to be with their parents and who had now gone back to them.

After Vespers, the remains were borne down the central aisle of the chapel, as if a great person were being carried in a grand procession. "Bear Hamlet like a soldier to the stage," Shakespeare had written of one of his great characters. There was no tragedy in Sister Peter's life, but there was something Shakespearean in its unity and depth. When retreat and Consecration of Virgins followed the funeral, the new sacristans found that a ten-day supply of flowers had already been cut and prepared and placed in cool places. And someone remembered seeing Sister Mary Peter, some days before her death, wheeling a wheelbarrow to cemetery and gardens where the best flowers were and returning with a grand array of pink and white and red.

1. Journal of Sister Clarita McGarrity.
2. July 14, 1953.
3. July 14, 1953.
4. Letter of July 27, 1953.
5. Mr. Kluenberg, the father of Sister Notburga and Laurentia, gave the first. Mr. Rohrer, brother of Sister Verene, gave the second. The statues remain the same. The new grotto is slanted a little toward the front entrance, so that all who came up the winding drive can see it. Sister Augusta Parle collected for it rocks from almost every country in the world.
6. Letter to the Abbot Primate, April 8, 1954.

IN ALL THINGS GLORIFIED

Anyone writing the history of Mount St. Scholastica from the vantage point of a thousand years would find in the time between 1956 and 1962 some very wonderful things. Probably, however, those who walked the convent halls, kept the mission schools going, cooked the meals, taught the classes, answered the telephones and doors, brought the pages of the Ordo to life, and watched the morning spread over the sky and the night come down had little time, if any, to think of what history would say.

Many events occurred in those years, and none of them was the single dominating element except perhaps the ringing of the convent bell calling people to the Work of God both within and outside the chapel.

So it is not possible, really, to arrange events in an order of importance, for everything was important. It is possible only to see what some of the events were. In those years from 1956 to 1962, for one thing, the mission world came in new ways to the convent and for another, the convent was called, imperiously almost, to go to the mission world beyond its accustomed pattern. Academy and college classrooms saw increasing numbers of students from Africa, China, Japan, India, Central and South America come with notebooks and textbooks to mingle with the usual students. There was no demonstration about any of it. With ordinary red pencils, teachers checked grammar and the position of commas in statements such as, "Freedom will come back some day to Cuba, like spring suns over crying flowers." Girls from midwestern states read letters from home side by side with girls ten thousand miles away from theirs. An English translation of a Chinese poem could now be turned back into its native tongue by a girl from Hongkong in the front row. The Mystical Body was becoming strangely tangible and very lovely as Mary Jo Wangari and Agatha Wangeci from Kenya stood in the sun of summer school sessions holding bouquets of marigolds, cosmas, nasturtiums, and blue bachelor buttons, their gleaming dark faces beautifully at home on a plot of Kansas ground. They had been taught English in faraway Africa by Irish Sisters with British accents.

It was the old Mount St. Scholastica that received them, the Mount St. Scholastica of Sister Thecla's day, when the grounds were covered with small girls as well as high school and college girls; it was the new Mount St. Scholastica, too, with building after building rising among the trees; it was the same Mount St. Scholastica, for there was only one.

"Sister, bless us before we sleep, as our parents do," the Latin American academy girls would sometimes say to the directress. And Sister Ambrose and her successor, Sister Theophane Reinecke, like Isaac, would invent a blessing.

The convent sent no additional Sisters to its Mexican daughterhouse in those years, but it tried to peer through the near future with the hope that more help could be given Mexico City and that some new foundation could be made in Brazil or Peru. Volunteer names accumulated on Mother Alfred's desk, while existing missions in the United States added classrooms, vacation schools multiplied everywhere, Saturday instruction classes grew, and letters from pastors building new schools in new places accumulated both hopefully and despairingly.

"You get the merit of having volunteered for South America," Superiors would learn to say. "But your mission this year will have to be still in South Nebraska, Iowa, Kansas, or Colorado."

Graduates of the college and of the missions answered the Papal Volunteer and lay missionary call. Almost overnight, it seemed to the people who had taught them, young men and women were teaching and doing social work and nursing in Brazil, Mexico, Peru, and Panama. Both the home college and Donnelly College were sponsoring courses in Christian Doctrine, Spanish, and Spanish American culture for prospective lay missionaries.

As if there were no time to listen to the mission summons, the educational world was crying for excellence. The convent had never really existed for anything else. The doctoral and masters degrees earned in those years were never enough to supply the demand. It was not too small, but too large a world, and in trying to meet its demands Mother Alfred once wrote to a Sister: "The more we forget ourselves and rely on God, the more will He bless our efforts." Even while the two colleges and the many schools staffed by Atchison were growing, the pioneer teachers of the college and academy were going into eternity, leaving the beautiful classrooms and the beautiful books for new people to handle. Sister Bernardo Brentano, Sister Flavia Hogan, Sister Ambrose Conway, Sister Regina Baska, great people who so helped to make the Mount, died during those years.

Political and scientific events had brought science and languages into such focus that in 1960 the American Conference on Higher Education considered the question: "Can the existing educational framework supply the national needs or should the federal government establish special schools?" Language laboratories mushroomed on the home campus and in the high schools, with foreign languages being taught also in some of the grade schools. On special study grants Sisters went for summer work to universities all over the country. The elementary education department of the college became accredited by the National Conference for the Accreditation of Teacher Education. But in its daily effort, its faculty meetings, and its summer community meetings, the convent continued to know that the strenuous teaching of real liberal arts offerings within the Christian philosophy of life could alone meet the national need, and the world need.

The use of tapes for excellence in teaching brought Mount St. Scholastica into the national educational spotlight when, at St. Walburga's Convent, Covington, Louisiana, Sister Mary Theresa Brentano pioneered in setting up a tape-classroom. The idea was that a teacher could conduct classrooms on three levels of progress with the help of machinery transmitting lessons directly to the ear of the listener. In 1959 and 1960, summer sessions included tape institutes, and some grade schools in the area were wired for testing the validity of the new aid to teaching. Cathedral School, St. Joseph, Missouri; St. Benedict's, Atchison; Guardian Angels, Kansas City, Missouri; and SS. Peter and Paul, Omaha, Nebraska, were some of the pilot schools.

But the convent's greatest resource was its Sisters, and their total strength was becoming more and more connected with the progress of Sisters everywhere. The need for greater unity of effort among Benedictine convents was evident.

There were many matters which required the concerted viewpoints and actions of Benedictine Prioresses who had been given a new bond of unity by the practice of biennial retreats.[1] One of these matters was the question of a school for higher studies in Rome. The notice of an International Congress of Mothers General in Rome, September 11–13, 1952, had come in a letter of late August that year. Unable to attend the Congress, Mother requested the Mother General at Casa del Cuore in Rome to represent the Congregation of St. Scholastica. It was at this Congress that the Holy Father made his appeal for better spiritual and apostolic preparation of Sisters. The proceedings of that meeting were sent to Atchison by Rev. Mother St. John Martin, Superior General of the Ursulines of the Roman Union, Rome, and secretary of the Executive Committee of Mothers General.

The result was a meeting of Mother Presidents. Mother Alfred of Atchison, Mother Carmelita of Clyde, Mother Rosamond of St. Joseph, Minnesota, and Mother Jerome of Yankton, South Dakota, discussed a school of higher studies. The matter came up for fuller consideration at the Superiors' retreat in 1955. It was decided, after correspondence with Superiors of other convents also facing similar decisions, that it would be better to open in the United States a Benedictine Institute of Sacred Theology which, through its summers of study, could channel to convents the learning sacred to all houses. The Convent of St. Benedict, St. Joseph, Minnesota, was chosen as the site, with St. John's University, Collegeville, primarily responsible for administration of the school. In the first summer session, 1958, Sister Kieran Curry and Sister Terrance Minton began the six-summer program. Sister Agnes Haganey joined them in 1960 and in 1962 Sister Mary Paul Ege began her studies there. Sister Simone Watson, Sister Auxilia King, and Sister Mary Edward Assenmacher came from Mexico and California.

At home the strengthening of its own Sister-education program went on. Outside needs seemed so great that the black veil at the altar on profession day had often to be accompanied by a train ticket at the Superior's office, and forty, fifty, or sixty children waited hopefully for every young Sister. The spiritual life, dogma, the Divine Office, the Holy Rule, chant, and modified liberal arts schedules were well taught in postulancy and novitiate. It was true that veteran teachers on missions helped the newcomer with her zeal, her new habit, and her new shoes. But it was so often not possible to keep young Sisters home to finish college or to receive the added knowledge of their religious life which the complexity of the modern world made necessary. There was small comfort in remembering that vocations of earlier, rugged days when even postulants and novices had sometimes to be sent out to teach had resulted in the persevering and flowering of vocation. The problem was to equip the Sister of the present with what the present demanded, just as the Sister of the past had been equipped to face the past.

In the summer of 1956, Sister Jerome Keeler joined the fifty sisters chosen to work on the so-called Everett Curriculum for Sister-Formation, meeting at Everett, Washington, for three months on a grant from the Ford Foundation.[2] The General Chapters began considering the question of extending the time for temporary vows to permit both study and mission experience before perpetual vows. And in 1962, the General Chapter voted to extend the period to five years and appointed Sister Jerome head of a committee to plan a Benedictine program of Sister education which would benefit all convents of the Congregation of St. Scholastica.

The face of the campus itself, where the dream would be actualized, was always changing a little.

Kremmeter Hall opened in 1958, a residence for girls, named

for the foundress who had come to teach what seemed to her a wild, lawless Kansas youth. To erect the building, two-thirds of the twenty-four beautiful maple trees which had provided an outdoor hallway for the meditating, the reading, and the reflecting student had to go. But they themselves had been only a stage in the century. They had stood there for years, together with the small railroad which had once delighted minims in the days of Sister Thecla's reign. Only the gay little ghosts of the minims in their small uniforms were there now. The last grade school classes had been discontinued in the 30's. Now the bases of two teeter-totters and of outdoor swinging chairs were all that bore witness to what had once been a reasonable Paradise for little girls. The St. Scholastica Academy of Atchison City, Kansas, which the pioneers had so proudly named on the day of their arrival, was now something of a city itself. It required new roads, a set of new streetlights, a new telephone system, and new tennis courts. Kremmeter faced Atchison, the Missouri river, and the dawn coming up over the Atchison hills and trees. Westward its windows looked over the sunset, and southwestward the cemetery in its majesty and sleep of peace.

Simultaneously Riccardi Center came into being. The Italian monk Placid Riccardi, the most recent Benedictine Beatus, had died in 1915 at the monastery of St. Paul Outside the Walls. Riccardi had proved sanctity to be quite at home in classrooms and Benedictine houses in the twentieth century. This Student Center with its dining rooms and club rooms, game rooms and parlors, seemed centered around the austere monk who had become a Beatus by the timeless means of prayer, study, a penitential life, and a kind of radiant love.

The oak parlor was especially dedicated to him. Its beauty focused on the oil portrait of the monk, retreat master, spiritual director, teacher, at whose death the Brother accidentally rang the chimes instead of the tolling bell, to earn the Abbot's decision: "Let them ring. If we cannot ring them for Placid, when shall we ring them?"

The community began holding its traditional July picnics in the dining room of Riccardi, to the sound of the taps, and the Star Spangled Banner, concluding with hymns to the Blessed Virgin under the direction of Sister Geraldine Jacobs or Sister Gertrude Marie Sheldon.

"Those new buildings do not have the tone of the old," said a visitor to the convent grounds in 1959. "You will have to do something about that."

Things were happening to give the tone, a tone proper to the new. In the summer of 1960, as the convent prepared to begin its next building, electric cables had to be strengthened to bear the weight of the needed current. A music recital had been scheduled for the evening, but when evening came there were no lights for the program. The department went ahead with its plans, and from a stage illumined by real candelabra musicians played and sang. Viewers of the concert would never forget it, particularly the girl from Tokyo who played Weber by candlelight. The girl was Kazue Shishido, educated in Tokyo by the Sisters of St. Paul through the first two years of college. During her junior year at Mount St. Scholastica she had been baptized a Catholic and she felt the current of gladness between herself and the audience that July night so much that she put in the picture poetry characteristic of the Oriental a new view of the Old Mount:

Candle Concert
Dark as black veil,
Calm as spring sea,
    in the audience.
Red velvet curtain as Arabian carpet
    Opens.
Shining candle light on the piano,
as a light-house of the sea in night.
Black key like dark eyes whispers
    what I am thinking,
White key like a pearl sings what I am
    feeling,
Shadow across keys reflects what a
    people is reminded.
Cheers are sound of waves
as warm as hands of mother,
as sweet as smile of mother.[3]

The convent was mother now not only to the students of the Middle West or of the nation or even of the western world. Imperceptibly it had embraced the world, and been embraced by it. Students and prefects, parents bringing their daughters to

267

school, new postulants walking up the front entrance, all were building the tone for the new buildings. "The new grass around the new buildings does better when there is some sod from our own ground with it," everyone began to notice. "It's easier than starting from new seed." The combination of the old and the new went on.

For many years the statue of St. Gertrude had stood in the administration building, holding the crosier of an abbess. "St. Gertrude was never an abbess," Sister Florence said one day to Mother Alfred. "What would happen if I took that crosier away from her?" Mother Alfred did not answer. And so the next day the crosier was gone and in its place a scroll, as more befitting the author of *Herald of Divine Love*. St. Gertrude was to reward the favor in a rather singular way.

On November 17, her feast day in the Benedictine Ordo, an interesting procession occurred. The librarians went out to the campus, covered with its brown grass, to break ground for the building which had so long been a dream. The Feeney Memorial Library was to be dedicated to Our Lady of Wisdom, but the librarians wanted to share it with the Benedictine saint who had so pronouncedly exhibited wisdom. Bulldozers came four days later, making their beginning on the feast of the Presentation of Mary. In eighteen months the great edifice had risen in stone and brick and glass, and on May 17, 1962, the transition was made from the second floor administration building where books had long ago spread like a pleasant epidemic out of the rooms into the halls. The college girls called the day, "Operation Backbreak," transporting the 40,000 volumes in one day. It was a wonderful day in Mount St. Scholastica history.

A small, solemn procession preceded invasion of Greeks, Romans, French, Spanish, Italian, English, and other great people of the past into their permanent home. The librarians with the Holy Bible, the statue of the Infant of Prague, and the image of Our Lady of Wisdom took first possession so that the Word of God might be the first item to enter the House of Wisdom.

The house was a beautiful one. Its windows facing north and south would never glare with heat. Its garden floor had spacious rooms for bookbinding. The old books were there in this new library, carefully rebound, often read and re-read, bearing honored names on their cards. The new books were there. A rare-book room housed Mother Evangelista's own Bible, well-used but unfortunately without a pencil mark. There was a photostatic copy of the Gospels in St. Jerome's Latin with an interlinear Saxon commentary by Adelfrith, Bishop of Lindisfarne from long ago seventh-century England. It contained the inscription:

> This is the work of Cuthbert and Aelfrith and
> Aedfrith the sinner; together with God we have done
> this work.

"There is so much in this room. If I could only stay home all year just to classify it!" a summer librarian said wistfully in the autumn of 1962. "But classrooms wait, and this will stay here, and some day someone will classify it all. We do not live as individuals only."

Sister Egberta Buening made the mural of Our Lady of Wisdom; Sister Sheila Rea carved the young St. Benedict, student, in wood, for the reference room.

And when the time came to schedule the observances of the Centennial Year, quite without design, only by seeming convenience the day of dedicating the library fell to November 17, St. Gertrude repaying the librarian for her gift of the scroll.

While new buildings were going up, other great works were going on in small corners of the old. In an office on the ground floor of the administration building, older Sisters, retired from the missions, and their helpers among the college girls, were grading papers, writing letters, and giving prizes in Christian Doctrine to children unable to attend Catholic schools. The work of the Confraternity went far. It resulted in careful syllabi made for vacation-school teaching. It spread the Word of God.

Always amid the planning and the laboring, there was the constant passage of the workman with his work completed to the heights from which God beholds the workman. "No one can replace them, but that is the way it should be," someone commented. "We only follow them."

The first months of 1956 had seen the deaths of Sister Opportuna Weissenberger, Sister Marceline Sinnott, Sister Gaudentia

Beimler. Sister Opportuna and Sister Marceline had been grade teachers for many years, in regular classrooms and in vacation schools. Sister Gaudentia had taught to within a very few months of her death from cancer. Kansas fields and Colorado mountains and the faces of many children had been part of their stewardship. Sister Prisca Pettinger and Sister Juliana Ostereicher followed; for many years they had been house-keepers, convent cooks, coffee-makers. Sister Mary Joseph Mc-Gerty put down years of grade school tack-boards and classes and said cheerily on the morning of her death: "Tell the Lord I cannot come to Mass but I will see Him soon."

In majestic succession, thirty-eight Sisters died in the next six years, taking some of the spirit of everything beautiful in the convent with them: Sister Henrietta Neuner, Sister Rose Scahill, Sister Basilia Franken, Sister Valentine Rosenwirth, Sister Claudia McGuire, Sister Relindis Plank, Sister Rita Callahan, Sister Barbara Schneider, Sister Flavia Hogan, Sister Theresita Wirth, Sisters Monica and Thecla Schecher, Sister Aurelia Scanlan, Sister Bernarda Brentano, Sister Appolonia Haug, Sister Crescentia Kragerer, Sister Stella Slattery, Sister Demetria Hopf, Sister Ameliana Beilman, Sister Virginia Kuckleman, Sister Nicholas Felten, Sister Vivientia Spohrer, Sister Ambrose Conway, Sister Alberta Stack, Sister Bonita Fibiger, Sister Cyrilla Miller, Sister Adelinda Salesky, Sister Agilberta Ketter, Sister Praxedis Still, Sister Ethelreda Henkel, Sister Regina Baska, Sister Generosa Stengel, Sister Petronilla Willems, Sister Lucina Ayers, Sister Timothy Marnett, Sister Anselma Manhart, Sister Francesca Pfrang.

"Pray for souls. We must pray for souls," was the refrain of the last of these.

Coif-makers, habit-makers, missionaries, expert seamstresses and menders and cooks, academy and college teachers, personalities made partly by the autumn color on the convent trees and the morning light through the chapel windows, they made a grand procession.

Some held, more visibly than others, certain aspects of the growth of the convent. In early June, 1959, Sister Barbara Schneider, manager of convent laundry and farms for forty years, put on sunbonnet over her veil and tennis shoes on her feet and walked over the grounds she had loved so long. Sixty-seven years of caring about the grounds, of speaking gently to the workmen in the laundry, of watching things grow, had made her feet sensitive to the hard summer ground and her eyes keen to see the progress of flowers and vegetables and new roses struggling for growth around the new buildings. She made her pilgrimage alone that Saturday afternoon. That night she lapsed into a coma and after a week of silence died on June 21. It was the middle of a dry June, and a few minutes after her death the sound of rain on the convent roofs made it seem that Sister Barbara was turning in her report. Her eyes had been blue and sure in measuring weather and in studying people. Her small hands, brown and strong and delicate on laundry or garden instruments and on Office books, made the convent often reflect that the combination of choir and lay Sister in American Benedictine houses had been indeed a happy thing.

On the following April 6, 1960, the convent had another reminder of days of harvest. Sister Luitgard Mengwasser observed the seventy-fifth year of her profession. Archbishop Edward J. Hunkeler said the Mass and heard the renewal of the vows. He gave a sermon of a few words in which, coming down to the front pew where she was sitting, he asked Sister Luitgard if she thought it right for a Sister to make a bishop shed tears.

One of her small hands had been curved since the installment of laundry machines in 1892 had brought a machinery accident. But her own face was wreathed in smiles as well as tears.

"The vows you made that day in 1885 were pretty good," a well-wisher said to her. "They lasted, didn't they?" The eyes of Sister Luitgard twinkled. "So far," she said.

They lasted two years longer. On March 2, 1962, about midnight, Sister Luitgard died. Watchers said she opened her eyes and smiled as if to say, "Why, You're here!" and died.

There were other signs of harvest near the close of the first century. Professed, Scholastic, and Novitiate scholars were taking their turns at singing the daily Proper of the Mass. Days of the long practices were over and the harvest was rich. Father Anselm was commenting with joy, in one of his rare summaries on the state of things: "There is a battle going on in some minds as to whether the Solesmes way is the best way. It is the best

I know for getting people to sing chant together." Looking back, it took effort to remember that pioneering had been hard. Now, things were different. "What key is it in?" someone asked Sister Mary Blaise Cilissen at the beginning of a summer practice. "Don't bother me with keys. Let me sing." It was not quite that automatic for everyone but it was on the way to becoming so.

There were other assessments to the community's progress. "Are there many now in the Novitiate?" Sister Josephine asked one afternoon when an autumn sun shone on the apple trees outside her infirmary window. "Are there new buildings? Are there many new students? Are all of you teaching for the love of God?"

It was a noble place. The flash flood of July 11, 1958, which crippled many old buildings in Atchison, had left the Convent standing washed and clear on that morning of the solemnity of St. Benedict, when the Introit sang: "I will make of thee a great nation." It had indeed kept a great deal of the old ways, but not to the exclusion of the new.

"Why, he has come into the Presidency like a knight in white armor!" Sister Ambrose Conway reported to the infirmary on the morning of January 20, 1961, when the community room for the first time in history admitted a television set, lent for the inauguration of President Kennedy. The stability of the Ordo, the changing of the seasons, the coming of the new, the maturing of the young, the interchange brought about by duty between God's world on the outside and His world within kept a basic pattern to which people could go for vision and from which they could go to daily work. Advent still followed the Pentecostal season, bringing days of peace, summary, and expectation.

Christmas came gently to Mount St. Scholastica in 1961. Through a blinding snowstorm in what became a four-hour trip the convent chauffeur Vincent brought a carful of Sisters from Kansas City, with veteran Sister Praxedis saying that she was not really afraid and that if the car came so did she. Gifts were wrapped for the poor and for benefactors. A circle of eight musicians played Christmas carols, and the community assembled in the traditional Christmas greetings to Mother Alfred. The solemn white-curtained dormitories welcomed missionaries home, and the chapel found place for them. Novices and postulants emerged from retreat to take part in the Christmas greetings, the lessons and chant for Matins were practiced. The summer dining room where the community assembled for the greeting was beautiful with the work of the hands, gifts from Sisters' recreation hours to be dispensed wherever they were needed. Halls and refectory were decorated with wreaths encircling Bethlehem scenes painted on cardboard.

"We are all rich in our poverty," Mother Alfred told the community. "We all have gifts to give. And tonight all our missions and the whole Christian world unite. In the great exchange of gifts between God and us, all are included."

At the midnight Mass Father David preached, and a tape recorder took his words to relay them to the sick. He said that Christmas is not an historical commemoration, but that since all things are present to God, God was at this moment coming to the convent, adding:

If we want to be persons whose lives are completely dedicated to God, we must take care not to be drawn by material things and considerations. There is danger that we will lose simplicity of soul and singleness of purpose. We are responsible for the example we give all our lives.

If we mean the giving of ourselves, we may be sure Christ will give Himself so the exchange of gifts continues. He became one of us so that we may become one with Him. We keep tonight the event in which God became human so that we could become Divine.

At two A.M. there was hot chocolate with rolls in silence in the Assembly Room. In the starched white and immaculate black of Christmas habits, Sisters kept a quiet and exultant joy. Sister Francesca was not home to ring the rising bell. Someone with a different touch rang it now, in place of the bell-ringer now at St. Margaret's Hospital beginning her special vigil for souls.

Morning Office and Masses followed. Wishing the community a Merry Christmas after the third Mass, Father David, its chaplain for twenty-five years, said: "At Christmas, when I know your good wishes and prayers for me, I feel my riches the most, grateful that I have the example of so many good people whom I may, in a sense, follow to God."

Six days after Christmas, on December 31, nine postulants received the habit and fourteen novices made vows. Hundreds of guests heard the Archbishop explain that the religious vocation means giving oneself to God. The feast day drew to late afternoon. Sisters in charge of kitchens were making statues and framing holy pictures for next June's religious vacation school children. The brightness of the afternoon began to fade. Upstairs in the Infirmary, Sister Josephine slept. Her face, to observers who came in and went out without speaking, was the face of one who seemed almost not aware of the world, yet still needing a little of it as she had always needed it to convey the greater realities to novices. Outside her room in the Infirmary hall, the clock ticked. It had been removed once as unnecessary at the installment of the main hall's electric clock, but she had missed its sound and it had been restored.

The giant oak doorways of the building, the linoleum floors, the clean bare woodwork seemed as if the old convent itself were asking observance, perfection, from everyone who lived there. It was the last day of the year, a day of prayer for the persecuted of the world, and in the chapel the Blessed Sacrament was exposed for veneration and Sisters were praying. At 4:15 the bell-ringer pressed her finger on the bell and five short peals sounded. The signal for the Work of God had been given and anticipated Matins would begin.

The first acolyte intoned: *Domine, labia mea aperies* . . . "Thou shalt open my lips, O Lord." The whole house was quiet except for the answer, *Et os meum annuntiabit laudem tuam* . . . "And my mouth shall announce Thy praise."

In a monastery everyone has his proper gift from God, St. Benedict says. By December 31, 1961, the convent had received more than a thousand lives into its keeping. Painting, embroidering, mending, caring for the sick, tending of house and table and garden, singing and writing, sculpturing and teaching had all been consecrated to God's glory, and the very bricks of the walls and asphalt of the drives seemed touched and toned by the passage of feet, the living of life. There was an atmosphere so palpable one could hold it, so invisible that it was like life.

The winter passed and turned into spring. The spring turned

into summer, and on the morning of June 5, 1962, the community assembled for the election of a new Prioress. Archbishop Hunkeler presided: "This is not a democratic right you are exercising," he said, "but a religious act you are performing."

At the close of the election, the Archbishop said: "I am pleased to announce that there has been an election. Will Sister Celeste Hemmen accept the office of Mother Prioress?"

A slight Sister with blue eyes who had become known to everyone as teacher and fellow-Sister, and as dispenser of community needs in her office as assistant-procurator, stepped out from the ranks and walked up the aisle. "This is an occasion of joy," the Archbishop said after he had congratulated her. Then Mother Celeste walked down the long aisle to the Superior's place. Smiling, Mother Alfred handed her the bell, that instrument with which the Prioress of a Benedictine house announces the time for beginning the Work of God.

"Let us go forward," said the new Mother to the community a few days later, "in the charity that at all times puts God first."

1. On the evening after Mother Lucy's funeral, in April of 1951, the Mother Superiors assembled had asked: "Wouldn't it be helpful if we could make retreat together?" The first such gathering was at Sacred Heart Convent, Lisle, Illinois; the second at Clyde, Missouri. This latter retreat, the fall of 1953, brought the enthusiastic attention of Abbot Primate Bernard Kaelin, who requested that the conferences be duplicated and sent to Benedictine convents abroad.

2. In the fall of 1958, Sister Mary Faith Schuster was sent to Marillac College, Normandy, Missouri, to teach for two years in the Sister-Formation College established there by the Daughters of Charity of St. Vincent de Paul.

3. Kazue Shishido, "Candle Concert," *Mount St. Scholastica Magazine,* Winter, 1961.

THE CONVENT'S WORK IN THE MISSIONS

To today's world, Kansas, Iowa, Nebraska, and Missouri schools are not frontiers. But in the 1860's and 1870's, the Middle West was still a mass of wagon trails. To travel seventy miles took longer than to go to Europe now, and to organize a parish school was missionary work.

Many of the Sisters who went to the convent's first missions had come from Ireland, from Bavaria and Austria, and from the eastern United States for what they considered real mission work. Some of the Sisters went as novices to teach, and almost one hundred per cent of these novices became the old of the house who would work for greater training of the young. Some indeed died very young.

In the century of its history, the convent took 117 schools. In 1963, it had seventy-four. The forming of new daughterhouses, the change in educational trends, the assimilation of small schools into larger ones account for the difference in number.

Wagon wheels over Kansas dirt roads, new trains over new railroad tracks conveyed the missionaries, until the conference of 1915 decreed that Sisters could ride in automobiles. In extending outside Atchison from its academy and its parochial unit which had opened several years later, the Sisters' schools tended to follow the missionary work of Atchison Benedictine monks, but not exclusively.

The two detachments which went to Seneca in 1876, to the parish school there and to the rural community of St. Benedict's nearby, rode out into beautiful, level, farming area. St. Mary's parish in the community called St. Benedict's had a colorful

276

history. It had been a mission place since 1864, and priests riding there from Atchison sometimes had their boots frozen to their feet. One of the first missioners remembered halting his horse at one juncture to allow a herd of buffaloes to go by. Feast days at St. Benedict's were held with great solemnity. The three Sisters would go into the prairies to gather flowers and would station themselves strategically to refill the children's baskets as they marched in the procession scattering blossoms. Children came on Saturdays for catechism instruction, and people walked miles to church when the drifts were too high for horses and buggies. When a death occurred, the parish was notified by having someone ride horseback, one rider in each direction from the church.

The St. Mark's procession in late April found the people taking part in a four-mile procession, "singing and praying. Sometimes," says Sister Celestine Nordhus, "it got very warm. The Sisters wore sunbonnets over their veils, which frightened the horses sometimes. It was a great demonstration." [1] The people built their own great church of St. Mary of the Assumption, carrying the rocks from distances.[2]

St. Joseph's in the apple country of Wathena, 1880; Sacred Heart, Atchison, 1882; St. John's, Hanover, 1883; were next. Sisters who recall the early days and the days of the 1900's speak of how beautiful were the trips in early harvest time through the tasseling corn, the country where shocks of wheat stood in the brown stubble of the fields and where ripening apples reached almost over the fences into the buggies and wagons.

Then followed the rest of the litany: St. Anthony's, Kansas City, Kansas, 1886; St. Joseph, Topeka, 1887–1892; St. Joseph, Kansas City, 1898–1902; St. John the Evangelist, Argentine, 1899; St. Theresa, Westphalia, 1900; Immaculate Conception, Valley Falls, 1902; St. Benedict, Kansas City, 1902; St. Bede, Kelly, 1903; Holy Name, Rosedale, 1903–1914; St. Gregory, Marysville, 1903; St. Leo, Horton, 1904; Sacred Heart, Paxico, 1905; St. Boniface, Scipio, 1905–1920; St. Ann, Effingham, 1906; St. Joseph, Shawnee, 1907–1912, and 1916 to the present; St. Mary Purcell, 1908; St. Patrick, Atchison, Route 2, 1909[3]; SS. Cyril and Methodius, Kansas City, 1909–1910; St. Joseph, Flush

(St. George), 1909; St. Bernard, Wamego, 1909; Sacred Heart, Baileyville, 1911; St. Bridget, Axtell, Route 3, 1912–1948; St. Peter, Mercier, 1913–1960; Olathe, 1915–1916 and 1917–1926; St. Joseph, Nortonville, 1916; Corpus Christi, Potter (Mooney Creek), 1918; St. Columbkille, Blaine, 1919; Annunciation, Frankfort, 1920; St. Augustine, Fidelity, 1920–1959; St. Theresa, Perry, 1920–1926; St. Casimir, Kansas City, 1922–1931 and 1944–1947; St. Louis, Good Intent, 1923; Holy Family, Eudora, 1925; St. Joseph, South Atchison, 1927; St. Patrick, Corning, 1929; St. Malachy, Beattie, 1929; St. Michael Axtell, 1931; Lillis District School, 1935; Christ the King, Welborn, Kansas City, 1940; St. James, Wetmore, 1946; St. Pius X Mission, 1956; St. Matthew, Topeka, 1958.

Mount St. Scholastica Academy and College, and Donnelly College, Kansas City, complete the Kansas schools.[4]

Some first fruits of the missions were religious vocations. Girls followed their eighth grade teacher all the way home in June, and mothers sewed their black dresses before they had even seen their little daughters in "party dresses." The missions brought the convent material for recreation, too.

"Now when the bishop comes in, you rise and say, 'Good morning, Your Excellency,'" one teacher told her group. "Stand now and see if you can say it when I come in. I'll be the bishop." She left the room, re-entered, and found the lesson learned. A little later, called out of the room to answer a telephone, she returned again. "Good morning, Your Excellency," they said, not only to her amazement but also to the amazement of the guest with pectoral cross who had himself entered without fanfare and was standing at the back of the room.

The mission schools brought other things to convent life. In her old age, when the past became the present to her, Sister Cyrilla Miller taught school the livelong day in her convent room. "John hasn't been so good today?" a visitor would say, coming in to her. "Oh, he's all right," Sister Cyrilla would rush to the defense of the little boy now grown to manhood somewhere in the busy world. "He just has trouble with arithmetic."

The fortunes of the schools changed. Some small schools became giants. St. Joseph's, Shawnee, grew from early times when pioneers lived at a nearby convent and rode the trolley to a small two-roomed school, to a sprawling city with 1700 pupils and thirty-eight Sisters. All schools were giants in some ways. Axtell once gave four of its nine high school graduates to religious life. And the gradual consent to the giving up of small schools for the Church's greater needs was never given because anyone really wanted to forsake places with names of such quality as Fidelity and Mercier.

"How is Sister Rose Scahill?" the vice-president of St. Louis University asked once. "She taught me in Mercier."

Nine Kansas schools developed high schools, of which six were in operation in 1963: SS. Peter and Paul, Seneca; St. Joseph, Shawnee; Flush Public High School; St. Benedict, Baileyville, and Kelly Public High Schools. These district schools developed in Catholic communities which, in depression years, saw a way of keeping Sisters and education through maintaining tax-supported schools. The absence of crucifixes and the maintenance of extra-school time for teaching religion have not been easy, but the schools have worked harmoniously with the State Department of Education for a quarter of a century.

Each school has its particular excitement but there is a common tone. "What I like best here," said a Kansas state inspector once at the close of the day's visit to a parochial school, "is the expression on the faces of those children studying religion. The devotion to the true and the good and the beautiful is a cult so easy to lose. You still maintain it."

At the root of the work lies a high and constant ideal.

"Do you believe your school helps students become better Christians, achieve the Christian *humanitas*?" The question was raised at the American Benedictine Academy meeting in Duluth, Minnesota, in the summer of 1959. "If I did not think so, I would close the doors tomorrow," answered the Rev. Quentin Schaut, then president of St. Vincent's College, Latrobe, Pennsylvania, now Newman Club director at Pennsylvania State College.

To achieve the Christian *humanitas* in the souls and lives of little children and of young people, the convent spread its mission work beyond the borders of Kansas to five other states.

St. Peter's Parish was first in Iowa near the railroad station, high on its own bluff in Council Bluffs.[5] St. Peter's was followed by St. Mary, Iowa, 1889–1900; then by St. Malachy, Creston, 1893, when the Benedictine motherhouse there was transferred to Guthrie, Oklahoma; then by St. Mary's, Danbury, 1900–1911. Six years later began the forming of a cluster of schools in the fertile country about fifty miles from Council Bluffs. St. Mary, Portsmouth, 1906; St. Mary, Panama, 1910; St. Paul, Defiance, 1917, are, in 1963, considering a merger into one large high school. Walks in the country on Sunday afternoons, Sunday adoration hours, a closely knit school and community, were some of the traits of the Iowa missions. It could get cold there, and the farmer who walked six miles to bring the Sisters milk one winter day when school was closed because of the weather was indicative of life there.

St. Boniface, Charter Oak, taken in 1914, was a boarding school as well as a parochial day school. During the nine years in which the community staffed it, Sisters watched with awed wonder as small boys devoured pancakes with a capacity not common in convents. Because of its distance from Atchison, the school was relinquished when it was possible for other Sisters to staff it. St. Mary's School, Des Moines, near the railroad track, was a mission from 1923 to 1953. Then both school and parish were dissolved as the population pattern in Des Moines changed and the old steeple visible from the trainstop became history closed.

Nebraska opened to the Atchison Sisters in 1888 when Mother Theresa took Annunciation Academy, Nebraska City. In 1911, St. Wenceslaus School, Wahoo, joined the list. It was a beautiful school, among Bohemian and Croatian people. A flourishing high school, it was taken over in 1923 by the School Sisters of Notre Dame, who were better equipped to conduct some classes in the native tongue of the people.

From 1913 to 1920, St. John the Baptist, Plattsmouth, was an Atchison mission. Then during World War I, in 1916, Sister Celestine Nordhus was sent to start St. Columbkill, Papillion, six miles from Omaha. It was a boarding and day school, a new building. Sister Joan Apley, writing the history of the community's Nebraska schools, tells:

About the middle of November of that initial year, a young priest brought Edward Clark — a little, neglected, homeless boy — to see

280

the Sisters as their first boarder. Sister Celestine, superior and principal of the academy, was deeply impressed. She said, "It was my first meeting with Father Flanagan. After I opened the door and saw the kind, lovable young priest with his arms around a little unfortunate boy, I guessed what his purpose was in coming to us. It was on this occasion that he said, "If it is ever in my power, I will some day make a home for boys like this one." [6]

Thirteen months later, December 22, 1917, Father Flanagan began his home at 25th and Dodge Sts., Omaha, on a borrowed $90. Later he moved his project to the present site of Boys Town, eight miles north and west of the little school he admired.

Farthest mission from the convent, St. Joseph's in northwestern Nebraska, Atkinson, taken in 1916, became a grade and high school. St. Anthony, Steinauer, built in Spanish mission style, joined the list in 1917. St. Joseph, Beatrice, 1918, developed into a high school in the 1940's. Some of the enterprise of the modern high school student, and some of the distinction a small school can achieve, was defined by one of its valedictorians:

From the scholastic angle none of us knew a thing about putting out a yearbook. From the financial angle we didn't have a cent; we had to raise the money ourselves. The enthusiasm, the fun, the sense of responsibility that first arose in the fund-raising drives and in the picture-taking and page-planning work were not confined to the yearbook . . . But Saint Joe has had yet a greater thing to offer us . . . the ideals and aims for which she was founded . . . I mean the Christian concept of education.[7]

Four other Nebraska schools entered Atchison history: SS. Peter and Paul, South Omaha, 1941; St. Mary, Dawson, 1923–1942; St. Anthony, Westpoint, 1937–1950; and St. Rose, Omaha, 1941–1943.

In 1889, the Franciscans of Our Lady of Sorrows Parish, Kansas City, Missouri, invited Benedictines to teach there. Atchison kept the school until 1899 when Franciscan Sisters of Oldenburg, Indiana, replaced them. Immaculate Conception, Higginsville, was another Missouri mission, from 1897 to 1899. And at Lamar, Missouri, birthplace of President Truman, the convent had for six years the dream of a flourishing southern Missouri academy. Some even saw the place as site for a future daughterhouse when the request came from Bishop Lillis to open a school there. But Sisters canvassing for boarders did not find the harvest great and the school closed in 1912.

Guardian Angels, Kansas City, became an Atchison mission in 1909; St. Patrick's, Maryville, and St. Mary's, Maryville, in 1910 and 1911. Both schools took boarders in days when children from the country had long trips to make in harsh weather over harsh roads. In 1961 the schools were amalgamated into one and a new parish, St. Gregory's, was established.

St. James School, St. Joseph, Missouri, opened in 1914; Immaculate Conception, Brookfield, 1915. And there were Immaculate Conception, Montrose, from 1917 to 1960, when Nevada Franciscan Sisters took it; St. Stephen's near Monroe City, 1917 to 1961, in Mark Twain country, a rural place noted for its love of music; St. Joseph in Palmyra, 1919, the closest to the route followed by the first Sisters from Hannibal to Atchison in 1863.

Cathedral School, St. Joseph, 1920; St. Benedict's, Clyde, 1920; Our Lady of the Angels, Wien, 1923; St. John the Evangelist, Bahner, 1931–1954; St. Joseph, Salisbury, 1938; St. Ludgers, Germantown, 1944–1959; Lillis High School, 1940; Bishop Le Blond High School for Girls, St. Joseph, 1960; and St. Bernadette's in Raytown, 1961, bring the present total of Atchison's Missouri schools to eleven.

Every mission school enters the convent's life.

"Here I am no great artist," a Sister may say, cutting away at ducks and saints' faces in a summer recreation, "but in my kindergarten class I am." And every mission becomes a person's life for a time. "Autumn came, and the leaves turned brown and fell," wrote the historian of the first year at St. Matthew's, Topeka; and, "You can know God is everywhere, but you can feel Him best in the mountains," says a teacher who has been west.

With every other convent in the United States, Mount St. Scholastica saw the day pass when every mission could have a specifically designated housekeeper. But the memory is still there, and in some cases the reality too, of the hands that bring a cup of coffee to some harassed activity sponsor or comfort a child at the Sisters' back door. Always sacred to mission history will be the person who, after the mission superior, was or still is the "heart of the house."

The curriculum of the community's high schools held, for the most part, to the core of classical studies. In some places, such as Seneca, the Catholic school shared public school classes in industrial arts and instrumental music. But even small schools kept to the core of religion, literature, history, Latin, English grammar and composition, science, and mathematics. The first Sisters had brought a love of these things. Mercifully, in many cases, they were more financially possible, too.

Atchison schools took some share in the many competitions in all areas of learning and performance which have been part of education since Homer and Aeschylus, and gold cups accumulated wherever there was a school, no matter how small the shelf. There were Merit Scholarship winners and graduates otherwise notable. But other rewards came too. "We send many of our high school boys to Lillis," a speaker from the Ozanam Boys' Home in Martin City, Missouri, once said, "because somehow the Sisters seem able to stand the guff."

The early schools were often boarding schools where parents brought their children over muddy roads on Monday mornings to leave them until Friday afternoons. The Sisters marshalled them into dormitories, baked multitudinous loaves of bread and pancakes, told them stories, and demanded reading, writing, arithmetic, and catechism.

"I know what your last name is," a diminutive six-year-old in one of these small boarding schools whispered one evening, as she helped her teacher with the boarders' dishes.

"You do?"

"Yes. I read it in the book on top of your desk. It said: 'D-E-S-K C-O-P-Y.'"

There were summer religious vacation schools too, and Saturday catechism classes. The religious vacation school with a plan of content and method began in the Kansas diocese in the summer of 1929, when twenty Sisters of Charity conducted nine schools enrolling 397 children. From Atchison, since 1930, an annual procession of suitcases and projects has gone each June to parishes for two- or three-week daily sessions. In 1961, the

Sisters taught fifty-two vacation schools with a total of 3134 pupils in Kansas, Missouri, Iowa, Colorado, and Nebraska. In addition, since September 1, 1944, the home college has sponsored religious correspondence courses for thousands of public school children during the school year, through the Confraternity of Christian Doctrine.[8]

The work of the convent in schools and vacation schools, directly by those who teach and indirectly by those who do not, goes on from season to season. Sometimes in the convent's history it has been given a rather clear view of what the work means.

In the fall of 1961, Sister Alberta Stack, teaching at St. Joseph's School in Atchison, became ill. On the morning of December 8 she asked, "The Mass!" The Sisters with her began, "I will go into the altar of God." Her lips formed the answer, "To God who giveth joy to my youth." The words of the Introit were read to her: "Let us all rejoice in the Lord, celebrating the festival of the Immaculate Conception," and, "The Lord possessed me in the beginning of His ways, before He made anything from the beginning."

She lived through the reading of the whole Mass, her own lips forming the words, "Who the day before He suffered took bread into His holy and venerable hands." With her eyes she joined in the prayers for the conversion of Russia, and then the fifty-two years of teaching children to know and sing the Mass and to serve at the altar were ended.

The mission world is like all the other worlds the convent touches and forms. It is like the Atchison parochial school world, where the Sisters come home to the motherhouse every night. It is like the academy and like the college. And yet it is different. Over every mission convent at night the world closes down in the distinct colors and spirit of those who live there and of the students they teach. There is some mystery in it, the mystery that puts a look of excitement on faces when it is mission time in August. The little girl who long ago grew excited because "the Sisters are coming," has something in common with the Sisters who are leaving home to go to her.

The excitement is both the responsibility and the reward of

those who, in accordance with St. Benedict's provision long ago, are sent on a journey to do the work of God.

1. Manuscript account, Summer, 1960.

2. Parishes in Nemaha County gave many vocations to the priesthood and Sisterhood, and to many Orders: Benedictine, Jesuit, Dominican, Franciscan, Sisters of Charity, Daughters of Charity, Sisters of St. Joseph, Missionary Sisters of St. Benedict. And when the first group of Papal Volunteers went from the United States to South America, Ronald Henry of Seneca and Rose Agnes Reinecke of nearby Baileyville were among them.

3. St. Patrick District School is one of the very early public schools which the community has staffed in Catholic areas of Kansas and to which Abbot Innocent referred in his counsel to Mother Aloysia.

4. Academy principals since the beginning in 1863 (although the academy was not formally incorporated under the laws of Kansas until March 19, 1873) have been Sister Ehrentrude Wolters, Sister Augustine Short, Sister Bertha Cotter, Sister Aloysia Northman, Sister Adelaide Cass, Sister Eusebia Rooney, Sister Theophila Tangney, Sister Angela Foley, Sister Ambrose Conway, and Sister Theophane Reinecke. The Academy, the oldest educational unit — although properly it had no high school classes until 1866 — saw girls come and go for a hundred years in the green and white pinafores of the first days, the Peter Thompson uniforms of the 1920's, and the varied styles of the last quarter of the convent's century. In 1963 it had an enrollment of 260 students.

5. The convent began staffing St. Peter's in 1888, and in its long history it became known for music pupils, for feeding the wanderer, and later for being one of the schools from which a teacher, Sister Bertilla Normile, took a spelling champion to the national capitol.

6. Unpublished master's thesis, Creighton University, p. 70.

7. Commencement speech, 1949. The speaker, John Geiger, is now the Rev. Bernard Geiger, O.F.M.

8. Sister Mary Patrick Reilly, "The Religious Vacation School in the Diocese of Leavenworth," unpublished master's thesis, Creighton University, 1947, has traced the history of this movement.

THE FINGER OF GOD

"It is summer in South America. The flowers are in bloom and the grass is green," wrote Mother Celeste Hemmen in a letter to the community, March 3, 1963. "Greetings from the top of the world."

An airplane over Peru and Brazil seemed a strange place for a Kansas Mother Superior. But she was on her way to plan a fourth foundation. "I feel that I go in obedience to the Holy Father," she had said the night before leaving.

The Benedictine Order, like the soul of every Christian, is essentially missionary. But Benedictine daughterhouses are not made quickly. Only after one place has become stable and formed a spirit which will transplant does a convent dare go to new fields. Atchison made its foundations slowly, and always at the call of some special need which found its way to the top of the Superior's daily mail and stayed there. Once the call was really heard, though, things moved quickly.

Mexico City was the first foundation, although Colorado and California had preceded it as mission territories. The morning after, the Chapter in answer to requests from Bishop O'Hara and Abbot Cuthbert, voted yes to a three-year trial period in Mexico, Mother Lucy wrote to Sister Helena of Incarnate Word College, San Antonio, February 29, 1944:

The generous spirit of self-sacrifice that your own community has shown in the pioneer work of that country [Mexico] makes me feel free to ask your assistance as regards our own initial steps. Will you permit our Sisters to come to your convent toward the latter part of May and arrange for a change of dress there? [1]

286

The response was generous, and Incarnate Word became a frequent stage in the trip to the distant mountains housing the site where the Mother of God appeared to Juan Diego four hundred years earlier.

After the blessing for pilgrims and the singing of *Salve Mater* from the convent front porch, the Missouri Pacific train took Sister Mildred Knoebber, Sister Chelidonia Ronnebaum, and Sister Anthony Payne to Kansas on the night of April 30, 1944. There they boarded a night train, and the next day Sister Mildred wrote:

St. Louis, Mo.
May 1, 1944

Dearest Mother:

We reached St. Louis after a good rest at about 9:00 A.M. and regretted having to miss Mass . . . We have come to a small hotel room right here in the station to make our change. Since we had so many bags, it will save us taxi fare and it is a $2.00 room, so we felt that would be easier. We explained our situation to the manager and he seemed very understanding, so I don't think there will be any scandal.

Sister Chelidonia and Sister Anthony are out shopping for Sister Chelidonia's watch. I went out to St. Louis U. to see Father Husselein a few minutes, and also had a brief visit with Father Scheller in the interests of the girls who wish to go on in Social Work, notably Mary Alice Walsh. I am sure she will get the fellowship next year if she wants it. I made a visit to the College Church where the Blessed Sacrament is always exposed. It was some compensation for having missed Mass.

We are full of the thoughts of how beautiful you made our departure. It is so good to feel that we have such a wonderful religious family to stand back of us in our work. Surely it is an impetus to do it all with more fervor for God's glory. *May God reward you* a million times for all the things you have done and are doing for us, dear Mother. We did not forget that the Mass today was for us.

In a short time now we must don the worldly appurtenances, but for God's honor. I assure you we shall try our best to keep the right spirit under the changed external. . . .

Devotedly yours in St. Benedict and Our Lady of Guadalupe,
Sister M. Mildred, O.S.B.[2]

The "worldly appurtenances" so significant to the beginners were to fade in prominence before more important sacrifices

287

as the years went by. But that day in St. Louis, where, contrary to previous plans, the exchange was made, giving up the habit blessed at the altar for ordinary clothing cost a great deal. Returning from their shopping trip that evening, Sister Chelidonia and Sister Anthony came confidently to their room only to draw back respectfully with, "Pardon us. We must have knocked at the wrong door," and then to burst into tears on realizing that the sedate lady in the blue suit was Sister Mildred.

Mexico laws prohibited teaching by anyone in religious garb. A few strange things were ahead for the Sisters. On the trip south by train, officials asked the travelers for birth certificates. The Mount St. Scholastica letterhead on stationery they had with them saved the situation, but Sister Mildred wrote: "Have Sister Augusta get our birth certificates to us soon so no further trouble about our American citizenship comes." One customs officer, very particular in inspecting papers, scrutinized biology tests which Sister Anthony had brought along to grade. He seemed puzzled and annoyed until she told him to "let her know if they passed or not. Then he had to laugh." [3]

Arriving in Mexico City, they were met by Father Anthony Reilman of St. Benedict's Abbey, stationed then at the Colegio Tepeyac, where the Sisters were to help teach. Sister Mildred writes of Father's relief at "how well-dressed we looked." With him were Señora Lanzagorta and two of her children, and Mr. Farley, principal of the Colegio Tepeyac. The Lanzagortas, who had been instrumental in bringing the Sisters to Mexico, received the pioneers as their guests. "We went first to the Oratory [in the Lanzagorta home] to say our Ave Maria to La Virgen." [4]

From that writing of Friday, May 6, 1944, through the weekly letters which Sister Mildred sent to the home convent, *La Virgen* appears to stay in the Mexico City correspondence.

It is impossible for someone not of the Mexico foundation to write the history of St. Benedict's Convent there. But the summary of how it has appeared to the motherhouse needs to be given. After a little more than two years, the Sisters moved to Colegio Guadalupe, their own school for girls, leaving Tepeyac now an all boys' school to the monks from St. John's Abbey, Collegeville, who replaced the Atchison monks when need at home recalled them. From kindergarten through secondary school, Colegio Guadalupe received more than 700 uniformed girls in 1947. The number swelled to 2,000 in a few years, with more than 6,000 being annually turned away for lack of accommodation. Sixty lay teachers helped the slowly growing community of Sisters staff the school.

Three other schools joined the works of St. Benedict's Convent — Juniper School for the children of United States parishioners of St. Patrick's Church, Mexico City; P. [Poza Rica] in Veracruz; and in the motherhouse's centennial year, 1963, a school for the very poor at Tulpetlac, on the site of the fifth apparition of Our Lady of Guadalupe, made to Juan Diego's uncle, Juan Bernardino, whom she cured of a serious illness, her first miracle.

The convent, a mansion near the school built in 1947, has grown in the nineteen years in Mexico from three to thirty-eight members. Fifteen of these are volunteers from the mother convent. One novice, a graduate of St. Joseph's High School, Shawnee, Kansas, entered the convent in Mexico after two years at Mount St. Scholastica College. Many of the new Sisters are from Colegio Guadalupe's long files of students.

The Mexico City convent has had its own brand of pioneer days. Novices have had to learn to prepare to receive the religious habit, and then to relinquish it for teaching, hours after profession. Mother Mildred, faced immediately with the requirement of formal dress for the school's graduation ceremonies in the Mexico City Bellas Artes (theater), solved it by appearing in the academic robes to which her doctorate in sociology from St. Louis University entitled her. The enigma of more work than their handful of Sisters could begin to do was solved by creating a deep bond of unity with "our family," the scores of lay teachers employed.

The Sisters became part of a vivid faith, the faith of a people who in a land forbidding the wearing of religious garb, yet walk hundreds of miles to form a pilgrimage to Our Lady of Guadalupe. And in exchange for their voluntary exile from their native land, they stood proudly in the Basilica in Mexico City while the American flag was raised there in 1960. They heard with mingled emotions the *Star Spangled Banner.* They listened as the United States ambassador saluted Mexico City in Spanish and the Mexican ambassador paid tribute to the United States in English. Mother Mildred had been requested to serve on the protocol committee for President Kennedy's visit to the Basilica, but when instead of a formal visit the Kennedys came simply to Sunday Mass at the Shrine, the Sisters were part of the throng who worshipped with them. They heard a woman from a far-off Mexican province say: "How wonderful. A President who is proud to pray."

Scrupulous obedience to the laws still on the statute books of Mexico has been from the beginning a convent rule. "We are happy to make the sacrifices entailed," said Mother Mildred to an interviewer, "in order to build confidence and dispel animosities." [5]

The union of a deep Mexican faith with instruction in doctrine is the purpose of the convent. But for the Sisters themselves there have been rewards in faith. The luminous devotion of the Mexican people has been a rich gift to the St. Benedict's Convent. "The surest way to win a child's attention," they say, "is to tell him a story of the Christ Child or His Mother." And, "The sheer love of the Mother of God is the endowment of Mexico. Our Lady of Guadalupe made no demands for penance. She simply promised to love the Mexican people." [6]

There was another reward for leaving country and convent. "You come to see how big the Church is. It isn't a little thing into which one must narrowly pigeonhole life. It holds us all." [7]

In the small chapel of St. Benedict's Convent, the full Divine Office has been chanted since 1950, with an increasingly Spanish accent in the Latin as vocations from Mexico slowly increase.[8] There in the first daughterhouse of Atchison, the old convent life shapes itself anew. The first death occurred July 19, 1961. Sister Alonza Sandoval, kindergarten teacher and convent procurator, said according to the pattern begun in 1880 in Atchison: "Mother, what do you think? Is it all right if I die?" And Mother Mildred answered as Prioresses had done in the high-ceilinged infirmary of Atchison: "Yes, Sister. I'll give you to Jesus. But are you sure you are completely content with what God wants for you?" Sister answered very firmly, "Yes, Mother."

Instead of the procession to the Atchison cemetery on foot, there were blocks of schoolbuses and automobiles, filled with small children and their predecessors who had been Sister Alonza's kindergarten pupils. And in the great city cemetery, in her religious habit and the silver wreath of her more than twenty-five years profession, the remains of the first Atchison Sister to die in Mexico were laid to rest.

"Mexico is different," the Sisters say, assessing their life there. In the Superior's office in Atchison there is witness to the difference, a gift from the Mexican convent of a small statue know as the Infant of Good Health. A serene and untroubled face, the Child has. His cult was begun in this land where tempers are explosive, crises dictate the order of the day, and a young convent has built its stability on the very crises. The Sisters learned of devotion to the Infant through Lupita Calderon, a friend of the community, and Pope John XXIII blessed the cult in the winter of 1958, when Mother Mildred had an audience with him.

That the statue of the Infant, given to the Mexico City convent, really sheds tears, no one needs to believe. But that the Child and His Mother are loved in Mexico is the permanence on which the convent rests.

In the summer of 1963, two more Sisters went from Atchison to the Mexico City community, to be part of the convent which believes, "As Mexico goes in the struggle against communism, so will all of Latin America go." There is work to do there. "Our only wish would be that each of us could do the work of a hundred," Mother Mildred says every time she returns to the Atchison house which sent her forth in such excitement in 1944.[9]

"St. Benedict's Convent is hard to describe," commented Abbot Leonard Schwinn of Canon City, Colorado, after a visit there. "It is courage and energy in a battle for the preservation and deepening of faith. It is Browning and Cervantes in a classroom. It is the finger of God at work."[10]

1. Copy of letter, MSS Archives.
2. MSS Archives. The "May God reward you" was written *Vergelt's Gott*, in accordance with custom still followed at Atchison, but exchanged for the English or Spanish in the daughterhouses.
3. Letter of May 6, 1944. MSS Archives.

4. *Ibid.*

5. Diana Cary, "Plain Clothes Prioress," *St. Joseph Magazine*, Vol. 61, (September, 1960), 5–6.

6. Mother Mildred in a talk to Sisters at the Motherhouse, March 26, 1963.

7. Interview with Sister Simone Watson, Summer, 1961.

8. Monks of the Priory which staffs the Tepeyac School are chaplains. In 1963, the chaplain is the Rev. Odo Zimmerman, O.S.B., former head of the classics department at St. John's University and present Prior of the monks.

9. Atchison Sisters who left their country for another, transferring stability to Mexico City through the years, were Mother Mildred Knoebber, Sister Chelidonia Ronnebaum, Sister Victorine Knoebber, Sister Vianney Kaiser, Sister Esther Dominguez, Sister Theta Bahner, Sister Alonza Sandoval, Sister Mary Gerald Markiewicz, Sister Althea Armstrong, Sister Mary Carmen Marshall, Sister Simone Watson, Sister Sharon Holthaus, Sister Mechtild Swearingen, Sister Hildegarde Marshall, and Sister Mary Frederick Lueb.

10. Interview in Atchison, March 27, 1963.

A CONVENT IN GLENDORA

"The veil that hides the future," writes Father Faber, "is a veil woven by the hand of mercy."

No one knew in the autumn of 1937, when Sister Augusta Parle began organizing the convent archives, selecting appropriate vestments for the new chapel, promoting quietly but strenuously the worthy worship of God, and becoming scholastic mistress, community secretary, and subprioress, that she would head a California daughterhouse fringed by palm trees, dedicated to an apostolate of the automobile among clamoring schools, and named for the convent's first driver as well as for the martyr who smiled in flaming colors from a window in the chapel Mother Lucy built.

St. Lucy's Priory was to have the rare combination of intense activity and intense quiet, of marketplace and desert.

The California daughterhouse began with a telephone call, June 5, 1943, feast of St. Boniface. Bishop Charles Buddy, now of San Diego, formerly pastor of Cathedral Parish, St. Joseph, Missouri, was inviting the Sisters to the land of palm trees and orange groves, of Marine and naval training bases, of small Mexican children who every morning crossed the border to the school of San Ysidro, named for a long ago Spanish Benedictine bishop.

The chapter voted "Yes" to the plea from the community's friend of many years, and on Saturday evening, August 21, the first written entry of the California convent history was made. Sister Alice Ann Kieffe wrote in the diary the Sisters had resolved to keep:

Saturday evening, August 21, 1943. After supper we entered Mother's office to get the Holy Cross [the Superior's blessing]. Mother said: "Don't consider yourselves as far away. This is always your home. If you need anything, just write. There are souls there who need your attention."

The next morning after Mass the exodus began. On the train, a conductor of the Missouri Pacific approached the five Sisters with a box of pencils: "Are you the Sisters opening that school in California? I've been saving these pencils for the children there."

Other travelers were Sisters Rosamund, Rose Angela, Mary Daniel, Regis, and Albertine. Western Kansas, the mountains of Colorado, the sunrise of New Mexico were beautiful sights from their train windows. Their diary reported:

Albuquerque: Time off to pray and meditate – not from a book either. One doesn't need a book while feeling so close to God up in His majestic mountains.

The train went past adobe huts and stores in Grant, New Mexico, past the carrot and cabbage fields made possible by irrigation. It hurried through Lamy, New Mexico, named for the great missionary archbishop of the Southwest, hero of Willa Cather's masterpiece; through the Navajo Indian reservations and on into Arizona, land of the Cliff Dwellers. Few travelers have appreciated more what they saw:

We just passed a huge pile of rocks that look like superman pancakes. The soil and puddles along roadsides are of the same redness as the pillars in the New Chapel. In Carizao, Arizona now. We had to put on colored glasses as the golden sun is going down on the monks of the West. I wonder what St. Benedict thinks of us.

At three o'clock, August 25, they saw the beginning of the San Diego diocese and by noon were in San Bernardino. A motor trip to San Diego afforded them their first mountain eagle hovering near a great height, and took them also to San Juan Capistrano mission where swallows perched on their heads, hands, and shoulders. Finally, Bishop Buddy's house in San Diego. The Diary records:

The Bishop was out on the front walk to welcome us to San Diego. He took us into the reception room where we knelt and kissed his ring. He asked us to come to see the Master of the House to thank Him for our safe journey. We followed Bishop Buddy to the Chapel where we spent a minute or two in silent adoration. Then the Bishop produced his book and recited the Te Deum.

San Ysidro, with lemon and olive trees in its yard, was new geography for Atchison Sisters. Almost ninety per cent of its pupils were from Tijuana, just across the border, with their special visas to troop across the line each morning. They were gracious little children. "What is your name?" the new Sisters asked them. "Mary Lopez, *a sus órdines*," was a typical answer.

Years passed in California, and schools mushroomed. National City and Chula Vista followed San Ysidro in the San Diego diocese. Then came beginnings near Los Angeles.

In October, 1951, Father John Flack of Baldwin Park invited Atchison Sisters "into a district bounded by the beautiful Sierra Madre mountains." Then Father Bernard Collins of Covina wrote Mother Alfred: "Following the advice of our Most Rev. Archbishop, through His Excellency Bishop Manning, may we invite the kind Sisters of your community, if it is possible, to staff our school." And Father Hugh O'Donnell of Azusa helped Sister Augusta in the search for a motherhouse location.

The Sisters also took schools at West Covina, Claremont, and Glendora, and helped staff the Bishop Amat High School. Some sixty Atchison community members went coast-ward.[3]

With the going west of Sister Valeria Willems in 1948, the California Sisters met at San Ysidro for the first Sung Vespers, July 11, feast of the Solemnity of St. Benedict, and the golden voice which had intoned the first solemn *Alma Redemptoris* at the motherhouse inaugurated the first solemn chant by Benedictine Sisters in California.

Finally, in 1952, the time was ready for a motherhouse. A nine-acre tract of land with an old mansion at the foot of the Sierra Madre Mountains became the site of St. Lucy's Priory. On July 16, Sister Augusta Parle and Sister Dolorosa Hoffmans left for California to make the purchase. The mansion had no furniture or lights but was equipped with rugs, drapes, billiard table, and player piano.[1] In the process of transforming what had been called the "Mall Villa" into St. Lucy's Priory, the billiard table became an altar, cue sticks the candlesticks, and cue balls trimmings on the candelabra. The snack bar became a sacristy and the wine bar a place for storing candles.

Sister Augusta and Sister Dolorosa returned to Atchison. Then, a few weeks later, in a special ceremony, Sister Augusta received a departure cross blessed by Pope Pius XII for the new foundation in 1950.[2] On the morning of August 28, 1952, the first Mass was celebrated at the new Priory on the nameday of Sister Augusta. Early that morning the San Ysidro bus began collecting Sisters from the southern missions to travel the 120 miles. The Rev. Francis Broderick, O.S.B., who had just finished conducting the retreat at San Ysidro, said the Mass and installed the statue of St. Lucy.

High Mass began at nine o'clock, followed by breakfast. Sister Augusta had brought silverware from the Motherhouse. It was a solemn moment when each Sister saw that symbol of stability, her own name embroidered in red on a linen napkin ring, transplanted from Atchison's huge windowed dining room with its view of grapevines, apple trees, and Novitiate grotto. Here in this California refectory, where forty persons formed a crowd, the windows looked out over orange and lemon trees, avocado orchards, and the mighty Sierra Madre mountains.

Four years of service and growth in California went by. All the California schools were from the beginning very large schools. Many children of Navy parents had seen the whole world. There were the parochial school's typical rewards, but in new settings.

"Sister, how can I get my marriage straightened out?" a young father asked one of the principals one Saturday morning. "I married during the war and didn't bother to do it right. But the other day flying over the Rockies, my little girl who is in your kindergarten here said above the conversation: 'Daddy, we'd better not crash. It would be all right if I was baptized. But we'd better not crash.'"

In the summer of 1956, the General Chapter admitted St.

Lucy's Priory to the Congregation of St. Scholastica. And on August 14, Cardinal McIntyre presided over the election which unanimously named Mother Augusta Parle first Prioress. Sixty-two Sisters were its founders.

The convent experienced its first death June 29, 1960, when Sister Edna Brokamp died at the age of forty-eight. Teacher and expert habit-maker, she was buried on the feast of the Visitation in the community's newly purchased lot in Resurrection Cemetery, Alhambra, the first Benedictine Sister to be buried in California. When St. Lucy's novitiate building, called St. Gertrude's, added to its portion the garage behind it, the novices christened the house "St. Edna's Hall" and placed over its door a mosaic cross made at Mount Angel Convent, Oregon, where Sister Edna had gone the previous summer with the Scholastics. "I'm glad now for every extra moment I spent helping Sisters who couldn't sew," Sister Edna smiled in the last weeks of her life.

St. Lucy's Priory built its traditions. Sung Compline every night, Sung Sunday Vespers on all missions, daily High Mass were some of its foundation practices. The first Sisters to make perpetual vows at St. Lucy's were Sister Esther Nagengart, Sister Mary Joseph Schneider and Sister Reparata Welsbacker, who had made their novitiate in Atchison. St. Lucy's summer classes are affiliated with the San Francisco College for Women. For the completion of college work and for graduate study, the Sisters attend also Mount St. Scholastica, San Diego College, and Loyola University.

Early in its beginnings, St. Lucy's fit itself into its environment. Its closer touch with the ocean and the world beyond Kansas borders was symbolized when a California pastor donated the convent bell, a bell from a ship once used to transport soldiers to the Korean area.

In the early days, Jesuit priests served as chaplains. With the official status of independent priory, Father Robert Salmon of St. Benedict's Abbey became chaplain, followed in 1956 by Rev. Daniel O'Shea and in 1962 by Rev. Francis Broderick. Monks from St. Andrew's Priory, Valerymo, a foundation from San André, Belgium, and monks from St. Charles,

Oceanside, a foundation from St. Meinrad's, serve as confessors and frequently as retreat masters.

St. Lucy's Priory has its own distinctive spirit. It was named in love for the truly great Mother who first sent Sisters to California. It was founded in peace in a hurrying, populous section of the United States. It brought unity to the Sisters scattered over the coast, teaching so far from home. To meet the educational challenge far beyond its own personnel's reach, it formed a Benedictine Club of lay teachers whose goal is to share the spiritual heritage of the Order with the valiant lay helpers who share their spiritual and intellectual work.

With careful saving by the Sisters and with the aid of benefactors and of St. Lucy's Guild, the Priory was able to break ground for its new academy in 1961, to open school there in September of 1962, and to plan the dedication of its new building for February 2, 1964.

Inside the chapel is the statue of St. Lucy which stood in the room where Mother Lucy spent the last year of her life, sitting in her chair and watching the stream of life go by. In the novitiate is the statue from Mother Lucy's own convent cell.

In the hearts of the Sisters who built the convent near the ocean is both the great shadow of the home mountain, which lies beyond the Sierra Madres to the east, and the expanse of the apostolate to which in God's grace it sent them. Here their own convent door is facing southward toward their own new fields of endeavor.

"Something dies in California," a Sister said returning home, tanned and older after years in the brave new convent near the coast. "There are so many children, there is so much to do, life moves so fast. Something dies . . . some absorption in self dies . . . and then something better is born."

Eight postulants, walking buoyantly up the steps of St Lucy's Priory in the September of 1963, presage the new convent's great hopes.

1. During the days of the initial purchasing, the Sisters were given hospitality by the Victory Noll missionaries in Glendora. On the last night of their stay, the Victory Noll Sisters came to the new St. Lucy's for supper, bringing the picnic with them.

2. Sister Augusta, with Mother Alfred, had had an audience with the Holy Father during their stay in Rome with the pilgrimage of Benedictine Prioresses in the Jubilee Year.

3. Some of the California Sisters volunteered. Others, like Sister Mary Angela Foley, were asked: "If you think you cannot go, just go back to your post as academy principal here at home." Sister Benedicta Howe, who long ago had given the sunflower that reached Pius X, and who for many years had conducted the college drama department, went west to teach *Julius Caesar* and the writing of poetry to eighth graders.

Those who transferred stability to the new daughterhouse, either as volunteers like St. Boniface or as designated missionaries like St. Augustine of Canterbury, were:

Mother Augusta Parle
Sisters
Simplicia Buchler
Valeria Willems
Anastasia Turinsky
Ludovica Schoirer
Aleides Harpenau
Eulalia Schoirer
Ruth Schoirer
Theophila Tangney
Thomascine Spaight
Anna Marie Beck
Irene Trompeter
Perpetua Kugler
Aimée Murphy
Emmanuela Garcia
Stephania Fox
Gabriella Schuele
Mary James Hribar
Vita Fox
Martha Wolken
Mary Angela Foley
Benedicta Howe
Emeran Saal
Mary Ann Wohletz
Aquina Brungardt
Carmela Quintano
Regis Sielman
Rosalita Grund
Winifred Cornwall
Clementine Portemeier

Mary Vincent Derks
Roberta Mellinger
Miriam Alfano
Celine Goodwin
Callista Herrman
Agnella Mayer
Rose Angela Farrell
Francita Marnell
Mary Thomas Furst
Lambertine Hermesch
Edna Brokamp
Mary Jude Merrians
Mary Raymond Eisenbeis
Serena Stein
Colette Smith
Mary Bride Gormley
Mary Hope Couhig
Rachael Henry
Giovanna Mapelli
Cabrini Hyland
Humbeline Wiesner
Rebecca Mondragon
Auxilia King
Padua Hartnett
Mary Aiden Murphy
Nathaniel Von Tersch
Ephrem Gonzales
Jarlath Keating
Thaddeus Schueren
Mary Edward Assenmacher
Fatima Tosh

Mary Dennis Peters

THE WEST

California is farther west than Colorado, but it is not the West to Atchison Sisters. That is something different. That is something older. That is something consecrated by years of poverty and love. That is something having to do with train bells and the entrance to Pueblo, Colorado, with Pike's Peak to the north and the Spanish peaks of the Sangre de Cristo range to the south.

Changing and permanent, christened the mother of a people by the Indians, the peaks hold together the state. Long beyond them, huddling close to the New Mexico border, is the San Luis valley with its devotion and sacrifice, its great and simple beauty, and all the history of Antonito, Conejos, Capulin, Monte Vista in its nest of snow peaks, and the sprawling religious vacation school where so many songs have been sung and sacraments have been received.

Above Pueblo is Colorado Springs with Sacred Heart School and Benet Hill, destined to be the new Benedictine motherhouse. And farther north is Denver and the hurrying feet of children to St. Cajetan's School. This is Atchison's map of Colorado.

"The West" in American history has meant many things to many different people. To Atchison it has been a new world for half a century. It has been the reward of those who filled the special westbound railroad cars or drove in yellow schoolbuses across Kansas into the mountains, ranch lands, silver mines, piñon trees, and potato and pea country. They always came home with impressions which set them a little apart, faces wind-tanned, memories of heights and of small dark-eyed children who looked so beautiful in First Communion veils, who loved art and music, who needed so little equipment when one offered them the Word of God.

Colorado's school life began October 3, 1859, with the opening of its first public school.[1] The first Catholic school of the state was taught in Denver, 1863, by a lay teacher. It was taken over the next year by the Sisters of Loretto.[2]

Atchison Sisters went first to Walsenburg. Founded in 1866, the parish had tried to establish a school in 1878 but had seen its building, along with church and rectory, destroyed by fire. Another church had been completed by 1882, and a subsequent and larger church, the one now in use, finished in 1900. But the school did not materialize until fall of 1913. In late December of that year, Bishop Matz of Pueblo appeared suddenly at the Atchison front door to implore and receive Sisters. The religious community which had begun his school had not been canonically erected and had been asked to discontinue.

Five hundred children were clamoring at Walsenburg doors. Colorado seemed a continent away in 1913, and it was with some excitement that Sister Etheldreda Neyer, Sister Mechtilde Stenger, Sister Humiliata Eccher, Sister Alma Brown, and Sister Adriana Stallbaumer, together with Sister Cunnigunde Bescher as housekeeper, went out to open St. Mary's School, January 3, 1914. It was with excitement too that they stayed through the first days when at the ringing of the bell children went to the outdoors they loved through every available exit, including windows.

Years later, Charles C. Brown, a former Colorado State High School inspector, himself not a Catholic, would say from St. Mary's stage:

I knew of some superior schools in Colorado, and . . . some Catholic schools were among them. I also knew of some average schools and some Catholic schools were among them. And finally I knew of some inferior schools, but no Catholic schools were among them.[3]

The Sisters of St. Mary's in those first days had no such hopeful vision. The pupils, ranging from seven to seventeen years, had not been long accustomed to classrooms. In the first year a coal strike, requiring soldiers from Fort Leavenworth, broke out, and Sisters from the patient farmlands of Kansas saw before them the dark-eyed children of union and scab worker. They learned sociology from primary sources.

But the school grew. Within a month, Mother Aloysia sent two more Sisters.[4] High school classes were added in autumn, 1915. The war years and their aftermath brought their own color, and children came with names such as Armistice, Liberty, Adam, and Eve. There was vitality in people and school. By 1928, a new high school building had been constructed at a cost of $95,000. In Walsenburg's half century of history its principals were Sister Etheldreda, Sister Hilda, Sister Victorine, Sister Theophila, Sister Ambrose, Sister Constance, Sister Arsenia, Sister Felicia, Sister Margaret, Sister Suitberta, Sister Suzanne. The school called its athletic teams "Crusaders" and its newspaper, *The Paladin*. It achieved North Central membership in 1947. It wrote a courageous history, its teachers gathering crowds of children for religious instruction on Saturdays. They also went every Saturday and Sunday even in the summer, to teach those in distant areas.

But Walsenburg entered Atchison history in another way. Tuberculosis had haunted the convent since the early 1880's, and in 1922 the community built an infirmary for invalid Sisters in Walsenburg. The building was separate from the Sisters' convent. There over the years Sister Ephrem was to make the lace for the Solemn High Mass albs, many Sisters were to prepare for and meet death, a book of poems by Atchison Sisters would be edited,[5] and many would recover health and return to teaching ranks.

Walsenburg weathered the years both in the school and in the infirmary. Sister Hilda Boos, superior and principal from 1915 to 1927, and again from 1929 until her death in 1934, kept her rod of iron and heart of gold through meager days when the school and convent were supported from the personal salary of Father Liciotti, through music lesson money slowly accumulating in the special jar,[6] and through help from the Motherhouse. Father Liciotti, Theatine priest, was everywhere, endearing himself to the convent history not only by turning his pastoral salary back into the school, but also by ministering night and day to the invalid Sisters sent to the Walsenburg infirmary. Both those who recovered and those who died knew the ministrations of the sunburned Italian-born priest. And when Mother Lucy died in 1951, the subdeacon at her funeral was the Monsignor who had been school director, chaplain, and early genius in general to the Atchison apostolate in Colorado.

St. Mary's was twenty-one years old when Atchison took its second Colorado mission. Down in the San Luis valley, 150 miles from Walsenburg and close to New Mexico, was the small town of Antonito, named for the San Anton peak and river near by. It had a public school, from 1890 to 1933, and a school newspaper, the *El Nuncidor*. Depression struck the beautiful valley among the mountains, and the potato and pea crops did not supply the adobe-house dwellers with enough money to pay their taxes. In August, 1934, Father Liciotti wrote to Atchison of the hundreds of Catholic children soon to be teacherless in the valley. Mother Lucy sent Sisters there who for two years lived in the home of Mrs. Mary Wasshar until their adobe convent was blessed May 25, 1936. They had turned their salary back into the treasury to build the school and faculty residence.

In the summer the Sisters taught thousands of children in catechetical schools. Antonito, composed mostly of Spanish-speaking children and children of Spanish descent, prospered in academic, artistic, and journalistic endeavors. One graduate, Virginia Trujillo, for meriting second in the nation with an essay, "Hire the Handicapped," was photographed with President Eisenhower.

Twenty-five miles from Antonito was Capulin, named for the chokecherries in abundance there. It had an old and sacred history. A country district, founded from New Mexico in 1868, its church had been built by the Jesuits in 1878, rebuilt and blessed by Bishop Matz in 1913, and staffed by Theatine Fathers since 1920. The Rev. Peter Ribas, C.R., was now its pastor. A school had been established in 1893, but depression had hit the small community and it needed Sisters who would teach for minimum wages.

On May 18, 1939, Mother Lucy received a call from Father Liciotti, convincing her that Capulin should also be taken. In August, Sister Placida Nordhus and her four companions found that the school consisted of a garage and church sacristy and ninety-two pupils. With $30, Sister Placida went to Denver to buy desks. Mr. Ball, director of the public schools, and Inez Johnson, state superintendent, helped her, and she returned with desks ordered and paid for. Perched on a height among barren hills, Capulin grew as a grade and high school. When its first class graduated, May 18, 1940, Father J. McCarthy of Alamosa was commencement speaker.

Historic Conejos was a mile away. There Our Lady of Guadalupe Church, the oldest in Colorado, had been built in 1854, by Bishop Lamy. Mass had been said there for the first time in 1857. The district had been settled in 1825 by Lafayette Head of Boonville, Missouri, a convert baptized by Bishop Lamy. A Father Monato had been pastor from 1858 to 1864. Jesuits had taken care of the parish from 1871 to 1920 and Loretto Sisters had taught the school. Now the latter were withdrawing from the beautiful site where the majestic, twin-towered church stood in lonely splendor against distant mountains.

Mother Lucy sent Sisters Cyrilla Miller, Ludmilla Kropf, Theonilla Stessman, and Walburg Rochel to Colorado's oldest church. They stayed at first with Antonito Sisters, until a one-story adobe convent could be built. Conejos was a mission now of Antonito, and memories of Sister Adelinda Salesky coming to Antonito for Mass over the brown roads in a jeep in subzero weather were recalled when she died in the chapel choir gallery after Communion, in 1962.

For a while nearby San Anton was also an independent mission staffed by Atchison, until it combined with Antonito and transported its children there by bus.

Meanwhile another mission had opened in Colorado. At 9th and Lawrence in Denver, Mr. and Mrs. J. K. Mullen built a new church. Near it, in 1937, a convent, school, and Ave Maria clinic were built by the same estate, and in September of 1937, ten Sisters went to the school to work with the Mexican children of Denver.

"Let us see what the Black Gowns will do," juvenile court officers were reported to have said. At the opening of school there were 320 children, and by March of 1938, the rate of delinquency in the area dropped ninety per cent.[7]

From St. Cajetan's the Sisters went to various parts of the city to catechize. Many lives built St. Cajetan's. In stately brick it stands close to the church. A newly built viaduct separates the convent and church from the school. But the children walk beneath it and the files grow longer. "It doesn't hurt much, Sister," a dark-eyed boy said in the summer of 1962, as someone bound his cut knee the day before First Communion. "Jesus' blood ran down His knee, didn't it? And now can I go back to class?"

At evening the recreation room is a small factory. "I put a little piece of cardboard now to make the pictures stand. They like them better standing," and Sister Alcuin adroitly adds another prize to her collection.

"How long have you taught in Colorado, Sister?" the visitor asks.

"Thirty-five years."

The lights are on in Denver. The city glitters for hundreds of blocks. But nowhere more brightly than at St. Cajetan's.

Monte Vista, high among the mountains, had been taught by the Sisters of St. Joseph of Wichita. When because of distance from other missions the community asked to remove its Sisters, Mother Alfred agreed in 1952 to take the school.

Cathedral School, Pueblo, was added in September, 1950, and a new school built to replace the huge building which had so long served in the long years when the Sisters of Loretto pioneered there. Sacred Heart in Colorado Springs followed in August, 1954. It seemed so idyllic that one of its teachers said she could think of no penance to do for Lent. In the spring of 1958, a new flag was given to the school and Bishop McSorley of the Philippines, together with two Army chaplains, officiated at the raising. At the ceremony some occasion for penance came up:

"Now all of you know what democracy means," the Bishop said, smiling, in his sermon. "No, Bishop," chorused the first grade, amid all the august company.

But the primary educational work in Colorado was with Americans of Spanish and Mexican origin, with their great gifts and their sometimes great economic problem. Because of this, Colorado had long been thought of as the site for a motherhouse whose particular devotion could be to Colorado's needs. When twelve acres were offered for sale on a beautiful elevation outside Colorado Springs, looking across the city toward Pike's Peak, Mother Alfred bought them, July 16, 1960.

On June 23, 1961, vigil of St. John the Baptist, Mother Alfred said: "If you wish to volunteer for the Colorado house, in the spirit with which you came to the convent, sign your name before July 11." When morning broke on that feast of St. Benedict's Solemnity, when the Introit speaks of the father of a great nation, more than the needed eighty names were in.

Events in Colorado moved toward decision. On May 7, 1962, at 5:20 in the morning, Frank McCuniff died at St. Joseph Hospital, Kansas City, Missouri, where his son was a doctor. He had been the great genius of the Benedictine mission to Antonito, the city druggist, president of the school board, "doctor" and friend to everyone through all the years of the Benedictine effort in southern Colorado. His body lay in state for a day in the auditorium of the junior high school. The Creighton layman-of-the-year in 1960, the man made Knight of St. Gregory by Pope John XXIII, had been loved most of all by his own people. Bishop Buswell of Pueblo, conducting the funeral at the small St. Augustine Church in Antonito, said: "What he has done for the Church will live as a blessing to us all."

"The Benedictine mission to Colorado was part of his life's work," wrote his widow to the Sisters. He was a symbol of its dignity to the outside world. He had been a knight unafraid to fight for the worth of education and of religion and of ordinary people. He had loved Colorado.

So did the Sisters to whom he had been so strong a friend. They had taught a long time in the classrooms of Colorado. They had taken high school girls on Sundays to fill mission churches with the chants dear to Atchison, Kansas. At the Church of the Sacred Heart, Gardner, and in the mission of Our Lady of Guadalupe at Chama, they had heard the mission pastor say: "I am glad we are out here in these mountains, the kind of people the Blessed Virgin came to 400 years ago." And the hymns, "O God of Loveliness" and "Jesu Corona Virginum" had sounded out from the small windows many times to the high silent mountains.

306

There was work in Colorado, and there was joy. On the first Saturday of September, 1962, volunteers named the motherhouse, which would channel the work and joy, "Benet Hill." On the feast of the Immaculate Conception, Mother Celeste named Sister Liguori Sullivan to head the Colorado venture. By that day also, volunteers had reconfirmed their intentions to transfer stability to the new place. And on the morning of April 3, 1963, in the early dawn Sister Liguori with Sister Clarita McGarrity began the long trip west to conduct registration for Benet Hill Academy, to open in September of the motherhouse's centenary year. The convent chauffeur, Vincent Snodgrass, drove a car laden with books with which, like Mount St. Scholastica itself, it would begin.

"The pioneers loved libraries as they loved altars and homes," Bishop John Wright of Pittsburgh said in an address the Monday evening before the departure.

Letters from Brazil meanwhile lay on the Superior's desk. "Some day there will be a Twin College establishment in Mineiros, Brazil, like the establishment of St. Benedict's and Mount St. Scholastica's here," Mother Celeste had said to community, college, and academy, on her return from South America. Mexico, California, Colorado, Brazil — all knocked at the door and the heart of the great convent. Its brightly tiled floor, leading down the main corridor past the choir chapel and the pictures of Mother Superiors, invited all newcomers to learn the Work of God, to stay to understand it, though the convent asked some to go out to the mission world to extend it.

1. Sister Irene Trompeter, O.S.B., "Colorado Schools Conducted by the Sisters of St. Benedict," unpublished master's thesis, Creighton University, Omaha, Nebraska, 1948, p. 9.

2. Ibid., p. 10.

3. Southern Colorado Register, 1953.

4. Sister Elfrida stayed forty years until her death, an anchor and guide to new Sisters who came West. Sister Louise taught several times but spent her long subsequent teaching career in Kansas.

5. Sister Bede Sullivan, Dove-Flights (St. Meinrad: The Grail Press, 1945).

6. Sister Everilda Baumgartner, interview, Summer, 1957.

7. The Denver Catholic Register, March 25, 1938.

THE NEW CENTURY AND THE
ATCHISON IDEAL

Amid the splendor and faith of the Second Vatican Council in Rome, while Indian summer was coming to Atchison hills, Mount St. Scholastica prepared to observe its centenary year. "Doing Christ's work in the world is the only mission of the Church," said the Rev. David Kinish in the sermon at the evening Mass, October 10, heralding the Council's opening. "If the works of the Church have no reference to salvation, they are unjustified."

The Mass was sung in the college auditorium because the St. Scholastica chapel was being prepared for the opening Centennial Mass and the pews were wet with new varnish. From the auditorium stage which forty years ago had been new, and from which speakers from almost all the world had addressed Sisters and students, the red velvet vestments gleamed. The Rev. Kieran McInerney, O.S.B., college chaplain, sang the Mass. Twelve novices and sixteen postulants ready to make the first vows and receive the first habits of the new century, sang the Proper: "The Spirit of the Lord has filled the whole earth."

Mother Celeste Hemmen's term of office had been in progress for four months. The daughter of Mr. and Mrs. John Hemmen of near Wichita, Kansas, was the convent's sixth Prioress. The convent's 552 professed Sisters and 36 Scholastics were teaching the 18,508 students in the convent's 74 schools and carrying on the work of the hands and prayer of the heart which are the convent's daily life. There was a community newspaper, the *Homelites*, and everyone not teaching was appointed to pray for some particular school.

The autumn sun was shining on the coasts of California, the valleys and hills of Mexico, the changing Spanish Peaks of Colorado, the plains and farms of the Middle West, and in all those places on the daughters of Mount St. Scholastica.

The convent was not very much different, as it approached its centennial. Mother Evangelista, walking into it now, would have found the same prayers at table, the same Divine Office. She would have seen the work of the hands expanded — the crocheting of albs, the making of lace, the tradition of hospitality on the faces of guest-mistresses and table-servers, the care of the house of God by sacristans and procurators, the attention to books and pianos and art, the ministry to the sick. She would have heard the familiar voices of teachers above the sound of chalk on blackboards and the less familiar staccato of typewriters and multilith machines. She would have seen fountain pens and paint-brushes, books and brooms, dishes and needles.

St. Benedict did not found his monasteries to imbed them in self-interest, but to set them free in the Church to work and pray.

"Every convent," the Rev. Paschal Botz, O.S.B., former editor of *Sponsa Regis*, has said, "has its particular ideal of holiness." Atchison has its ideal. Everyone who calls it home knows it, although she might define it with a shade of difference — in fact it is part of the ideal that she must define it with her own shade of difference. Entering postulants are encouraged in the special seeking for God to which He has called them. Yet they are told to love the community, to find their perfection in it and with it, and over the years many have perhaps wondered that they were asked to risk their shining ideal among a group so human.

But there is a common, almost stern, belief here that sanctity consists in personal union with God, in unflagging devotion to obedience, in great mercy to those who fail, in the realization that one who seeks God finds Him, entirely for herself and yet entirely for all the lives she touches, that everyone in the convent is responsible for everyone else.

The task laid on Benedictines by St. Benedict was to "prefer nothing to Christ" and never to put anything ahead of the "Work of God," by which he meant specifically the Divine Office. Probably Benedictines of all ages have asked themselves if they were real, if they were the kind of Benedictines their founder would claim, or if they were only a transitional, stop-gap sort of monk or nun holding the ideal until the proper kind of world climate would make the real thing possible.

In Atchison not everyone can always be at choir. There are classes to be taught, and not all the hours can be perfectly arranged. There are the sick to care for. But all through and to the end of the first century, the Work of God has been the preferred thing: the whole house knows when Office is in progress, the whole house knows that from five to six is Matins hour. And deep in their hearts Atchison Sisters, when they take up their Antiphonals, as when they take up other books and other instruments of service, feel like real Benedictines not like compromisers. There is in the great house which a hundred years have built the conviction that all the works ought to praise the Lord and all saints bless Him.

And it seems to those who have lived there a while that there is an appreciation of the human, a joy in being human, a lessening of worry over God's compounding of spirit with dust. Perhaps joy in the human and trust in the Divine is another way of stating the Atchison way of life. "Put it in the book that unless we trust in Divine Providence as the early Sisters did, we will all fail," one of the Sisters said in the summer of 1962. "Be sure it is there, someplace."

In the century, Mount St. Scholastica learned that it could build nothing alone, that he who tries to do so lives only to weep among the ruins of his efforts. But it learned also that it could build everything if it built with God. It learned never to lose the vision of the holy mountain given by the century, the mountain where Moses stood and knew his God, the mountain to which each seeker of God is called. The young inherit the vision and bring their own as a contribution. The middle-aged and the old constantly rebuild the vision out of the seemingly trivial events of the day through the power of the Spirit of God.

In the year of the second Vatican Council, the convent prepared to keep its centennial. It began to take stock of what
had been at Mount St. Scholastica so long. Every picture and
statue, every brick and woodframe, every block of marble and
yard of terrazo had a history. It seemed at night that every
thing in the convent was holy, the long spotless halls with
statues so familiar that one had to stop to remember who they
were, the long halls filled with the voices of postulants in the
chapel practicing the Proper of the Mass.

On one such night, a cool October night, the ancient melody
of praise poured out of the consecrated chapel through the
silent house. No mechanical record machine was capturing it.
It was escaping whatever earth is and going into whatever
Heaven is. Tomorrow it would all be expended in the singing
of one Mass. "Dilexisti justitiam et odisti iniquitatem." It was
the Mass of the Virgins which Benedictine postulants were
practicing to honor the great Carmelite, St. Teresa. "Thou hast
loved justice and hated iniquity. Therefore God has exalted
thee."

It seemed as if all time were standing still and had come to
a great rest. The old century was ready to meet the new one
with a timeless refrain which said that God is in time and yet
beyond time, and that He will lead all of us into His timelessness.

The pictures on the first-floor hall proclaimed that this place
had a regard for human history, for all the efforts of men and
women. The architecture and arrangement of the buildings
said that this place had built gradually on its past for its
present duty and its future hope. There was a belief written
into the pattern of the day that love of learning is part of the
desire for God, that all kinds of work are sacred, that for those
who live by faith the pattern of the day brings grace.

The Centennial opening day, November 11, 1962, dawned.
"Rejoice that you belong to a city whose architect is God," the
Rev. David Kinish said in his early morning conference to
the community. The new Abbot of St. Benedict's, Abbot Thomas
Hartman, sang the Pontifical High Mass. The Very Rev. Eugene
Vallely, Vicar-General of the Archdiocese, gave the sermon,
emphasizing the graces given the community. At the evening

banquet, Abbot Cuthbert McDonald proposed a toast to the convent from the Office of Virgins: "With thy comeliness and thy beauty, proceed prosperously and reign."

A week later, Nov. 17, the Feeney Memorial Library was dedicated to Our Lady of Wisdom. Sisters, students and guests sang Solemn Vespers before the blessing, remembering the handful of pioneer Sisters who had sung to the Virgin Mary one November day a hundred years earlier and who had made their first expenditure for books.

Christmas came and on the clear cold days before the feast Sisters practised the Office and adorned the house. Then on the night of December 24, 200 Sisters, novices, and postulants of the home choir, in pressed scapulars and veils solemnly assembled at ten o'clock. Typewriters, mangles, and sewing machines were quiet. There sounded only the organ and the voices while the community longed for and praised the Word made Flesh.

At two o'clock in the dark morning, after Mass, a great power seemed still to be in the empty choir stalls.

January 3, and the monks of the Abbey filled the north side of the chapel as the combined communities sang a High Mass of gratitude. In the Riccardi Center dining room, Abbot Thomas blessed the banquet which both communities shared. "Perhaps this has never before happened in American Benedictine history," Abbot Cuthbert said when the day was over.

The feast of St. Scholastica came. Archbishop Hunkeler celebrated the Mass. "Let us hold out our hands for more, even as we thank God for the gifts of this century," he said.

There were trumpets accompanying the organ and the singing of Sisters, students, and parents of the students. In the parlor near the chapel, the remains of Sister Annette Beschler lay in the solemn state a convent gives its dead. A plain gold ring with the letters IHS, a rosary, a silver wreath for her twenty-five years and more as a Sister adorned her.

On March 21, in the pageant summarizing the convent's meaning, David Boyer of St. Benedict's College, as the young Benedict, wore a scapular and cowl which had been Abbot Martin's.

Out on her mission at St. George, Kansas, Sister Felicitas

Banks died one Sunday evening; at home in the convent Sister Hyacinth Wapp slept away. Sister Hedwige Hinrichs, 89, followed. On Ascension Thursday Sister Mauritia O'Shea died an hour after Holy Communion, and on July 2, Sister Maximilla Rilinger ended her years of seeing to it that all who came to her home-or-mission kitchen found provision.

A harvest of commencement-exercise invitations from mission schools reached the Superior's desk. It was summer now, the Centennial summer, and the Community began to gather. Of the 905 Sisters who had persevered in vows there, 231 were already listed in the framed necrology outside the chapel door as those "purchased from among men, following the Lamb wherever He goes."[1]

There were eloquent names on the list: tall Sister Benigna Barnett, infirmarian; mission superiors like Sisters Isabelle Triska, Euphrasia Coleman, and Susanna Seidl; young Sisters who spent their lives quickly like Sisters Victoria Hopf, Julia Coleman, Gabriella Goracke, Eustochia Haug, Mildred O'Keefe, Vivian Scanlan, Placida Hetscher, Anne Jennings, Cornelia Schalz, Aleidis Rank, Agnella Thillen, Georgina Gareis, Benno Jermaine, and Pulcheria Obstmeier; veterans who bore the day's heat for many years like Sisters Columba Meyers, and Mathilda Mayer; teachers like Sisters Clarissa Weber, Clementina Hammes, Mary Grace Peppard, Nicholas O'Connell, Isidore Wapp; those given the special grace of manifesting their desire for God like Sisters Ernestina Dehner, Baptista Wagner, Magdalen Reichel, and Rosina Baumgartner; housekeepers who made life beautiful like Sister Callista Hurla; Sister Madeline Arkfeld with her apostolate of prayer for priests; brave people like Sister Julitta Hochgrafe, who waited to come home to die until the diocesan examiners had found her school in good pedagogical condition; home-makers like Sister Digna Staab who washed spoons, attended concerts, and lived so long approving of all things, her paralysis included.

There are all kinds of reasons for remembering all of them: Sister Catherine Owens who came from New York at the recommendation of a pastor who had heard once of the place; Sister Herkentrude Roeder, widow and tailoress; Sister Richardis Heitz, whose uncle gave the convent its Christmas crib; Sister

Martha Zimmerer, who enlivened recreation with her German stories; Sister Aquilina Skinner, who ruled dining-room cleaning with busy hands, stern face, and vulnerable heart.

There are those here who suffered much: Sisters Adela Beedo, Carlotta Philipps, Elfleda Devine, Auxilia Becker, Abundantia Brunner, and Dafrosa Wahler; Sister Margaret Mary Portz, who never found anything hard enough to keep her from smiling; Sister Ebba Kramer, at whose funeral Abbot Martin departed from custom to speak a small eulogy for the infirmarian who came to the Abbey in flu-epidemic days to help the sick.

Looking at the list, one recalls Sister Irmengard Beedo's question in her old age while night winds blew the leaves against the sky and the orchard outside the infirmary was quiet: "Sister, do we go to Purgatory?" "Oh no, Sister, aim for Heaven." "All right. I just wanted to know."

For all the daughters of Mount St. Scholastica, Sister Chrysostom Koppes had written a Centennial song:

> The Lord has fashioned us a song to sing.
> From the summit of our mountain we will sing it:
> The glory of His praises
> Who has shaped the overflowing years,
> The overflowing years to peace.
> Let there be laughter in the song we sing,
> Let it be measured to the lilt of prayer
> Old in its beauty, and in beauty new, with gladness fair.
> The Lord has given us a song to sing,
> A song of ripened fruit and harvest gathered home,
> Of wind and rain and patient sorrow,
> Storm and rain and quiet brooding care
> Waiting for the morrow's spring.

The convent had been built both for today and for tomorrow. In the peace formed of its effort to serve God were the instruments of its battle for God. "The world is too sophisticated today to kill those who believe," a speaker had said at the school year's close. "But the communication of truth is nevertheless the daily martyrdom. And truth is God." For this daily work every Sister from the youngest postulant to oldest Infirmary

Sister was needed. And only glorious springtimes were waiting beyond the rim of the battle.

1. Of these, 726 were from 28 of the United States; the remaining from 13 foreign countries. Kansas and Missouri led in numbers of vocations with 328 and 153; Germany led foreign countries with 137. The names of twelve Sisters were not yet mentioned in this history complete the rostrum of those who died within the convent's first century: Sisters Artemia Biernacki, Seraphine Laib, Mary Paul Goetz, Ricktrude Kampert, Verona Schmidt, Madeline Arkfeld, Regina Hasselwander, Oliva Metzger, Alphonsa Wolken, Methodia Broz, Pia Haefele, Mary Kevin Enright.

With them is the word, "benefactors," for all mankind. There, too, are the names of the abbots of St. Benedict's, the bishops of the diocese, and the single word, "parents." The necrology was painted by Sister Celestine of the Chicago Benedictines and erected by Ed Eccher.

Its summation tells the story of both the bareness and the glory of the Christian's passage to the Creator. "Use the Kleenex on my face again. Don't waste it," one old Sister said to the nurse at her bedside. And, "Doesn't God want me?" Sister Aurelia said. "Yes, but He doesn't want the clock," the Infirmarian answered, of the friendly timepiece which loudly kept track of the night and which Sister kept with her. "Take the clock."

"When you go to heaven," the nurse went on, "see that I get the room next door painted." And minutes after the great transition, the convent Procurator said, "By the way, Sister Fortunata, have the furniture moved out of that room next door. I want to have it painted."

THE HOLY MOUNT

St. Anthony's entrance at Mount St. Scholastica is guarded by two doors. It is marked by suitcases, by a statue of St. Anthony, and frequently by a novice cleaning the stone steps between the outer and inners doors, or smiling to hold a door. For St. Anthony's is the back door, the home door to returning missionaries.

Inside the door an atmosphere meets the one who returns. Something of the taste of what it was when she first entered, a sense of intense individuality and personality, is there. Directly ahead is the choir chapel, bearing the whole history of the place and all its hopes in the wonderful windows. Down a corridor to the left is the St. Scholastica Chapel, mother church of eighty-six small convents.

The Mount is the place where each Sister came to be a saint. Everyone finds, therefore, on returning to it, the young girl who left father and mother, the postulant whose veil kept slipping off her hair, the novice wearing her habit self-consciously, the Scholastic treasuring the first "Good morning" of her first pupils, and the wonderful anonymity of the long professed years.

The Mount is a holy place. Despite all the failures, the mediocrities, the endless need for new beginnings, the halls near St. Anthony's entrance breathe a sacredness grown familiar. Down the corridor is the statue of St. Benedict, given long ago by Abbot Boniface Wimmer, down past the pictures of mother superiors, Abbot Martin, and the bishops who saw to the direction and consecration of the lives committed to this place.

Beyond is the monotonous spotlessness of the dining room where the crucifix Sister Ethelburg's father gave still presides over the Chapters in which Sisters meet, and where the lazy August sun looks in from grapevines and parsley beds upon the depleted missionary ranks when the summer is over.

Across from the dining room are the serving rooms and the kitchen, shining with chrome and newly scrubbed linoleum squares. Beyond it is the porch to which the poor find their way, and where every morning a circle of aprons pray over vegetables "with all the angels and saints in heaven and the just on earth."

Outside there are flowers and gardens, strawberry patches, the shrine of Fatima, the novitiate building, and the Way of the Cross leading to the resting place of the bodies with wreaths on their heads and cheap black cucullas, laid to rest in the ground by which, to some degree, they had themselves been made holy.

Around the cemetery, peonies and clover bloom. Above it the sunset sends fire and light over the whole hill, transforming rooftops, carefully mended and painted through the years. Near the cemetery is the cupola of the first convent, glittering with white paint, housing a bench on which no one ever sits but which people dream of going to for a moment some day. Beyond at a long obtuse angle are the college buildings, and the library dedicated to reading, study, and the long work of education.

Inside the convent, below the kitchen, the sewing machines hum. Coif machines whir, turning yards of linen into the circular headgear which invests twentieth century nuns with medieval dignity. The bakery diffuses the fresh bread, every loaf of it blessed with holy water, the fresh buns of Wednesday and Saturday, the feast day rolls of every Sunday, the "Poor Souls" bread of November 2, the ordinary fare for ordinary days.

Life is a mystery, and a mystery is a truth we cannot fully understand. Mount St. Scholastica is a mystery, unfathomable, but one with which all her daughters are completely at home. They do not explain her, but they know her. That all are made for holiness and happiness is part of what she communicates to those who come; receiving them as they are, she helps them to become what they want to be. Her mystery is part of the legacy with which she sends them out to the world, with black veil, office book, briefcases, and good shoes. It is the embrace with which she receives them whenever they return through St. Anthony's entrance to the shining halls, the smile of a novice, the scent of fresh bread, and the endless majesty of the St. Scholastica Chapel, mother church, holder of the heart, terrible in its sweetness, vast in its understanding, heart of the holy mountain.

No religious history has any real significance except in the area of what it really does for religion. And religion is simply the tie between men and God.

One of the first prayers a new postulant learns at the convent is:

O holy father, blessed by God both in grace and in name, who standing in prayer with thy hands raised to heaven did most happily yield thy angelic spirit into the hands of thy creator, and has promised zealously to defend against all the snares of the enemy in the last struggle of death those who shall daily remind thee of thy glorious departure and they heavenly joys, protect me I beseech thee this day and every day by thy holy blessing that I may never be separated from Our Blessed Lord and the society of thyself and of all the blessed.

The prayer enfolds the family of the convent and links it with the world for which is prays and works. It contains the reason for the lights that go on at night on the hill south of Atchison, where there was only hazelwood brush when Mother Evangelista and six Sisters crossed the river by ferry a hundred years ago.

Sometimes in seeking the pattern of the century, one asks if that is enough. With the world's billions waiting for the Word of God, here is only a novice with exceedingly young face polishing a corridor. Here is only a Sister who has spent seventy-eight years in vows of poverty, chastity, and obedience, stability, and the conversion of morals, praying her rosary in the back pew of Mount St. Scholastica chapel.

The justification is not in the fact that daughterhouses have gone out from here to Mexico, California and Colorado, and will soon begin in Brazil. It is not in the fact that thousands of children are taught daily to know God and His world, and all the beauties of intellect and will He has made possible. It is not in the fact that books and magazines have been published here, laundry washed, and mending done. It is not even in the fact that the convent is looking southward to the needs of the Church even as it tries to answer the demands of its archdiocese and region.

Near the end of His life, Christ said over the spilled ointment: "The poor you have always with you. Me you have not always."

Every morning the Sisters stand in the choir stalls between the glowing windows before the tabernacle under the mosaic of the King, personally to serve the Holy Trinity. They sing: *Deus misereatur nostri et benedicat nobis. Illuminet vultum suum super nos et misereatur nostri*, and *Benedicite omnia opera Domini Domino . . . Laudate Dominum de coelis . . sol et luna . . . ignis et aestus.* The justification of the century is in the fact that God is personally praised and loved.

From this service it follows that the convent cannot rest until all mankind praises and serves.

The convent, silhouetted against the evening, exists to be a citadel of God. It represents in a special way the gift of many parents who saw their children go or who brought them. It stands between the world and God, a meeting place, and that is all it is or ever needs to be in order to remain a holy mountain.

The theme of a story emerges only when the whole story has been relived by the reader as it was first lived by the people who made it. The theme of this story is that life on earth does matter, that people can build something if they try to work with God. It is His work primarily, but it is theirs too. It is important to know that, in the joy of the morning and in the heat of the day. For God is a good God who has put work in our hands, freedom to do it in our wills, and light and grace in our hearts.

The tone of a story is what remains when the book is closed and the century is over. It is intangible but real. It is like the impalpable but real awareness of frugal but white linen, mended many times and folded by novice hands for the dining room table. It is like the sudden shaft of sunlight on the grapevines or the ordinary summer flowers which hide the rocks in the rock garden. It is like the quality in the singing which drew the night watchman with his flashlight and raincoat to ring the front doorbell and ask, "Who is singing the contralto in that hymn?"

Somehow it is beauty. And beauty is what should remain, together with love, when people have tried to build a house for God through which they and others can learn to love and serve Him.

St. Benedict longed for the holy mountain where he would see God. In the Prologue to his Rule, he asked the Lord who would dwell in his tabernacle and rest in the mountain, and he found his answer in the prophet, "The innocent of hand and the clean of heart." So he built houses on earth where men could prepare themselves, and he provided that the energy resulting from the effort, the energy through which the victory itself would come, should be expended in good works.

The Sisters in Atchison, Kansas, over the period of a century, constructed such a place, too. They built it strong and durable, so that it could sustain the battle involved when human beings try to become and remain innocent of hand and clean of heart. They took care of their house of strength and peace, hoping that God would use it to call many to His final holy mountain in His light of glory. And because they knew He would help them remain faithful to prayer and work and would make it His tabernacle, even on the earth of shadow and struggle, they called their home "Mount" Saint Scholastica.

INDEX

DATE DUE

UE 26 '64			
JY 23 '64			
DEC 1 0 '99			
JAN 2 1 01			
GAYLORD			PRINTED IN U.S.A.